JUL - 6 1994

The Oxford
Guide to
Heraldry

The Oxford Guide to Heraldry

THOMAS WOODCOCK
Somerset Herald

JOHN MARTIN ROBINSON
Fitzalan Pursuivant Extraordinary

Oxford   New York   Melbourne   Toronto
OXFORD UNIVERSITY PRESS
1988

Oxford University Press, Walton Street, Oxford OX2 6DP

Oxford New York Toronto
Delhi Bombay Calcutta Madras Karachi
Petaling Jaya Singapore Hong Kong Tokyo
Nairobi Dar-es-Salaam Cape Town
Melbourne Auckland

and associated companies in
Berlin Ibadan

Oxford is a trade mark of Oxford University Press

British Library Cataloguing in Publication Data
Woodcock, Thomas
 The Oxford guide to heraldry.
 1. Great Britain. Heraldry
 I. Title   II. Robinson, John Martin
 929.6'0941
ISBN 0-19-211658-4

Library of Congress Cataloging in Publication Data
(Data available)

Typeset by Pentacor Ltd., High Wycombe, Bucks
Printed in Great Britain by
Butler & Tanner Ltd., Frome, Somerset

Acknowledgements

THE authors would like to thank the following for their assistance with the text and in obtaining photographs:

The Chapter of the College of Arms, for permission to quote from the College Minutes and reproduce illustrations from the College Library; Mr William Chandler of the San Diego Museum; Mr John Cherry of the British Museum; *Country Life* for illustrations on pp. 141, 148, and 185; Mr Peter Day and the Trustees of the Chatsworth Settlement; Miss Rachel Fairhurst; the Hon. Janet Grant, especially for picture research and work on the Glossary; Mr Peter Gwyn-Jones, Lancaster Herald; Mr Jonathan King; Mr Michael Maclagan, Richmond Herald; Miss Olive Middleton; Mr Godfrey New, for photography; His Grace The Duke of Norfolk, Earl Marshal; Mr Robert Parsons, for the drawings that accompany the Glossary; Photographie Giraudon for illustration on p. 11; Mr John Rose, for photography; Mr Colin Sheaf of Christie's; Mr George Squibb, Norfolk Herald Extraordinary; Sir Anthony Wagner, Clarenceux King of Arms; and Mr Robert Yorke, Archivist at the College of Arms.

Contents

List of Colour Plates

Introduction

THERE are many books on heraldry. So many, that it might be queried whether yet another is necessary, or indeed whether heraldry is a very 'relevant' subject to write about. To deal with these two questions separately, it might be best to concentrate first on why this book fills a gap when several others already exist. Many of the standard works on heraldry still in print date back to the late nineteenth or early twentieth centuries. Fox-Davies and Boutell immediately spring to mind. Though constantly updated, these tend to reflect the state of heraldic knowledge, historical research, and the general theories current at the time of their original inception, added to which they are on the large side, and perhaps rather daunting for the general reader. Though there are several smaller, popular books on heraldry, many of them are based on, if not actually cribbed from, Fox-Davies/Boutell, and they tend to repeat the same old facts and stories, and even the same illustrations, which makes for dull and repetitive reading. It seemed to us, therefore, that there was a need for a short guide to heraldry which contained all the basic technical information about arms, using reasonably simple layman's language rather than the (often bogus) heraldic vocabulary invented by heralds between the sixteenth and nineteenth centuries. Also, the subject could be made more intelligible if set in its wider historical context, covering the evolution of the College of Arms and the Court of the Lord Lyon over the centuries, and the way that heraldry has been used at different times as a form of architectural decoration. This, at least, is the aim of this little guide. Whether or not it succeeds is for the reader to decide.

It seemed particularly worthwhile to try to illustrate our book with historically interesting and/or beautiful examples of heraldry which are not already well known to the public, and to draw for this purpose on the library of the College of Arms which contains the most important collection of heraldic manuscripts in the world, most of which have never been reproduced in print. This is the reason why, wherever possible, the illustrations in this book have been chosen from examples in the College library, and it is hoped that this will give the book an additional attraction.

The aim has been to provide the type of heraldic information that an interested, educated person, not a specialist, might want to know. As an officer of arms one is often asked questions about heraldry. Such general questions have been borne in mind, and the attempt to answer them has been made in the following chapters, and especially in the glossary of heraldic terms incorporated at the back of the book.

Anybody who buys a guide to heraldry is probably already largely converted, so does not need to have its interest and importance pointed out. Others, however, may have at the back of their mind the sneer of Lord Chesterfield, or some other eighteenth century sceptic, dismissing heraldry as the 'science of fools with long memories'. Heraldry is indeed a science, with its own rules and terms, but also an art, and a beautiful one at that. Perhaps more importantly it is the 'shorthand of history'. Alexander Nisbet in his *System of Heraldry*, published in 1722, had some very sensible things to say about the subject: 'Knowledge thereof is worthy of any gentleman. If properly understood it is as useful as it is interesting', because it illustrates through symbols the history of prominent families, and therefore of the nation in general. The purpose of heraldry since its inception has always been partly 'show and pageantry', and these are important features of any civilized society. It has also long had a practical function in 'distinguishing, differencing, and illustrating Persons, Families and Communities'.

Through heraldry it is possible to trace the origin of noble families and the various steps by which they 'arrived by greatness', and to distinguish the different branches descended from the same families and the relations between families. Even a slight knowledge of heraldry therefore can make all the difference in looking at old houses, churches, and monuments, and add greatly to the pleasure to be derived from them, quite apart from its intrinsic interest or its relevance to genealogical studies. To quote Nisbet again: coats of arms 'represent the heroick Achievements of our Ancestors and perpetuate their memory'.

*The Oxford
Guide to
Heraldry*

I   *Origins of Heraldry*

ERALDRY, defined as the systematic hereditary use of an arrangement of charges or devices on a shield, emerged at about the same moment in the mid-twelfth century over a wide area of Europe. Between 1135 and 1155 seals show the general adoption of heraldic devices in England, France, Germany, Spain, and Italy. The question is why? There has been much debate about the origins of heraldry, but the subject remains obscure, and no definite or convincing conclusions have been reached.

It is often stated that heraldry in its early stages had strong military associations, and that its original purpose was the identification of knights in armour on the battlefield. In the eleventh and twelfth centuries the normal tactic of European warfare was the massed cavalry charge with lance and shield. This great set-piece formation could only be executed once, and if the enemy was not completely overwhelmed by the first charge, the battle then broke up into a hand-to-hand mêlée where some symbol or device, it is argued, was necessary to identify the combatants. A man in armour was very hard to recognize. William the Conqueror, for instance, was forced to remove his helmet in the thick of the battle of Hastings in order to identify himself to his followers who thought he had been killed. Victorian heraldic theorists claimed that a man's arms came to be painted on his shield so that he could be recognized by his followers in battle, and that such a mark of identification became essential after the development of the closed helmet which completely concealed a man's face.

This argument has been elaborated to show how heraldry was a product of the feudal system of land-tenure in Europe. A man held his land in return for military service, and was bound by personal allegiance to his lord under whom he must serve in war. Arms came to be used so that knights could be distinguished by their 'followers' in battle. The hereditary nature of heraldry is also a result of the feudal system. If service in war was the rent by which land was held, the right of inheritance by the natural heir was an understood condition of feudal tenure. In Sir Anthony Wagner's words: 'The hereditary succession to the crown of France or England was not more firmly based in law than that of the pettiest knightly house to its ancestral fee.' At a time when the right to lead or the duty to follow in battle was inherited, the coat of arms was likely to become hereditary too. In this way, it is argued, heraldic devices became a symbol of the owner's identity and also a mark of his status. Knights needed to be distinguished by shields and coats of arms, so arms thus became a mark of knightly status or noble rank.

The military theory of the origin of heraldry is developed in its most elaborate form in such early twentieth-century works as *The Complete Guide to Heraldry* by A. C. Fox-Davies. But while there may be some truth in it, there are also strong grounds for scepticism. J. H. Round, in his entertaining essay 'Heraldry and the Gent', demolished the Fox-Davies theory as long ago as 1910. He pointed out that only the limited class of 'barons' or tenants *in capite* had followers to whom they needed to identify themselves in battle. The great body of those who held land by military service, the 'knights', or gentry, had no followers. The service due from a military tenant in the feudal system was well defined. He held his land by service of two knights, one knight, or half a knight, and as time passed these fees became progressively subdivided. Long before closed helmets made the adoption of arms necessary for recognition in battle, men were already holding land by the service of one-third, one-quarter, one-fifth, or even one-twelfth of a knight in the twelfth and thirteenth centuries. A single knight, let alone a fraction of a knight, had no band of followers, so had no need to identify himself to them. The single knight, in fact, went to war not to lead but to be led. Yet heraldry indubitably became the distinguishing mark of this class. Many landowners, great and small, who bore arms did not in any case hold their land by military service at all. Military service was only one of many forms of feudal tenure; there was also tenure in serjeanty, tenure in socage, and tenure in frank-almoin. Even such a leading twelfth-century magnate as William d'Aubigny, Earl of Arundel, held his vast estates in Norfolk and Sussex by grand serjeanty—the duty to serve as butler at the coronation banquet—not by military service. Many landowners went to some lengths to shield themselves from the burden of knight's service. Round quotes the particular example of Ralph FitzOrm (ancestor of the Okeovers of Okeover in Staffordshire), who held estates at Okeover, Ilam, and Stretton under the Abbot of Burton, at Mayfield under the Prior of Tutbury, and at Callow under Robert Ferrers, Earl of Derby, none of which properties were subject to knight's service.

Even if the need for identification in battle had existed, the shield was hardly the most practical choice to meet it. The surface of a shield, being two-dimensional, can only be viewed from a very limited angle. Also, being held at body height on the battlefield, it would have been obscured by other combatants in the course of a struggle, and would, in any case, have rapidly been obscured by cuts, dents, mud, and blood. These difficulties would have been exacerbated by the nature of the heraldic charges, many of which closely resembled each other. The earliest English rolls of arms, dating from the thirteenth century, show many very similar charges, or even duplication of charges; a quarter of the thirteenth-century English shields of arms, for example, contain the lion, which would not have made for an easy identification. It seems, therefore, that the identification with any certainty of arms on a shield on a battlefield would have been so difficult that it must be assumed that such was not the practical purpose of arms.

It seems much more likely that the depiction of arms on a shield was a subjective demonstration on the part of individual warriors, a form of individual 'vanity' and display rather than a practical military device. Nevertheless, even if marks by which knights and lords might be readily known were not absolutely called for by military needs, the social and military order of the twelfth century was such that, once invented, they found a ready market as military status symbols, and were popularized probably by the tournament rather than in real warfare. The tournament is supposed to have been invented in the mid-eleventh century in France by Godfrey de Preuilly, and it developed as a popular form of regular training in the handling of weapons and horses. It rapidly became highly organized and hedged around with rules and elaborate pageantry. Ambitious knights travelled round Europe fighting in tournaments at fortnightly intervals. It provided the means for warlike young men to make their fortune, as is demonstrated by the career of William the Marshal who rose from a simple knight to become Regent of England. He and another knight, Roger de Gaugi, entered into a partnership in 1177, and travelled from tournament to tournament gaining much renown. By their skill at arms they captured no fewer than one hundred and three knights in ten months, making a large profit in ransoms. It is probable that such itinerant participants in tournaments helped to spread the usages and conventions of heraldry across Europe. Later in the Middle Ages the bearing of arms came to be accepted as an essential prerequisite of participation in a tournament. In 1389, for instance, when John de Kyngeston was challenged to a joust by a French knight, in order to enable him to accept the challenge Richard II 'received him into the estate of Gentleman and have made him Esquire, and will that he be known by Arms, and bear them henceforth'. The growing importance of military pageantry and its association with the tournament would have excluded those of insufficient social standing who were unable to meet the expense, and this would have helped to restrict the use of arms to the knightly class. Thus, arms came to be seen as a mark of noble status, and were granted by the Holy Roman Emperor and the European kings as a corollary to ennoblement. In early days,

The ordinances statutes and rules made and inacted by John Erle of worcestre constable of england, by the kinges comandement at windesore the xxix daye of may in the vj yere of his noble reigne, to be obserued and kepte Jn all maner of Justes of peace Royall, within this realme of England, before his highnes or lieutenant by his comandemēt or licence, had fro this tyme foorth, reseruing alwais to the Quens highnes and to the ladies there present, the attribution and gifte of the price, after the maner and forme accostomed, the merrites and demerites attribute according to the articles followenge

Joust with heralds in attendance. Drawing of *c.*1560 illustrating ordinances made by John Tiptoft, Earl of Worcester, Constable of England, for jousts of peace royal 1466 (Coll. Arms, M 6, fo. 33).

however, most arms were self-assumed, and their owners sometimes changed them at will. In about 1195, for instance, Richard I altered his arms from either two lions combatant or a lion rampant (only half the shield is visible on his first Great Seal) to the three gold leopards or lions passant guardant on a red field, which remains the Royal Arms of England. But even in the twelfth century, and before the rapid proliferation of armorial devices led to a growing measure of royal control, there was some equation between nobility of blood and armorial bearings.

This clue suggests an alternative theory for the origins of heraldry. Although heraldry came to have strong military associations, it may have developed from the civil personal mark, the seal device, of certain north European ruling families descended from Charlemagne, who perpetuated some of the administrative organization and poss-

Knight in armour with shield of arms and heraldic horse trapper on seal of Humphrey (de Bohun), Earl of Hereford and Constable of England, *c.*1275 (PRO E42/65).

ibly the symbolic devices of his court. The latter included the sun and the moon, the fleur-de-lis (which later became the symbol of royalty in France), and the symbols of the Evangelists: St Mark's lion and St John's eagle.

This is the argument put forward by Beryl Platts in her recent book *Origins of Heraldry* (1980). Though Miss Platts's argument is not supported by any positive evidence, it may, as a tentative theory, help to throw new light on this obscure subject. But far more detailed research still needs to be done on the European dimension before her argument can be accepted in all its aspects. She claims that personal family identification in a recognizably hereditary form was practised in certain courts of northern Europe, especially those of the Counts of Flanders, Boulogne, and their allies, before the Norman Conquest, and that members of those families who accompanied Duke William to England brought their own devices with them, and passed them on to their heirs who transferred them to shields. In England, all heraldry, she thinks, is either a survival of those original Flemish devices or an imitation of them, while in Scotland they remain today 'the chief foundation of that country's heraldry system'. Such devices survived because they were treasured as links with the lost world of the Carolingian monarchy, especially by the descendants of Charlemagne among the Boulonnais nobility, and this is the real reason for the reverential status of arms in the Middle Ages.

Consequently, the origin of heraldry was not Norman but Flemish. The Normans were not in a position to know about the symbolic devices of Charlemagne's court. William the Conqueror himself was only four generations away from the Scandinavian pirate Rollo. Whatever Rollo's standing might have been in his own country, it is virtually certain that he had little or no knowledge of the patterns of social behaviour surviving out of the old kingdom of the Franks. It is argued by Miss Platts that William the Conqueror's army contained many men who were not Norman. His invasion force included a large contingent from Brittany led by Alain Fergent, son of the reigning duke Hoel V, and more importantly a contingent from Flanders and its dependencies. William's father-in-law was Baldwin V, Count of Flanders, one of the most powerful princes in north-west Europe. Although Baldwin himself did not personally lead a contingent of troops to Hastings in 1066, nevertheless a large number of knights came from his Flemish *comté* and its neighbours: Guy of Ponthieu, Gilbert of Ghent, Arnold of Ardres (the hereditary seneschal of Boulogne), and the sons or nephews of the Counts of Guisnes, St Pol, and Hesdin. The overall commander of this Flemish contingent was Count Eustace II of Boulogne.

It must at once be said that only Eustace II of Boulogne is in the accepted list of fifteen men known to have fought under William at Hastings (see *Complete Peerage*, XII/1, app. L). The army was, however, of about seven thousand men, so the others may have been there too. Whether they were present at Hastings or not, all these nobles were interrelated, all were linked to the family of Count Baldwin of Flanders, and all were directly descended from Charlemagne. Through the troubled years after the death of Charlemagne, Flanders and its subsidiary *comtés*, unlike the rest of the Frankish Empire, had managed to retain something of the character of his rule. Boulogne in particular, with its Roman lighthouse and ramparts, and the international trade of its port, was rich and sophisticated. Its count, Eustace II, who was definitely at Hastings, had the strongest Carolingian ancestry. Through Ponthieu and Guisnes, he was descended from Charlemagne's favourite daughter Berthe, but more importantly, through his mother, Maud of Louvain, he was the great-grandson of Charles, Duke of Lorraine, the last male heir of the Carolingians. Not only was Count Eustace a descendant of the Frankish emperor, but his court at Boulogne copied the synodic pattern laid down by Charlemagne; it comprised a seneschal, an advocatus, a master of hunting, a constable, standard-bearer, marshal, and butler, supported by four chatelains, two viscounts, and twelve barons. Beryl Platts argues that not only did some of the administrative and hierarchical character of Charlemagne's court survive at Boulogne, but so also did its most rarified and colourful symbolism. She states that such a sophisticated and elegant *comté*, with its complicated international fiscal, military, commercial, and social connections, must have had badges of identity which would provide instant recognition for the Count and his officers within or without his territories. Although it cannot be proved it is suggested that such devices, of their nature, could not have been changed on the death of the reigning count, but must have been hereditary in the family. Furthermore, if Boulogne employed hereditary devices in the eleventh century to identify its ruler and officers, so also must the other linked *comtés* of Flanders, Hainaut, Louvain, Alost, Ponthieu, Guisnes, Hesdin, Lens, and St Pol.

Miss Platts claims that such proto-heraldic devices were displayed, not on shields at that stage (many similar shields are shown on the Bayeux Tapestry), but on seals and banners. Even if this were so, what evidence is there for her claim that in 1066 the Counts of Boulogne used as their personal symbol three red balls (torteaux) representing the sun on a gold ground? That the second son of the Boulonnais house used three red crescents (representing the moon) on a silver ground? That the Counts of Flanders used black and gold triangles in a gyronny pattern? That the Counts of St Pol used a wheatsheaf as their device, and the Count of Hesdin, the escallop? The three red balls on a gold ground of the Counts of Boulogne can indeed be seen in the Bayeux Tapestry, on the banner or lance flag carried by one of the leading cavalrymen, but this does not necessarily identify it as a symbol of Boulogne, and Count Eustace himself (in the famous scene where he identifies Duke William in the helmet-removing incident) is shown carrying a banner with a device of a cross and four smaller crosses (mistaken by Miss Platts for four small balls), said to have been used later by his sons at Jerusalem, on the First Crusade in 1096, and so proving that these devices were already hereditary in the eleventh century. In other words hereditary devices may have been known in 1066, and symbolic banners seem to have been carried at the battle of Hastings and in the First Crusade.

However, Matthew Paris, the compiler of England's first roll of arms, shows Count Eustace's sons as kings of Jerusalem bearing the famous arms of *Or a Cross Argent* when he records the death in 1100 of the elder son, Godfrey de Bouillon, and the coronation of his brother Baldwin I in the same year. Also, the banner carried by Count Eustace in the Bayeux Tapestry is usually identified as the Papal banner granted to William, and the device of a cross and four smaller crosses is not associated with the kingdom of Jerusalem till the mid-thirteenth century, when Hugh de Lusignan, whose descent from the Counts of Boulogne was remote, took the title. Again, if the Counts of St Pol already had a hereditary device of a wheatsheaf by 1066, why was Guy III de Chatillon, Count of St Pol (died 1289) recorded on 'Walford's Roll' with arms of *Paly Vair and Gules on a Chief Or a Label Azure*? Nor does there seem to be any evidence for the suggestion that the 'St Pol wheatsheaf' was brought to England by Robert de Comines; its use by the Comyn family in Scotland is an example of canting or punning heraldry, the garbs representing three sheaves of the plant cummin which, if anything, positively disproves Miss Platts's assertion.

The thirty or more lance flags on the Bayeux Tapestry with proto-heraldic devices should not, however, be completely dismissed. For instance, one appears to show three buckles, and three buckles or formalets were the arms later attributed to the Malet family, one of whom, William Malet, seigneur of Graville, is in the accepted list of those at Hastings. Lance flags or pennants appear in early equestrian seals, and certain groups of coats depicted in this way can be traced back to a time very close to the Conquest. Certainly, there is evidence of charges which became hereditary being used by different members of a family whose common ancestor lived in the eleventh century, traditionally thought of as a pre-heraldic period. For instance, variations of checky (see Glossary for this and other heraldic terms) were borne by descendants of Isabel de Vermandois by her marriages to

Seal showing the checky coat of the Warennes used by John (de Warenne), Earl of Surrey, 1318/19 (PRO E42/101).

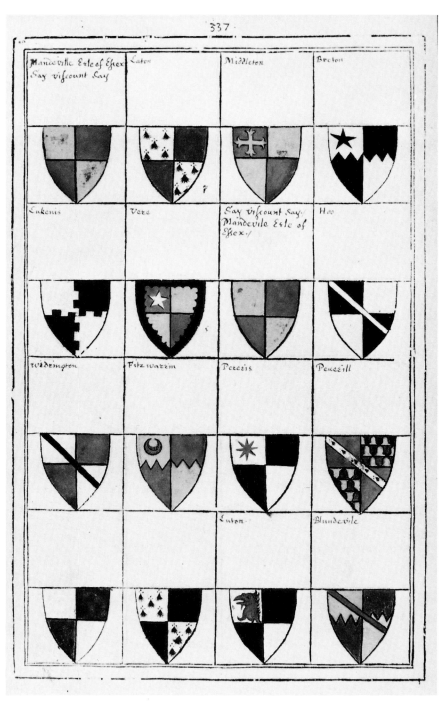

'Holles's Ordinary': shields of quarterly arms, many of families related to Geoffrey de Mandeville, Earl of Essex, on mid-seventeenth-century Ordinary of painted arms (Coll. Arms, EDN 31, p. 337).

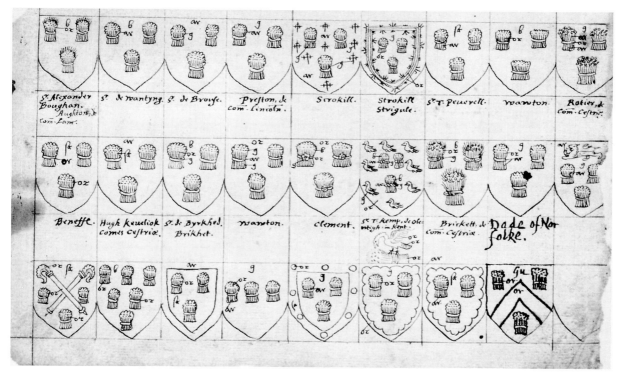

Shields of arms with garbs, including Earls of Chester and the Comyn family, from the Book of Sutes or Ordinaries, collected and finished in 1599 by William Smith (c.1550–1618), Rouge Dragon Pursuivant. Purchased by Edward, Duke of Norfolk, for the College in 1759 at the sale of John Warburton, Somerset Herald's library (Coll. Arms, Smith's Ordinary, EDN 22, fo. 43v).

both Robert de Beaumont, Earl of Leicester (died 1118), and William de Warenne, Earl of Surrey (died 1138), and this is the origin of the Warenne arms (still quartered by the Duke of Norfolk as Earl of Surrey). J. H. Round, in *Geoffrey de Mandeville* (1892), pointed out that Geoffrey de Mandeville, Earl of Essex killed in 1144 was the central figure in a group of families related to him, including FitzPiers, Lacy, Vere, Beauchamp of Bedford, Clavering, Say, and Sackville, who all bore a quarterly coat. The descendants of three of the four children of Count Hugh II of Clermont-en-Beauvaisis (died 1103) by his wife Marguerite de Ramerupe bore garbs (wheatsheafs): the three children were his son Reynold and his daughters Marguerite, wife of Gerard de Gerberoy, and Ermentrude, wife of Hugh d'Avranches, Earl of Chester, and garbs are associated with Cheshire to this day. The descendants of their sister Adèle, wife of Gilbert de Clare (died 1123), bore chevrons, as did her mother's family of Ramerupe. In the early thirteenth century, Gilbert de Clare's great-nephew, Robert Fitz-Walter, bore a *Fess between two Chevrons* in the same tinctures as Clare, and his brother-in-law Gilbert Pecche bore *Argent a Fess between two Chevrons Gules*, changing the field from Or to Argent.

The origins of these families' arms must be so close to the Norman Conquest that it would seem highly likely that the use of heraldic devices began with lance flags before being transferred to shields to become 'true heraldry'. After the Conquest, William rewarded his

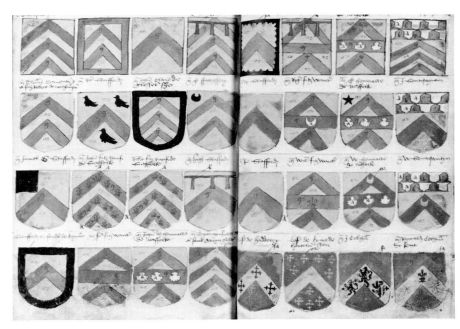

Banners and shields of arms with chevrons of Clare and related families, mid-sixteenth century (Coll. Arms, Flower's Ordinary, 2 G 9, fos. 155–6).

non-Norman allies, as well as his own Norman followers, with grants of land. The cadets in England of the Flemish families, and the devices used by them, must have influenced the development of heraldry in England and in Scotland, where some of them migrated. If the undoubted links of the ruling families of Flanders with Charlemagne had any heraldic connotations, the political decline of Flanders in the twelfth and thirteenth centuries and the misfortunes that overwhelmed its ruling houses, would have given their descendants in England an additional urge to preserve their heritage and promote their armorial devices.

Whatever its origins, it is clear that what had been, in the late eleventh century, the inheritance of a small group of interrelated families in north-west Europe, spread through the upper ranks of society in the twelfth century. This widespread adoption of colourful devices and symbols was one aspect of the twelfth-century renaissance, that 'great age of renewal after a long night of the mind', when 'the seed of a happy thought was carried far and quickly to take root and grow in other minds than his who first thought it', to quote Sir Anthony Wagner. Once symbols were transferred to the shield, they gave rise to what is uncontroversially accepted as heraldry, and this practice spread across Europe in a period of less than thirty years.

So much for theories; what of facts? The oldest documented example of arms on a shield in Europe is, uniquely, recorded both in written and pictorial form. A chronicler, Jean de Marmentier, tells us that when Henry I of England knighted his newly-wed son-in-law Geoffrey (Plantagenet), Count of Anjou, in 1127, he hung about his

Enamel portrait of Geoffrey, Count of Anjou (formerly over his tomb in Le Mans Cathedral), showing the arms bestowed on him by his father-in-law, King Henry I of England (Musée Tessé, Le Mans, France).

neck a shield painted with gold lions on an Azure ground. (The earliest seal showing an heraldic shield dates from 1136.) Geoffrey died in 1151, and was buried in the cathedral at Le Mans in Normandy. Preserved in the museum there, is an enamel portrait of him which used to hang above his tomb in the cathedral, which shows him holding the shield with lions. Furthermore, a blue shield with six golden lions appears on the tomb of his bastard grandson, William Longespee, Earl of Salisbury (died 1226), in Salisbury Cathedral, showing that the arms were treated as hereditary.

The earliest shields of arms were essentially simple. Many knights adopted unadorned stripes or crosses which, it has been suggested, may have had their origins in the bands of leather or metal which were used to strengthen wooden shields, and which offered an obvious surface for painting a simple pattern. For instance, it has been suggested that chevrons originated in battens on the shield which evolved into 'V's due to the pointed convex surface of the shield. Others adopted specific objects such as the crescents, suns, wheat-sheafs, lions, and eagles which, as we have seen, may have descended from the symbolism of Charlemagne's court via the Flemish *comtés*. Others chose punning or 'canting' arms. An important factor is the use of common charges by groups of families linked by blood or feudal tenure. There is evidence that the second tier of the feudal structure in Westmorland, for example, took arms which were variations on those of their overlord, the Vipont family of Appleby Castle. The Vipont arms comprised black annulets (or rings) on a gold ground, and variations of these are borne by those surviving West-morland families whose descent can be traced to the reign of Henry II, such as the Lowthers, Earls of Lonsdale, and the Musgraves, formerly of Hartley and Edenhall.

From its simple origins in the twelfth century heraldry developed in complexity and elaboration. By the thirteenth century it was acquiring

(*left*) Reverse of seal with the arms of Aymer (de Valence), Earl of Pembroke (1296–1323), showing *Barry (of fifteen) an orle of nine martlets*, a combination of bars perhaps derived from the wooden battens on the shield and martlets often associated with the Crusades (PRO E329/87).

(*right*) Seal of Gilbert Basset, his shield composed of *barry wavy of six*, an excellent example of the simple geometrical character of early medieval heraldry (PRO E42/36).

Seal dated 1275 of Edmund Plantagenet, Earl of Cornwall (d.1300), nephew of Henry III. An early use of the lion rampant (PRO E329/191).

the rules and terminology which are the basis of its present laws and language. As time passed, it became increasingly complex in its design with the introduction of a number of fabulous and chimerical creatures, and patterns which moved far away from the simple vigorous geometry of the early days. A later development, originating in Spain, was the incorporation of quarterings of other arms inherited via heraldic heiresses, creating ever more complex patterns. More will be said about this in the chapter on marshalling. Many shields of early sixteenth-century origin were very complicated, with chevrons and chiefs covered with different charges. Eventually, arms came to include pictorial scenes 'proper', sometimes referred to as 'landscape heraldry'. This can be seen in the arms of several of the generals, admirals, and governors who built up the British Empire in the eighteenth century. The arms of Lord Nelson, for instance, show the battle of the Nile on a chief, while those of the Lords Harris include a chief of augmentation showing the fortress of Seringapatam with the drawbridge let down and the Union flag of Great Britain hoisted over that of Tippoo Sahib, all proper, to commemorate the conquest of that Indian city in 1799. This sort of pictorial elaboration in heraldry, however, came to be seen as 'degenerate', and in the nineteenth century, as an aspect of the general Gothic Revival, there was a reaction against 'bad' heraldry and the reinstatement of medieval standards, with clear, vigorous arrangements of simple charges. And this taste for 'real' heraldry has continued to govern most of the design of arms in the twentieth century.

II

European Heraldry

N its early stages heraldry was remarkably uniform through-out Europe. Similar armorial bearings were adopted in the middle of the twelfth century in most western countries. The sudden and widespread emergence of heraldry is thought to have been associated with the Crusades and the rise of tournaments, which brought together knights from all over Latin Christendom, and emphasized the universality of western civilization. During the thirteenth century the science of heraldry crystallized into approximately the form we know today, with the same range of colours, metals, and furs, and the same rules for marshalling arms. The principle that arms were personal property and could not be used by another was generally accepted throughout most of Europe, though this was only enforced nationally, so that similar arms do appear in different countries. Gradually all the leading ruling houses came to have officers of arms or heralds, whose job it was to regulate heraldry and to record arms. It is thought that the heralds originated as roving minstrels who attached themselves to tournaments, and gradually acquired special knowledge of arms by this means. As a result they came to exercise supervision over arms, and were called upon to adjudicate in cases of dispute. In the fifteenth century in France and England, the heralds were formed into colleges with permanent headquarters and libraries. The establishment of officers of arms and heraldic records led to the rules of heraldry becoming formalized and regulated, to be handed down from generation to generation in the European kingdoms.

The science and system of heraldry developed as part of European rather than national culture, and was coterminous with Latin Christian civilization, but as time passed characteristics peculiar to individual countries or areas began to emerge. Thus in Germanic Europe—Germany, Austria, Switzerland, and Scandinavia—the use of the crest developed its own rules, leading to a proliferation in the number of crests. A single German coat of arms might display four or five crests on top. This contrasts with the practice further west. In Holland, England, and Scotland, for instance, except in rare circumstances, it is unusual to display more than a single crest above the shield, while in France the use of the crest above the shield died out entirely in the later Middle Ages. In eastern Europe, especially Poland, whole territorial areas or groups of families not related by blood adopted the same armorial bearings, a form of clan affiliation not met with further west.

Similarly, in the east there was a more restricted use of colours, with a marked preference for simple gold or silver charges on red or blue fields, whereas in France, England, and Scotland there was a preference for more elaborate arrangements of arms, with small charges peppering the whole of the shield, and the use of elaborate patterns of furs. The adoption of marks of difference also developed in different degrees in different parts of Europe. In the east the practice is almost unknown, whereas in *ancien régime* France, or in Scotland, differencing was developed with a high degree of elaboration.

In the later Middle Ages regional variations in heraldry tended to become more emphasized. With the growth of nationalism, the emergence of strong organized monarchies, and the gradual dissolution of universal medieval civilization, the heraldry of individual countries absorbed and developed its own local characteristics and practices, and emphasized individual aspects of the armorial achievement in different degrees. Thus, Scotland and France placed great emphasis on mottoes, often incorporating them above the crest on top of the shield, whereas in Germany mottoes were used sparingly. England came to make more of supporters (the figures or animals who support the shield bearing the arms) than any other European country, all peers, the knights of certain orders, and important corporations being entitled to them as an integral part of their arms. Italy evolved its own form of crest wreath, which is thinner than that used elsewhere. In Flanders (now Belgium) there emerged the practice of suspending the shield by a strap from the helmet. Similar distinct national variations can be found throughout Europe, leading to particular heraldic characteristics in different regions.

German, or Teutonic, heraldry extended its sphere of influence from Austria and Switzerland in the south to Scandinavia in the north. The Germans, as might be expected, were more thorough in the marshalling of arms than any other European nation. The most striking characteristic of German heraldry, however, is the design and treatment of crests. These often reflect the shield by repeating the charges and tinctures in a manner virtually unknown in English heraldry. Many of the ancient nobility (*uradel*) whose arms, dating from the thirteenth century, comprise simple designs of a bend or fess on the shield, repeat the same on their crest. For instance, there are two bars on both the arms and the crest of the Kreys family of Ratisbon. Sometimes the charges on the shield are repeated in the crest. The Monnich family of Basle, whose arms depict a demi-monk, likewise incorporate a demi-monk in the crest. When several arms were marshalled on the same shield each corresponding crest was placed on a helmet on top, leading to the typically German arrangement of rows of different crests above the shield. This was copied in new grants of

German heraldry: early fifteenth-century 'Povey's Roll', executed by a German artist illustrating Bohemian arms with simple bold charges often repeated in the crest (Coll. Arms, Povey's Roll, B 23, fos. 47v–48).

arms. Those of the Prussian field marshal, Von Blücher, granted in 1814, have four crests of which only one is the Blücher family crest of cross keys; the others are augmentations of honour, namely, the Prussian eagle, a crossed marshal's baton and sword in a wreath, and the Iron Cross. Prince Albert's Garter stall plate at Windsor illustrates German multiple crests.

Other characteristics of Teutonic heraldry are by-products of the loose political organization of the Holy Roman Empire with its comparatively weak central monarchy and powerful local authorities. Many of the towns, for instance, were semi-independent, especially the free imperial cities. Thus, from early times civic arms came to be a prominent aspect of German heraldry. Like personal heraldry, the origins of civic heraldry are not entirely clear, and have been the subject of much controversy. One view is that town arms developed from the civic seals of the twelfth and thirteenth centuries. The contrary view is that civic coats of arms developed independently of

(top left) German heraldry: engraving of the Garter stall plate of Prince Albert (the Prince Consort), with crests dexter to sinister for Marck, Thuringia, Saxony, Meissen, Julich, and Berg (Coll. Arms, Garter Stall Plates [1801–44], fo. 85).

(top right) German heraldry: a manuscript given to the College by Sir William Dugdale, Norroy, on 2 June 1676, illustrating the arms of the seven original Electors of the Holy Roman Empire, namely the King of Bohemia, the Prince Palatine of the Rhine, the Duke of Saxony, Marquess of Brandenburg, and the Archbishop of Mainz, Cologne, and Trier (Coll. Arms, L 14, pt. I, fo. 1).

(bottom right) German heraldry: volume of German and Venetian nobility executed in 1580, depicting the arms of the Duke of Saxony (Coll. Arms, Vincent 171, fo. 16).

seals, with which they have nothing in common. What is clear is that civic arms, like personal arms, were originally self-assumed but came to be granted and controlled by the Holy Roman Emperor or his delegates. It became the rule that when a village was raised to the status of a borough, or on the founding of a new town, it was granted a coat of arms.

Over the greater part of the territory that was once the Holy Roman Empire the arms of towns bear remarkable similarities, making use of fortifications, gateways, ramparts, towers, and so forth as charges. Another common feature of German civic arms is the augmentation of an escutcheon of the arms of the town's overlord. Thus, Wittenberg

German civic heraldry, showing the common use of fortifications as charges. The five-volume collection of Hector Le Breton, King of Arms of France, was given to the College of Arms by George Holman of Warkworth in 1686 (Coll. Arms, Hector Le Breton, Armes de Princes de l'Europe, shields nos. 375–80).

has an escutcheon of the arms of the Dukes of Saxony, and many Austrian towns have an escutcheon with the Habsburg arms of a silver fess on a red ground (*Gules a Fess Argent*). The free Imperial cities emphasized their status by displaying the imperial eagle, as in the cases of Aachen, Vienna, and Krems. Most German civic arms do not use helms, crests or supporters, but the placing of a mural crown on top of the shield is standard practice. Another peculiarity of German heraldry is the use of twin arms side by side. There was no restriction to a single shield, and twinned arms were considered to be perfectly acceptable. In civic arms this practice is represented in the arms of such cities as Fulda, Essen, and Nuremberg which have two shields couché side-by-side.

A further aspect of the strength of the towns *vis-à-vis* the monarchy was the emergence of burgher arms in emulation of noble arms, but separate from them, and not recognized as bestowing nobiliary status. Prominent citizens were able with impunity to assume armorial ensigns similar to those sported by the feudal nobility in states where the emperor's authority was distant and weak. These burgher arms came to be treated as a different species, and were differenced from noble arms by the use of a closed tilting helmet to support the crest. Noble arms, by contrast, sported open helmets with bars. Burgher arms spread to Scandinavia, where they were freely assumed by merchants in the trading cities of the Baltic (many of whom were of German descent), but they failed to become hereditary there, unlike noble arms.

Burgher arms were also a feature of the heraldry of the Low Countries in the later Middle Ages. The rich towns and cities of Flanders were the most advanced commercial and industrial centres of Europe, and enjoyed considerable independence from their distant overlords, the Dukes of Burgundy. In present-day Belgium arms of burgher descent are differenced from noble arms by the absence of helmets. Noble arms are further distinguished by gold medallions on chains. In Holland only noble arms, amounting to approximately those of four hundred families, together with civic arms, are recognized by the Hoge Raad van Adel (the High Council of Nobility), and protected by law. Burgher arms are self-assumed and uncontrolled. Nevertheless, Dutch heraldry is noted for its pleasant simplicity, many shields having a single charge only. In general, unlike German heraldry, one shield, one helmet, and one crest is the norm in Holland. The practice of marshalling arms in the form of quartering is rare, and mottoes are not normally used. In Belgium, on the other hand, there is considerable later German influence as the country was ruled by the emperor in the eighteenth century, and on the establishment of an independent kingdom in the nineteenth century the royal family was

German. Until the First World War the royal arms *Sable a Lion rampant Or* (derived from the arms of the former Duchy of Brabant) were charged with an escutcheon of Saxony: *Barry of ten Or and Sable a Crancelin in bend Vert* (familiar to English eyes from the arms of Albert, the Prince Consort).

In France the choice of charges and their arrangement bears a close similarity to British heraldry, though it is perhaps not fanciful to see in French heraldry in general a certain Gallic elegance. The major difference between the two countries is the absence of crests in France. From the sixteenth century onwards, French families tended to place coronets of rank only on top of the helmet, and in the eighteenth century the helmet, too, disappeared from general usage, the coronet being placed directly on top of the shield. Supporters are also comparatively rare in French heraldry. For example, though the king used different supporters at different times, the Royal Arms were as often depicted without. A pair of angels was the best-known of the royal supporters; these were sometimes shown wearing dalmatics charged with fleurs-de-lis, and sometimes not. The most common depiction of the Royal Arms was just the shield of fleurs-de-lis (originally semy all over, but reduced to three in the second half of the fourteenth century by Charles V) and the crown, encircled by the collars of the two French Orders of Chivalry, St Michael and St Esprit. A good surviving example of the French Royal Arms with the angel supporters is the carving on the pediment of the French church of St Luigi dei Francesi in Rome.

Supporters and crests were as rare in French civic heraldry as in royal and noble arms, though the mural crown was frequently used. French civic arms are distinguished by the incorporation of chiefs of the arms of their former overlords. Thus, Dijon has a chief of the arms of the Dukes of Burgundy, Nancy those of the Dukes of Lorraine, and many towns, including Paris, the royal fleur-de-lis. Mottoes were very popular in France, and a coat of arms often sported two; one above the shield and one below. This is true of the Royal Arms which displayed the ancient French war-cry *Montjoie St Denis* above the shield and the biblical Latin tag below, *Lilia Non Laborant Neque Nent*.

An interesting, if exotic, offshoot of French heraldry occurred in the early nineteenth century in Haiti, where Henry Christophe, an illegitimate black slave, proclaimed himself king in 1811, and set up a full-scale court on the royal French model with a titled nobility and French-style heraldry. King Henry of Haiti instituted the Royal and Military Order of St Henry, and established a King of Arms and thirteen heralds. The carefully graded nobility took their names from places on the island, leading to some delightful and improbable titles including a Count of Lemonade and a Duke of Marmalade. The Royal

Arms of Haiti depicted a phoenix, symbolizing the King's resurrection from the chains of slavery. Unfortunately this fascinating and original heraldic experiment enjoyed only a brief existence. King Henry shot himself on 8 October 1820. But the arms of the short-lived Court of Haiti are recorded in all their francophile elegance in a manuscript preserved in the library of the College of Arms in London.

From the seventeenth century up to 1789 the control of arms in France was hereditary in the d'Hozier family as *Juges d'Armes*. The Revolution saw the abolition of French heraldry, as of the monarchy and nobility. Fifteen years later, however, a new imperial heraldry was instituted on lines carefully laid down and precisely regulated by Napoleon. The arms of the nobles and of towns were organized into several degrees, all with appropriate charges and differences. Civic heraldry was divided into three classes of 'good towns', each category

(*right*) French heraldry: *Armorial général de l'Empire Français*, pl. 5 (1812), showing Napoleonic augmentations for noble ecclesiastical and civic heraldry.

(*below*) Armorial general of the Kingdom of Haiti compiled for Henry Christophe, an illiterate black slave who proclaimed himself King of Haiti in Mar. 1811. He instituted the Royal and Military Order of St Henry, the collar of which surrounds his arms (Coll. Arms, JP 177, fo. 1).

5

sporting its own appropriate canton or chief of Napoleonic symbols,
'N's, eagles, bees, and the imperial crown. After the Restoration in
1814, most towns reverted to their ancient arms, but Fontainebleau
has kept in use the Napoleonic arms of a 'good town' of the second
class, with an 'N' in a canton. Napoleonic noble arms were similarly
graded. Their charges reflected Napoleon's military campaigns, with
weapons and 'items of warmongery'. Crests, supporters, helmets,
and mottoes were all excluded, but a system of plumed hats or toques
on top of the shield was adopted to indicate noble rank, together with
various carefully graded augmentations to the shield itself. The arms
of a *Chevalier d'Empire*, for instance, contained a red *pièce honorable* (a
fess, bend, chevron, and so on) charged with a simplified design of the
Légion d'Honneur. Knights not of the *Légion d'Honneur* placed an
annulet argent on the ordinary. Barons bore a red sinister canton and a
toque with three plumes of ostrich feathers and a counter-vair edge;
counts, a blue dexter canton, five ostrich plumes and a counter-ermine
edge to the toque; dukes a red chief semy of silver stars, seven ostrich
plumes, and a toque edged with ermine. Princes of the Napoleonic
empire bore a chief semy of bees and a toque with seven ostrich
plumes and an edge of vair. Thus, specific charges and arrangements
of design were laid down in 1804 for the several grades of nobility,
officials, and civic heraldry throughout the Empire. The Napoleonic
system, in turn, was largely abolished on the fall of the Empire ten
years later. Today there is no formal control of arms in France, but the
nobility use their pre-revolutionary arms in the same way that they
use their titles, despite the lack of official recognition by the Republic.
Civic heraldry continues in general use, and has been augmented in
this century. An innovation of the last hundred years is the addition to
the shield of some kind of military decoration to demonstrate bravery
under enemy fire.

Iberian heraldry, as is to be expected, has many strange characteristics of its own. The Spaniard and the Portuguese glories in the
antiquity of his pedigree and considers his to be a very superior kind of
nobility. There is a vast amount of Spanish writing on genealogy and
heraldry, partly because this was a branch of learning which did not
attract the hostile interest of the Inquisition. (The arms of the Spanish
Inquisition, by the way, are *Sable a Cross Vert dexter an Olive Branch
sinister a Sword* with the Motto Esurge Domine et judica causam
tuam.) In Spain, scarcely a family of eminence has sprung from any
origin connected with law, commerce, or the Church, those 'copious
fountains' of the aristocracies of England, of Venice, and of Rome.
The Spanish nobility is based almost entirely on military service. The
great families of Spain fought their way to their rank; their 'coronets
were gained by the sword only'. They are divided into two classes, the

Grandees and the nobility of Castile. The latter were originally life peerages, unless otherwise specified. In the eighteenth century under the Bourbon monarchs they were usually rendered hereditary by their patent of creation, but were greatly multiplied and further devalued in that way. The number of Grandees, on the other hand, tended to contract by intermarriage, with the result that they became very inbred. A young bodyguard at the Royal Palace in Madrid in the late eighteenth century asked whom he should salute, and received the reply 'My friend, the safe rule is to suppose everybody in the Palace who looks like a monkey to be Grandees of the first class.'

The descent of Spanish arms and Spanish titles differs from much of northern Europe, in that there is general inheritance through females, and unlike England, France, and Germany with their strict rules, illegitimacy is no bar to the correct descent of arms or titles. In the words of Richard Ford, 'Gluttony and drunkenness are the besetting sins of the people of the cold chaste North; more violent passions those of the burning temperate South', and there is suitable heraldic allowance for the results. In general it was considered that a family pedigree could be more damaged by misalliance than by illegitimacy, and the patents of nobility of many Spanish families contain remainders to illegitimate branches in default of legitimate heirs. The Dukedom of Medina-Sidonia, for instance, under a patent of Henry IV of 1460, can be inherited by illegitimate descendants. Illegitimacy in Spain was divided into three branches. The first class of illegitimates were 'Natural Children', those born of single or widowed parents who could be legitimized by the subsequent marriage of their parents or just by declaration of their father that they were his heirs. Olivares, for example, recognized his natural son as his heir. The second class of illegitimates, known as 'the Spurious', were those whose parents for whatever reason were not in a position to marry. These bastards had to be legitimized by a petition of royal ratification. The third class, called 'the Incestuous', were the offspring of those who were either too closely related in consanguinity or who were bound by religious vows. They required a papal dispensation to inherit their parents' property or arms. But these were granted in so wholesale a fashion that every Spanish diocese had a stock of signed blanks ready to fill in the appropriate names where necessary.

The charges depicted on Spanish armorial bearings have several peculiarities. Many record particular historical events or deeds of war. The arms of Columbus, for instance, incorporate anchors and islands in the ocean commemorating his discovery of America. The miraculous cross which appeared to the Spanish army at the battle of Las Navas de Tolosa in 1212 embellishes the arms of thirty-two families. The Gusmans have a snake on their arms because Gusman el Bueno killed a snake in Africa. Spanish titles are often equally literal. The Pizarros were created Marques de la Conquista. The admiral who brought Charles III across the sea from Naples to Barcelona was created the Marques del Real Transporte (Royal Transport), and Godoy was made Prince of *The* Peace (after the Treaty of Basle).

Some of the legends associated with Spanish arms need to be treated with a certain degree of caution. To take two examples from the quarterings of the royal achievement: the arms of Aragon, which comprise four red stripes palewise on a gold ground, are said to record the legend of Geoffrey de Vela, an ancestor of the Counts of Barcelona, upon whose shield the Emperor is supposed to have drawn four lines with his fingers dipped in blood. This is almost certainly a fanciful posthumous explanation, and there is equally no particular reason to believe an alternative story that it was a king of Aragon who marked his own shield in this way before the battle of Las Navas de Tolosa in 1212. The same is true, alas, of the chains of Navarre (which appear in the arms of twelve Spanish families as well as on the royal arms). According to legend, these represent the chains which hang above the tomb of Sancho VII of Navarre at Roncesvalles, and which he broke through at the same battle of Las Navas de Tolosa where they surrounded the tent of the Moorish captain. It seems equally likely, however, that the chains of Navarre are a canting coat, a chain being called in Navarre '*una varra*' or in the local patois '*na varra*'. The argument in favour of a canting coat is weakened by the fact that the early Kings of Navarre used an eagle on their seals, and Sancho VII who is said to have adopted the coat used an escarbuncle on a heraldic seal; his nephew and successor Theobald I (1234–53) added the chains between the limbs of the escarbuncle to produce the distinctive coat.

Spanish and Portuguese heraldry is characterized by the widespread use of orles and bordures round the edge of the shield. This custom originated as a form of marshalling the arms of a man's wife; in early times it was the custom for the husband to surround his own arms with a bordure charged with single heraldic devices taken from the arms of his wife or with her complete arms arranged as a series of seven or eight little shields. This manner of perpetuating female arms in an hereditary coat is almost unique in European heraldry, occurring only in occasional cases of compounded arms in France and Britain. Later grants of arms often included a similar bordure as part of the original design. The same practice is also encountered in civic arms, many towns having bordures to their arms displaying the castles and lions of the Royal Arms. Madrid has a bordure with seven stars, and the national arms of Portugal have a bordure with seven towers.

As well as bordures, Spain and Portugal also marshal arms in the more conventional way by quartering. Indeed this practice began in

Spain, and spread from there to the rest of Europe apart from Poland. The practice was introduced to England by Eleanor of Castile, wife of Edward I, as is demonstrated on her tomb at Westminster Abbey. Highly complicated schemes of quartering have evolved in Spain and Portugal over the centuries, for it is held there that a woman may transmit the arms of her family whether or not she is an heraldic heiress in the sense accepted in the heraldry of Britain and other countries.

Another peculiarity of Spanish heraldry is the introduction of words and letters on the shield itself, a practice which would be deemed 'incorrect' in northern Europe. Very often these comprise the opening line of the 'Hail Mary', as in the case of the arms of the Mendoza and Garciliasso de Vega families, both of which bear the

Spanish noble heraldry: the Mendoza arms exhibit the Spanish foible for incorporating the opening line of the 'Ave Maria' (Coll. Arms, Hector Le Breton, La Noble Ordre de la Toison d'Or, fo. 71).

words *Ave Maria Gratiae Plena*. This is a manifestation of the Iberian devotion to Our Lady, as is the frequent use of the crescent as a symbol of the Immaculate Conception, and the display of her arms on all cathedrals, namely a branch of lilies issuing from a vase with two handles (symbolic of the Incarnation of Christ born of a virgin).

The Royal Arms of Spain are among the most interesting in Europe, and form a potted history of the country. They are still displayed on all public buildings as a matter of course. Over the centuries they have undergone many changes. In the earliest shields the lion of Leon and the castle of Castile were quartered without supporters. After the union of the crowns of Aragon and Castile by Ferdinand and Isabella in the late fifteenth century, the shield was further divided. The first and fourth quarters were given to the arms of Castile and Leon, the second and third to Aragon and Sicily. Navarre and Jerusalem were introduced subsequently. At the bottom tip of the shield the pomegranate of Granada was squeezed in to commemorate the final defeat of the Moors. The shield was supported by a single supporter behind it, the eagle of St John, the patron of the Catholic Kings (*San Juan de los Reyes*). Under the emperor Charles V, further quarterings were introduced as part of his vast inheritance— Austria, Burgundy, Brabant and Flanders. The columns of Hercules were added on either side as additional supporters or badges, and the single-headed eagle gave way to the double-headed eagle of the Holy Roman Empire. This was discontinued by Philip II, who reverted to the eagle of St John and reduced the quarterings. The Bourbon monarchs, from Philip V onwards, added the three fleurs-de-lis of France as an escutcheon of pretence. Today the arms of the kingdom of Spain are usually depicted supported by the eagle of St John and the pillars of Hercules, with a crown and the motto *Una Grande Libre* over the shield, and the flanking badges of the yoke of Ferdinand and the bundle of arrows of Queen Isabella beneath the shield. The shield itself is quartered into: I and IV quarterly 1 and 4 Castile, 2 and 3 Leon; II and III per pale 1 Aragon, 2 Navarre, with the pomegranate of Granada in the triangle at the point of the shield.

Compared to the complexity of Spanish heraldry, that of Italy is a model of simplicity. For centuries the country was split into dozens of states, and had no overall heraldic authority to supervise the use of arms until after the unification of the kingdom in 1870. As a result, the country escaped the over-elaboration caused by too much supervision and differentiation (seen at its worst in English nineteenth-century civic heraldry). Many Italian arms retain a medieval simplicity, often just comprising a simple cross on a plain field or the division of the shield per fess or per pale into two colours, and as a result there is a good deal of duplication of arms. The troubled history of Italy is also

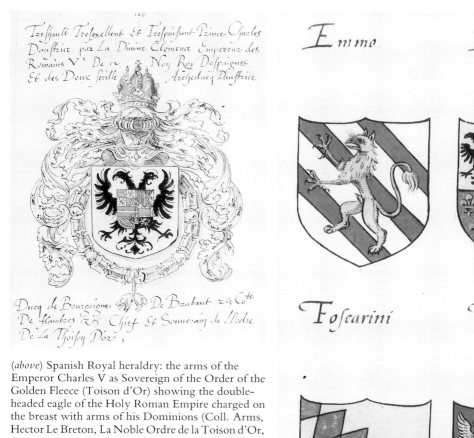

(*above*) Spanish Royal heraldry: the arms of the Emperor Charles V as Sovereign of the Order of the Golden Fleece (Toison d'Or) showing the double-headed eagle of the Holy Roman Empire charged on the breast with arms of his Dominions (Coll. Arms, Hector Le Breton, La Noble Ordre de la Toison d'Or, fo. 63).

(*right*) Italian heraldry: the arms of the Roman family of Este allude to their political allegiances, France and the Holy Roman Emperor, while the ombrellino and crossed keys indicate that they produced a Pope. The arms of the Venetian family of Foscari incorporate the Lion of St Mark (Coll. Arms, Vincent 171, p. 65).

reflected in its heraldry in the influence of waves of invaders, German, French, Spanish, and Austrians, all of whom have left their mark. The chief on the top half of the shield often represents a political allegiance, the most frequent being the lilies of France with a label for the House of Anjou, the eagle of the Holy Roman Empire, or the cross keys and triple tiara of the Pope. Those Italian families who have produced a pope are also entitled to display a gold *ombrellino* with their arms. Some arms combine several allegiances. The arms of Prince Odescalchi, the head of a great Roman family, for instance, have an imperial eagle in the fess and a gold *ombrellino* over the shield.

In spite of foreign intervention and influence, Italian heraldry has evolved several characteristics of its own, some of which parallel developments in Italian Renaissance art. It differs from the more stylized heraldry of the Gothic north in displaying charges of a more naturalistic or classical nature, reflecting the classical and naturalistic qualities of painting and sculpture. The most distinctive characteristic of Italian heraldry is the use of almond-shaped or horse-head-shaped shields. The latter derives from the armour worn on the foreheads of horses at tournaments and resemble the shape of a horse's head as seen from the front. As in French and Spanish heraldry, crests are rare, but thin crest wreaths are borne with coronets of rank on top of the helmet, a combination not found in the heraldry of other countries. The arms of dukes and princes are placed on a *manteau* of 'purple' (actually red), fringed with gold and lined with ermine. The *manteau* is a feature of princely and royal arms to be found throughout Europe except Britain. It has been suggested that the *manteau*, a sort of heraldic tent, had its origins in the seals of princes in the fourteenth and fifteenth centuries, in which purely ornamental carpets are spread out behind the armorial bearings, sometimes held by small figures. A more likely explanation, however, is that the *manteau* is an heraldic depiction of the 'cloth of estate' or drapery baldachino suspended over the throne or chair of state of a great magnate. They became regular accessories of princely arms throughout continental Europe in the seventeenth century. In its most pompous form the *manteau* becomes a 'pavilion', and is reserved for the arms of sovereigns only.

Heraldry in central Italy is inextricably intermingled with that of the church, the Pope for centuries having been the ruling sovereign of the papal states as well as head of the church. The papal arms themselves, with the crossed keys of St Peter, the triple tiara, and the rare combination of two metals, gold and silver, are perhaps the most widely familiar example of Italian heraldry. The great Roman princely families derive their titles and arms from the papal monarchy, and in the more exalted cases impale, or display on a fess, the papal insignia. The Vatican has continued to grant occasional titles and arms to laymen since 1870, but today its heraldic authority is largely restricted to regulating ecclesiastic heraldry throughout the Catholic world. All the major churches of Rome, and several of the princely palaces, still display painted shields of the arms of the reigning Pope, just as they did before 1870. The casual tourist sipping coffee in the Piazza Navona, for instance, will note that the façade of Borromini's Church of St Agnes in Agone bears shields of the arms of the Doria Pamphili family (who own it) and of Pope John Paul II.

The strictly ecclesiastical aspects of Roman heraldry were revised by Pope Paul VI in 1969. He abolished the use of mitres and croziers in episcopal arms, and substituted a graded system of ecclesiastical hats ranging from red hats with fifteen tassels on either side for cardinals to a black hat with two tassels for a simple priest. Croziers continue to be included behind the shield in the arms of abbots, while archbishops, patriarchs, and bishops place a cross of their rank behind the shield of their arms. Tasselled hats have long been used in ecclesiastical heraldry, but for centuries the number of tassels on each side was not considered to be important. It was only in 1832 that the number of tassels for cardinals was definitely fixed at fifteen on each side. Pope Paul VI's new regulations carried the system to its logical conclusion by proclaiming exact rules for all grades of cleric. (The use of mitres and crossed croziers on the medieval model, of course, continues in English heraldry for archbishops and bishops of the Church of England.)

The personal arms of Pope John Paul II designed in 1978 by Archbishop Bruno Heim have an ugly off-centre gold cross on a blue ground and the letter M for Mary; they owe more to the traditions of Polish than of Roman heraldry. The heraldry of Poland is unique in Europe because of the pre-heraldic runic signs, thought to be ancient clan property marks, which were absorbed into its heraldry, and adapted to form charges. Some remained strictly geometrical charges of curved or straight lines, while others evolved into more conventional charges such as crosses, lances, scythes, horseshoes, and crescents. As well as being different in design, Polish heraldry is different in usage from that of western Europe, due to the fact that Poland did not develop a fully fledged feudal system. Its aristocracy was organized into clans, which varied in size and importance; some contained hundreds of different families not related by blood. Polish heraldry, as a result, has tribal characteristics not found elsewhere. As a general rule, one clan had the same coat of arms for all its members. This clan system disintegrated in the sixteenth century, and different clans broke up into several family groupings, but all of them retained the original clan arms without brizures or cadency marks. Nearly six hundred unrelated Polish families, for example, are known to bear the same arms of a horseshoe enclosing a cross. This is a situation unlike any other in western Europe. Indeed, it has been computed that of one thousand two hundred and thirty-eight coats of arms used by the Polish nobility, only seven hundred and forty-nine are individual ones belonging to one family. The other four hundred and eighty-nine serve twenty-two thousand families! A second peculiarity of Polish heraldry is that each coat of arms had its own name, usually the ancient rallying cry or name of the clan. As a result the need for blazoning did not exist in Poland.

There is very little foreign influence in Polish heraldry. Quarterings, partition lines, and fantastic beasts are rarely found. Hungarian heraldry, though like Polish heraldry in that it never uses quarterings, is by contrast much more closely affected by Austrian and German heraldry. But it, too, has particular national characteristics dictated by the history of the country. One of these is a preference for charges relating to the Turkish wars which lasted from the fifteenth to the eighteenth centuries. Many of those ennobled and granted arms in this period were the fighting soldiers. Sometimes a whole garrison was ennobled at one time, and granted a single coat of arms. An extreme case is the collective grant of armorial bearings by Prince Stephen Borskai to 9,254 mercenaries in 1605. It has been calculated that fifteen per cent of all Hungarian armorial bearings incorporate a gory decapitated Turk's head, usually with moustaches and a turban. Sabres, swords, and lances brandished by arms in armour were also popular, and commemorated the warlike achievements of the Hungarian soldiers. The frequent use of lions, bears, and griffins, on the other hand, is supposed to have derived from the ancient tribal insignia of the Magyar nobility.

Further individuality is given to Hungarian heraldry by its extravagant, even eccentric, complexity of design. The arms of Hajduboszormeny, for instance, are charged with a firing gun with a friendly sun above and a bonfire of burning logs below, the whole encircled by a dragon holding a patriarchal cross. The arms of the town of Debrecen show a paschal lamb carrying a cross and pennant, its feet placed on a pair of open books, and a palm tree in the background. The most common colour for Hungarian shields is blue, and the charge has to stand on firm ground, which is why ninety per cent of Hungarian arms have little green hills at the base of the shield.

Russian heraldry developed late, and evolved under external rather than internal forces. It should be seen as an outwork of German and French heraldry rather than an indigenous creation of its own. There was no medieval heraldry in Russia, and the simple divisons and charges of that period are absent. The earliest Russian heraldry is found in the west of the country, where the nobility started to adopt arms of the Polish type in the sixteenth century. The widespread adoption of civic and noble heraldry in the country as a whole did not occur until the early eighteenth century, and was a manifestation of Peter the Great's westernizing policy. Peter established an heraldic office under a Master of Heraldry at St Petersburg in 1722 and imposed western-style arms on the nobles, either by adapting their traditional symbols and devices or by completely new grants. New nobles were granted arms as part of their ennoblement, and three hundred and fifty-five grants of arms to new titled families were made in the course of the eighteenth century. As well as the shield, Russian arms comprised crests on western-style helmets worn affronte for old nobles and in profile with a raised vizor by new ones. Supporters were optional, and used indiscriminately by titled and untitled nobility alike. The Nabokovs, for example, used lion supporters though they were untitled, while many titled families did not have supporters at all. Peter the Great's heraldic policy was extended likewise to civic heraldry. The arms of Moscow were derived from a late medieval seal showing a mounted horseman. To this was added a dragon, and in 1730 the horseman was defined as St George, and the design formally designated as the city's arms. St Petersburg, as a new town, received a completely new grant. It comprised a pair of crossed anchors with a gold sceptre alluding to the new city's role as a great seaport and the seat of the imperial government.

In the early nineteenth century, under Napoleonic influence, the Russian heraldic system was reorganized on much more hierarchical lines, with appropriate insignia decreed for different grades. Already in 1797, by order of Tsar Paul I, the huge noble class had been ranked and regimented into six grades: the Old Aristocracy (noble before 1686), the Titled Nobility, Naturalized Foreign Nobility, Noblesse de cap (civil servants of high rank), Noblesse d'épée (army officers of the rank of colonel upwards), and Untitled Nobility, each with their own appropriate arms. Most Russian arms dated from the nineteenth century, and later in the century there was some attempt at Russification of heraldry. Muscovite pointed helmets were substituted for European medieval helmets. The only really distinctive feature of Russian heraldry, however, was that heraldic animals faced in the opposite direction to the rest of Europe, sinister rather than dexter, although there was some attempt to bring things more closely into line with western usage. St George and his horse in the arms of Moscow, for instance, were reversed to dexter in 1856. The Russian Imperial arms themselves were unusual, as they comprised a double-headed eagle, deriving from Byzantium, studded with individual shields of cities and provinces. The 'Small Arms' of Imperial Russia, as revised in 1857, comprised a double-headed eagle with the arms of Moscow in the centre surrounded by the Collar of the Order of St Andrew; the arms of Kazan, Poland, Taurida, and Kiev, with Novgorod and Vladimir, were displayed on the dexter wing; the arms of Astrakhan, Siberia, Georgia, and Finland on the sinister wing. All Russian heraldry, even civic heraldry, was abolished in 1917, though Stalin thought of reviving it in the 1930s. A sign of renewed interest in heraldry in Russia was the publication in Moscow of a book on Russian civic heraldry by N. N. Speranzov in 1974; this is the first Soviet work on heraldry, and in it reference is made to 'new coats of arms being worked out for Soviet cities'.

(*right*) Banner engraved in 1867 depicting the 'small arms' of Alexander II, Tsar of Russia, a double-headed eagle with a central shield showing the arms of Moscow, and on the wings smaller shields of different provinces of the Russian Empire (Coll. Arms, Young Collection, vol. 922).

III

Grantees of English Arms

I N C O U N T R I E S under the jurisdiction of the Earl Marshal of England a right to arms is acquired almost exclusively either by proving descent in an unbroken male line from someone registered as so entitled or by a new grant from the Kings of Arms. Technically it is also possible to acquire a right to arms by Act of Parliament, by grant of the Sovereign, by prescription, meaning use from time immemorial; and rights can be acquired by office and marriage. An example of arms by grant of the Sovereign is the grant by Royal Charter of 26 August 1790 to the Royal Society of Musicians of Great Britain. The arms granted are not registered at the College of Arms, and despite the contravention of one of the basic rules of armory by placing a colour on a colour the arms would seem to be valid. They are blazoned *Azure on a Cross Gules the Imperial Crown of England—the first quarter charged with a Syrinx Or—the second quarter charged with the Royal Harp of King David proper—the third quarter charged with the Pythagorean System—the fourth quarter charged with the Aretine Scale of Music proper.*

In Northern Ireland the English Kings of Arms have continued the practice of Ulster King of Arms, in that they will confirm arms to British subjects whose paternal ancestors were domiciled in Ireland and continued so domiciled at least down to the birth of the grand-father of an applicant, and whose use of arms can be proved prior to the year 1820. This was stated in a letter from Garter King of Arms to the Chief Herald of Eire in 1945 and entered in the Chapter Minutes of the College of Arms in 1959 (C.B. 26,36). The position whereby a right to arms, other than of office or by marriage, is acquired, namely, with the rare exceptions noted above, either by proof of descent or by new grant from the Kings of Arms, is the result of the evolution of the Law of Arms, a branch of English law interpreted by civil lawyers in the Court of Chivalry. Sir Edward Coke in his *Commentary upon Littleton* (1628) wrote that 'gentry and armes is of the nature of gavelkinde, for they descend to all the sonnes'. Arms in England, therefore, belong to families passing down all male lines, and not to the senior male heir alone. This contrasts with the position in Scotland, where junior male members of a family must matriculate a variation of the arms, which then passes to their heir male. Although the property of particular families arms do not belong to surnames, as is sometimes imagined. Before the incorporation of the College of

Arms examples of different devolution of arms can be found, for instance in the 1404 confirmation of lands at Haywode in Stratfeldsay, Hampshire with the arms which belong to the lands by Walter Haywode to John Fromond. But such an example of arms appertaining to a particular estate is very rare.

Arms were originally largely self-assumed, although celebrated early examples of formal grants exist, such as that already described of the knighting in 1127 by Henry I of his son-in-law Geoffrey Plantagenet, when he hung around his neck a shield painted with gold lions. This is borne out by the medieval cases in the Court of Chivalry, of which the best known is that of *Scrope* v. *Grosvenor*, which lasted from 1385 till 1390. Questions as to the authority on which they bore arms were not produced. Both sides were attempting to establish that they had borne arms from time immemorial, which in the Court of Chivalry was deemed to date from 1066 (before arms were used) rather than 1189, from whence it was deemed to date for the purposes of the Common Law. In the early fifteenth century the Crown moved against self-assumed arms that did not date from time immemorial, and in writs of 1417 to the Sheriffs of Hampshire, Wiltshire, Sussex, and Dorset, Henry V ordered them to proclaim that no one should use arms on the forthcoming expedition to France unless entitled to them in right of his ancestors or by a grant from a competent authority. The writ commences by admitting that divers men had assumed unto themselves arms on previous expeditions, and forbade the use of arms except by right of ancestors or valid grant, and also '*exceptis illis qui nobiscum apud bellum de Agincourt arma portabant*' a clause that has been variously interpreted, but which might perhaps be most reasonably considered to mean that those who self-assumed arms at Agincourt might keep them.

The earliest pictorial and occasionally blazoned records of arms are the rolls of arms, a chronology of which commences with the shields used to illustrate the works of the thirteenth-century monk and historian Matthew Paris. Of these the first is probably the sheet of arms in the *Liber Additamentorum* (BM MS Cott. Nero D1) painted in or before 1244. Rolls might be general or local in content, were often books rather than rolls, and might be occasional or in the form of an Ordinary. Occasional rolls relate to those present on a particular occasion, such as at the battle of Falkirk in 1298, and Ordinaries are collections of arms, crests, supporters, or badges arranged according to design. The definition of documents as rolls of arms ceases in the early sixteenth century with the commencement in 1530 of the county surveys known as the Heralds' Visitations, initiated by commissions from the Sovereign to the Kings of Arms. These record many medieval arms as well as new grants, although the present system, whereby the complete text of every new grant is registered, was only initiated with the record of the grant of arms and a crest to Nevinson Fox on 21 July 1673.

The volume of new grants in the early sixteenth century can be judged by the fact that there are between four and five hundred identifiable grants by Sir Thomas Wriothesley (Garter 1505–34). In the mid-sixteenth century William Hervy (Clarenceux 1557–67) was for three years making at least sixty grants a year, and Robert Cooke (his successor as Clarenceux from 1567 to 1593) is reputed to have been the most active sixteenth-century granting King of Arms. A count of Cooke's patents for which there is evidence at the College of Arms produces over nine hundred, whereas between four and five hundred attributed to Sir William Segar (Garter 1606–33) appear in a manuscript entitled *Aspidora Segariana* or *Sir William Segar's Grants, Confirmations, etc.*, collected by Simon Segar, his great-grandson. As Segar wrote that Cooke 'confirmed and gave Armes and Creastes without nomber to base and unworthy persons for his private gaine onely without the knowledge of the Erle Marshall', Cooke may have been responsible for more than twice as many grants as Segar. The large number of patents issued by Cooke may in part be accounted for by those which confirmed both arms and crest, such as that of 18 March 1576/7 to Henry Stanley of Sutton Bonnington in Nottinghamshire and his wife Anne. Whereas Cooke made many grants of crests to existing arms, as did other sixteenth- and early seventeenth-century Kings of Arms, the confirmation of both by Patent seems to be particularly associated with Cooke, although examples by Segar exist.

Segar's contemporary, William Camden (Clarenceux 1597–1623), also made about four hundred grants, of which three hundred and nineteen are listed in Sylvanus Morgan's *Sphere of Gentry* (1661). Most of these were made alone and not with one of the other Kings of Arms, as the basis of the present system, whereby Garter and Norroy grant together north of the River Trent, and Garter and Clarenceux grant together south of the Trent, was only agreed in 1680. The disruption of the Civil War, when some heralds supported the King and some Parliament, and the end of the Visitation system, led to a decline in the number of grants, and in the first ten years of the new recording system, between June 1673 and March 1683, only seventy grants were made. In 1684, five years before the end of the Visitation system, eight grants were made. Thereafter the numbers picked up, and between ten and twenty grants a year were made from 1690 till 1770. In the decade to 1780 an average of over thirty grants a year were made and between 1780 and 1790 the numbers rose to between forty and forty-five a year. Under Sir Isaac Heard (Garter 1784–1822) there was a marked increase; from 1790 to 1800 there were over seventy grants a year, over eighty a year in the next ten years, and under the Regency and subsequent reign of George IV more than a hundred grants a year, reflecting both the interest of the Sovereign and the Gothic revival. The reign of William IV witnessed a drop to slightly over eighty grants a year, and between seventy-five and eighty a year were made under Queen Victoria. The first ten years of the twentieth century coincide with the reign of Edward VII, and the number of grants increased to between one hundred and thirty and one hundred and forty a year; after 1910 between one and two hundred grants a year were made until the early 1980s, when the number approached two hundred a year, being a few over two hundred in 1986.

Despite the variation in numbers, the grantees have remained much the same. The Kings of Arms are authorized in their patents of appointment to grant with the consent in writing of the Earl Marshal, arms and crests by Letters Patent to 'eminent men'. This phrase first appears in the 1741 patent of appointment in English of Stephen Martin Leake as Clarenceux. Earlier patents in Latin only refer to the consent in writing of the Earl Marshal (a clause first inserted by the Earl Marshal in 1677) without specifying the grantees. Grants have also always been made to eminent women and corporate bodies; and lawyers, physicians, clerics, members of county families, office holders, those associated with the Court, and corporate bodies such as livery companies are to be found amongst grantees of arms in every century as, inevitably, through the College being in the City of London are Lord Mayors, Sheriffs, and others eminent in the City. The wealth and position of the Church prior to the Reformation can be judged from the recorded grants by Sir Thomas Wriothesley, Garter, and Thomas Benolt, Clarenceux, who both died in 1534. They include grants to Banham, Essex, Hampton, Gardebys, Hawke-borne, Malyn, Melford, Parker, Westbury, and Whyting, respectively abbots of Tavistock, St Augustine's Canterbury (both Essex and Hampton), Ramsey, Cirencester, Waltham, Bury St Edmunds, Gloucester, Cerne, and Glastonbury. Archdeacons of Richmond, Nottingham, Durham, Wiltshire, Huntingdon, St Stephen's Canterbury, and Leicester are listed as grantees of these Kings of Arms, as is Thomas Wolsey and many other priors, deans, canons, and bishops, all of whom were effectively having grants for their own lives alone as their celibate profession precluded legitimate male issue. Other grantees of the early sixteenth century include lawyers such as John Caryll of Warnham, Sussex, Serjeant-at-Law, and John Hales, a Baron of the Exchequer, Robert Amydas, Master of the Mint, William Burch, Gentleman Usher to the King, Thomas Magnus, the ambassador, Richard Pace, Secretary to the King, most if not all Lord Mayors and Sheriffs, and a few foreigners resident in London,

(*left*) Impaled arms showing Thomas Wolsey as a Cardinal, Archbishop of York, Bishop of Durham, Bath and Wells, and Lincoln, Abbot of St Albans, and Edmund Grindall as Bishop of London, with pen-and-ink sketch of arms of Matthew Parker as Archbishop of Canterbury. Early Tudor book of arms formerly belonging to William Hervy, Clarenceux (Coll. Arms, L 10, fo. 67).

(*right*) Arms of eminent ecclesiastics before the Reformation, including the Abbots of Cerne, St Augustine's, Canterbury, St Albans, St Mary's, York, and Bury St Edmunds; the Prior of St Mary's Hospital; the Archdeacon of Wiltshire; the King's Secretary Dr Richard Pace; the Ambassador Thomas Magnus; Dr Young; and Trinity College, Cambridge. The inclusion of Trinity College dates the painting to no earlier than 1546 (Coll. Arms, L 10, fo. 71v).

whether as emissaries or merchants, amongst whom were Sir Ferdinand de Vielelobos, Sir Rey Van Auville, Sir Dego Sermyent, and Anthony Cavalier.

The current policy of only granting to those who are subjects of the Crown, and making honorary grants to those descended in an unbroken male line from people who were subjects of the Crown with the consent of the country of which they are now subjects, has only evolved in this century. This enables a limited number of honorary grants to be made to eminent Americans who can trace either descent in an unbroken male line from someone resident in a British-

American colony in 1783, when Britain recognized American independence, or from a subsequent emigrant. The granting of arms to foreigners when commanded to do so by the Sovereign was historically one of the perquisites of the Office of Garter. Unfortunately there were insufficient perks attached to the Office of Garter, and jurisdictional disputes between the Kings of Arms affected the College till the eighteenth century. Details of the disputes which centred on Garter's lack of a province in which to grant or conduct Visitations will be found in Sir Anthony Wagner's *Heralds of England* (HMSO 1967). For most of his career as Garter, Wriothesley made agreements with Clarenceux and Norroy that he should grant in their provinces either with them or in their stead. The apparent contrast of attitude between grants of arms to subjects of a foreign Sovereign and grants of honours by a foreign Sovereign to a subject of the British Crown can be seen at the end of the sixteenth century in Elizabeth I's reaction when the first Lord Arundell of Wardour was created a Count of the Holy Roman Empire by the Emperor Rudolph II. She remarked: 'I would not have my sheep branded with another man's mark; I would not have them follow the whistle of a strange shepherd.' The sheep in question spent two months in the Fleet Prison, and was banished from Court. Creation as a Count of the Holy Roman Empire is a far greater thing than a grant of arms, but logic suggests that if a great honour is unacceptable so should be a lesser one. Elizabeth I's approach is a forerunner of the current Foreign and Commonwealth Orders Regulations which govern the use and recognition in this country of foreign awards or honours conferred on British subjects.

An initial view of grants made by Robert Cooke does not immediately show the base and unworthy persons to whom Segar referred. Amongst churchmen are Thomas Godwin, Bishop of Bath and Wells, and John Whitgift, Archbishop of Canterbury. Lawyers include the Lord Chief Justice of the Common Pleas, Sir James Dyer, Matthew Ewens, a Baron of the Exchequer, and members of the Bar such as Hugh Browker of the Inner Temple, one of the Prothonotaries of the Common Pleas; examples of Doctors of Physic are Isaac Barrow of Cambridge, Thomas Larking, and John Simminges. The Queen's Surgeon George Baker was a grantee of Cooke's, as were Sir Francis Drake and the astrologer John Dee. Perhaps Sir William Segar viewed with less pleasure the Queen's two Master Cooks Cordell and Pindar, and the Sergeant of the Pastry John Dudley. James I did not adopt as strict an approach as his predecessor, and recognized Lord Arundell of Wardour's Imperial title, and a case even exists of Segar approving a foreign grant of arms to an Englishman. In 1625 he confirmed arms granted in a letter of safe conduct of 1603 by Sigismund Bathori, Duke of Transylvania, to John Smith, descended from Smith of Cuerdley,

Lancashire. The arms *Vert a chevron Gules between three Turks heads couped proper turbanned Or* were granted in memory of three Turks heads which John Smith cut off before the town of Regal in Transylvania when serving under Henry Volda, Earl of Meldritch. Segar was apparently happy to confirm a red chevron on a green field, which by placing a colour on a colour, transgressed the rule of armory in England, if not those of Transylvania. He also confirmed arms and a crest to a man named Guevera from Lincolnshire, descended from Nicholas Velez de Guevera of Segura in Spain, the validity of the armorial bearings being confirmed by the Spanish ambassador.

(*below left*) Grants and confirmations by Robert Cooke, Clarenceux, including a grant with a crest to John Whitgift, Archbishop of Canterbury, dated 1588 (Coll. Arms, B EDN, fo. 26).

(*below right*) Record of confirmation of arms and crest, dated 19 Aug. 1625, by William Segar, Garter, originally granted 9 Dec. 1603 to John Smith by Sigismund Bathori, Duke of Transylvania (Coll. Arms, Vincent 169, p. 131).

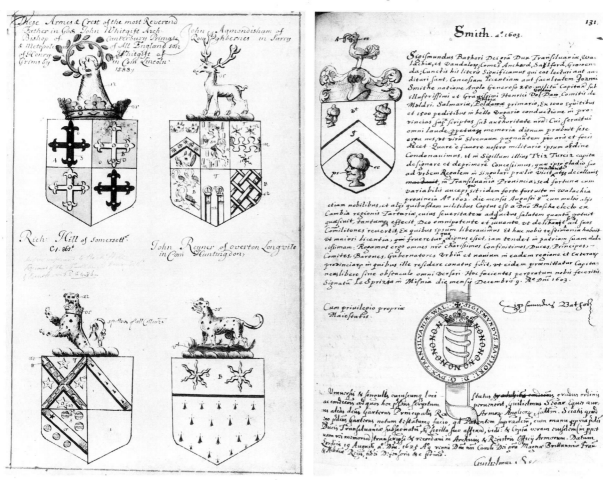

Richard Netter, Gentleman Usher to Anne of Denmark (Queen of James I), John Sutcliff, Groom of the Privy Chamber to Charles I, and Thomas Sackville, one of the Gentlemen Ushers were all early seventeenth-century grantees. Thomas Cadiman, Doctor of Physic to the Queen, was granted arms in 1633. Those who collected money for the Crown appear as grantees under the early Stuarts, examples being Joshua Gallard, one of the Receivers of the Revenues of Charles I, John Halloway, Controller of the Custom House, and in 1616 William Harrison of Aldcliffe, Lancashire, described as father to Sir John Harrison, Farmer of the Customs; this is probably an instance of a son having the grant made to his father, as was the grant made to Shakespeare's father, John Shakespeare, in 1596 by Sir William Dethick, Garter. George Broome, Sub-Prothonotary of the Court of Kings Bench, and Richard Colchester of Gray's Inn, Cursitor of the Court of Chancery, are lawyers who were granted arms, as was a schoolmaster Alexander Gill, Chief Master of St Paul's School. John Weddall of Stepney, Captain of the *Rainbow*, a principal ship of the King's Navy, was granted arms in 1627, and an example of confirmation of both arms and crest by Segar is that dated 16 August 1632 to Henry Ashton, described as Colonel to the mighty Prince Michael Fedrovitius, Emperor and Conqueror of all Russia, and descended out of the ancient right and noble family of Ashton. Sir John Ogle, Colonel of a Regiment of Foot, and Toby Massey, one of the Captains

Confirmation of arms and crest by Sir William Segar, Garter, to Henry Ashton, dated 16 Aug. 1632 and recorded in a pre-printed book collected by Sylvanus Morgan (1620–93), the herald painter and author (Coll. Arms, Miscellaneous Grants 6, fos. 91v–92).

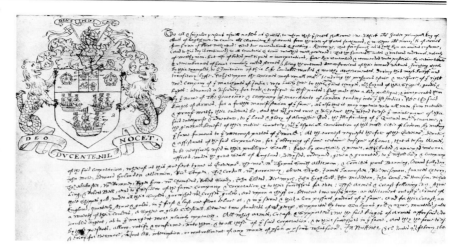

Grant by Garter, Clarenceux, and Norroy to the East India Merchants, dated 4 Feb. 1600/1, of arms, crest, and supporters with two mottoes; a single fleur-de-lis and lion passant guardant from the Royal Arms of England appear quartered in centre chief, and the supporters are two heraldic sea lions (Coll. Arms, I 9, fo. 84).

of the Militia, are other military examples, and lesser ecclesiastics are represented by Richard Ball and Benjamin Carrier (the Catholic convert), both Doctors of Divinity. The Earl of Thanet received supporters from Segar, as did Viscounts Valentia and Wenman, and examples of barons are Lords Deincourt and Goring. Segar granted arms, crest, and supporters to both the Merchant Adventurers Company and, as Norroy in 1600 with William Dethick, Garter, and William Camden, Clarenceux, to the East India Merchants.

Norroy always made many fewer grants than Clarenceux, as he had a less populated province, and his presence in London, except whilst on a Visitation, when those subject to his jurisdiction were resident north of the Trent, must have reduced the numbers, as must Clarenceux's ability to grant to natives of the north living in London, an instance of which is Cooke's 1589 grant to Simon Blakey of Blakey in Lancashire. Examples of the reverse are rare and sound doubtful, such as Gilbert Dethick's 1547 grant to George Toke of Worcestershire who 'hath at alltymes used hym self so manfully and discretly and inespecially under Therle of Warwyk as then the Kings Ma[jes]ties Lieftenant at the battaill of Mustelbrough'; there is nothing odd about this, but the justification of the grant being by Norroy rather than Clarenceux seems to be that it was 'geven and graunted at Newcastell upon Tyne'. Norroy's grants give much the same picture as Clarenceux's. There is a list (R 21/57) in the College of Arms of all those granted arms by William Flower, Norroy, from the time of his creation in February 1561/2 till 1583. For a period when Cooke made several hundred grants, Flower only made thirty-one. The list contains a Dean, Whittingham, and a Bishop, Barnes, of Durham; a Serjeant-at-Law, Robert Pickering; and two Aldermen of Hull. A Royal Warrant of 1660 (I 25, 82v) declared grants by the usurping

Commonwealth Kings of Arms Bysshe, Squibb, and Ryley, null and void. Grantees such as Colonel Thomas Horton, Commander-in-Chief of all South Wales, granted arms and a crest by Ryley, Norroy, in July 1649 would have to have a further grant if they wished to establish a legal entitlement to arms. William Dugdale, Norroy from 1660 to 1677, subsequently Garter (1677–86) kept an annual record of his patents which gives an impression of Restoration grants. In 1662 he made seven grants: three of the grantees, Rawlinson of Carke in Cartmel, Lancashire, Lightbowne of Manchester, and Wilmot of Osmaston in Derbyshire, were of Gray's Inn, to which Dugdale had been admitted in 1660; Degge was of the Inner Temple; there was an attorney, John Scattergood of Ellaston in Staffordshire, a Justice of the Peace for Derbyshire and late a merchant of the East India Company, and William Orme of Hanch Hall, Staffordshire, who recorded a pedigree at the 1663–4 Visitation of that county. The fourteen grantees in 1663 show that analyses of single years should be treated with caution as the preponderance of lawyers in 1662 is not typical. William Sancroft, Dean of York and subsequently (1678) Archbishop of Canterbury, was granted arms in 1663, as was Robert Thoroton of Nottingham, Doctor of Physic and author of *The Antiquities of Nottinghamshire* (1677). John Conde, Clerk of the Peace for Nottinghamshire, Atkinson, Captain of a Troop of Horse, and Thomas Shipman, Captain of a Foot Company in the Trained Bands in Derbyshire, and his brothers William and Gervase, were further

Record of four grants in 1663 by William Dugdale, then Norroy, to Robert Thoroton (the historian), Samuel Clarke, Thomas Scott, and George Gregory (Coll. Arms, Dugdale's Grants, fo. 3).

grantees. Gervase Shipman's brother-in-law George Gregory, High Sheriff of Nottinghamshire in 1666 and ancestor of Gregory Gregory, the builder of Harlaxton in Lincolnshire, also had a grant, as did Thomas Cholmondeley of Holford in Cheshire, natural son of Robert, Viscount Cholmondeley. Of the remaining seven, their only distinguishing features are that three recorded pedigrees at the Visitation of Derbyshire of 1662–4, two at the Visitation of Staffordshire of 1663–4, and one at that of Nottinghamshire of 1662–4; the final grant was made with Clarenceux to three brothers named Lascoe, citizens of London, whose eldest brother lived in Nottinghamshire.

At the end of the seventeenth century, the collapse of the Visitation system tended to concentrate the grantees in London, and the insertion of the requirement of written permission from the Earl Marshal further reduced the numbers of new grants. After 1676 those wishing for grants were required by the Earl Marshal either to be holders of public office or to produce certificates from two gentlemen that they were well affected to the government and could support the condition of gentleman. The period of December 1704 to December 1706 when there were no grants is often considered to be the lowest ebb of the College, though there were nine grants in 1704 and over twenty in 1707, so that there is an average of about eight grants a year for the four years 1704–7. In 1720 more than half the grantees were resident in London or Middlesex. They included the Paymaster of the Queen's Lottery, a Commander of several of His Majesty's ships of war, a baronet, a knight, and Henry Wise of Brompton Park, Middlesex, Master Gardener of all His Majesty's Gardens, responsible for the layout of Hampton Court and Kensington Gardens. His crest, appropriately, contains a damask rose. A corporate grantee of the 1720s was the Royal Exchange Assurance in 1723, and an example of a grant to a family of foreign extraction is that in 1728 to Thomas Smith, whose ancestor named Le Fevre came from France in the reign of Queen Elizabeth. The grantee's great-great-granddaughter Emily Smith married the 7th Duke of Beaufort in 1822. Thus, though grants of arms in the early eighteenth century tended to be restricted geographically, they never dried up entirely.

An examination of two years in the late 1740s shows a continuing dependence on City and mercantile grantees, with considerable business in granting supporters to existing arms and a crest for new peers and Knights of the Bath. Of the fourteen grants in 1747 six were of hereditary supporters to Lords Anson, Archer, Feversham, Folkestone, Ravensworth, and Rolle, and one of supporters for life to Sir Peter Warren. Sampson Gideon, father of the 1st Lord Eardley, described in *The Complete Peerage* as a Portuguese Jew of immense wealth, Arthur Griesdale, and John Brownsword were all successful

London merchants who had grants. Of the remaining four there was one corporate grantee, the Foundling Hospital, set up by a seaman, Captain Coram, with a group of Tory backers under the title of the 'Hospital for the Maintenance and Education of Exposed and Deserted Young Children', an alteration of a crest granted to Simcoe of Chelsea in the previous year, a grant and confirmation of the arms and crest borne by his family to Just Henry Alt, resident upwards of twenty years in England as Minister from Hessia, and a solitary northern grantee George Eastwood of Flockton Nether in the parish of Thornhill, West Riding of Yorkshire. In 1748 there were fifteen new grants, and supporters for peers dropped to two, Lords Monson and Powis. The City representation remained much the same, with grants to Peters, Acworth, and Milward, and John Brownsword came back for more in the form of a grant of arms for his wife Jane. Edward Garthwaite of Shackleford in Surrey had connections with Jamaica, and other merchants representative of this period of great expansion in England's overseas trade were Michael Atkins of Bristol and William Sitlington of Wigton, Cumberland, whose grant states that he was born on 21 July 1722 at six o'clock in the afternoon in the Forest of Westwood, and having been round the greatest part of the globe, had acquired a sufficient competency to support the condition of a gentleman. The Law was represented by Hezekiah Walker of the Middle Temple and John Aspinall of Preston, Lancashire, subsequently Serjeant-at-Law and Recorder of Preston, whose patent states that his ancestors had been possessed of a considerable freehold estate at Standen in the said county for above five hundred years, and had used arms and a crest not registered at the College. The Chapter Clerk to the Dean and Chapter of Canterbury had a grant, as did the Principal Clerk of the Survey in Deptford, and there were two naval grantees, Vice-Admiral Sir Edward Hawke and Rear-Admiral John Gascoign. On 31 March in the first week of 1749 (before 1752 the year changed in England on 25 March and not 1 January) Henry Flitcroft, the architect, had a grant. Other eighteenth-century architects who applied for grants of arms included James Wyatt in 1780; and, not surprisingly as he was Clarenceux King of Arms, John Vanbrugh had one in 1714 though he waited until the year of his knighthood, ten years after he was appointed to the College. Vanbrugh's appointment was indicative of the low state to which the College fell in the early eighteenth century, as he ridiculed both heraldry and genealogy.

The substantial increase in numbers of grants in the late eighteenth and early nineteenth centuries reflected once more a wider geographical spread of grantees caused by the more general revival of interest in heraldry. Contributing factors were grants of supporters to Knights of the Bath and peers and of arms to Esquires of the Bath, augmenta-

Grant of arms in 1840 to a widow, Elizabeth Greenwood, on assuming the name and arms of Holden pursuant to a Royal Licence. The arms are displayed on a lozenge for a widow, and are differenced with a gold canton, as the petitioner was not herself descended from the family. Her children as descendants were authorized to bear the arms without the canton (Coll. Arms, Grants 44, p. 374).

tions of honour granted to naval and military commanders encouraging them to have arms to which such additions could be made, the use of arms by High Sheriffs (to display on the banners of their trumpeters), continuing grants to illegitimate children of armigerous families, and assumption of the name and arms of another family pursuant to a Royal Licence usually obtained as the result of a name and arms clause in the will of a childless relation. Royal Licences were also occasionally obtained on voluntary application, as in the Licence granted to Elizabeth Greenwood in 1840 to enable her and her issue to assume the name and arms of Holden, recorded with other material in the 'Earl Marshal's Books', a series classified in the College library under the letter I. The increase in this type of business can be gauged by the number of volumes used in different periods. Two concurrent volumes, one on vellum and one on paper, numbered I 25 and I 26, cover the seventeenth century. One volume covers 1705–59, the next 1760–82, and thereafter the number of years tend to decrease: 1782–91, 1791–5, 1795–1800, 1800–3, till the five years of 1824–8 are covered by three volumes numbered I 45–I 47. In the reign of Queen Victoria each volume covers an average of four years, marking a significant drop in Royal Licences. The general impression gained from Royal Licence cases in their heyday is that they related to County families failing in the male line. Two examples of assumption of names and arms, both in 1813, and both with literary associations, are Jane Austen's brother Edward's assumption of the name and arms of Knight, and John Salusbury Piozzi's assumption of the additional name and arms of Salusbury at the desire of his aunt Hester Lynch Piozzi, relict of Henry Thrale and friend of Dr Johnson. In the previous year ordinary grantees included John Fisher, Bishop of Salisbury, and Benjamin Hobhouse, MP, scion of a Bristol merchant dynasty. 1813 was also the year of the grant of arms to Harriet, first wife of John George Lambton subsequently 1st Earl of Durham, and natural daughter of George James, 4th Earl of and subsequently 1st Marquess Cholmondeley. Seven years earlier, in 1806, the guardian of the three natural sons and four natural daughters of Thomas Peter Legh of Lyme Park near Stockport obtained seven grants, one for each child. They are followed in the College record by a grant to Lady Hamilton, described as Dame Emma Hamilton of Clarges Street and only issue of Henry Lyons of Preston, Co. Lancaster. The text of the grant recites part of the codicil dated 21 October 1805, the day of his death, to the will of Horatio, Viscount Nelson, which states that, 'the eminent services of Emma Hamilton, widow of the Right Honourable Sir William Hamilton, have been of the very greatest service to our King and Country'. There were grantees on other continents, such as in 1814 to Thomas Fanshaw Middleton, Bishop of Calcutta, and the town of Kingston, Jamaica, in 1803. Edward Chambers of the parish of Hanover in the County of Cornwall, Jamaica, whose ancestors were established there soon after the conquest by Venables and Penn, was granted arms in 1771. High Sheriffs include Matthew Boulton, the famous industrialist of Soho in the parish of Handsworth near Birmingham, nominated High Sheriff for Staffordshire in 1794, and the son of Boulton's partner James Watt, also James Watt, the restorer of Aston Hall, Birmingham, and High Sheriff of Radnorshire in 1826. Another son of a distinguished father was John Angerstein, only son and heir of John Julius Angerstein, the Chairman of Lloyds and great collector, whose pictures form the basis of the National Gallery; he was granted arms, long borne by his family in Germany, in 1827. The father of a more distinguished son was the 81-year-old John Gladstone, granted arms in 1846 when his son William Ewart Gladstone was aged 36. Disraeli, incidentally, was a grantee in 1876, when he was raised to the peerage as Earl of Beaconsfield.

The number of grantees in the nineteenth century is so great that a limited examination can only give an indication of the role of heraldry in England if small groups are chosen, such as Lord Chancellors and Archbishops of Canterbury. Between 1805 and 1896 there were six Archbishops of Canterbury: Manners-Sutton, Howley, Sumner, Longley, Tait, and Benson. Manners-Sutton was a grandson in the male line of the 3rd Duke of Rutland, and entitled to arms by descent. Howley was granted arms in 1813 when Bishop of London. Sumner used arms registered at the Heralds' Visitation of Kent in 1663 for a family of Somner living in Canterbury, but never proved his descent. Longley had a grant for the See of Ripon when Bishop of Ripon in 1836 but used personal arms to which he had no entitlement as confirmed by the subsequent grant in 1924 to his great-nephew Sir John Raynsford Longley. Tait's grandfather, John Tait, a Writer to the Signet, had grants from the Lord Lyon in 1791 and 1795, and Benson had a grant in 1877 when Bishop of Truro, also obtaining a grant for the Bishopric in the same year. From 1807 till 1905 thirteen individuals held the office of Lord Chancellor, namely Lords Eldon, Lyndhurst, Brougham and Vaux, Cottenham, St Leonards, Cranworth, Chelmsford, Campbell, Westbury, Cairns, Selborne, Halsbury, and Herschell. Lord Eldon, formerly Sir John Scott and son of a Newcastle coal barge proprietor, was granted arms, a crest, and supporters in 1799. Lord Lyndhurst had a grant in 1827, with an extension of the limitations for the arms and crest to include the descendants of his father John Singleton Copley, RA, the portrait painter who was born in Boston, Massachusetts. Lord Brougham and Vaux had a grant of arms and a crest in 1831. Lord Cottenham, previously Sir Charles Christopher Pepys, was entitled by descent to arms and a crest registered at the Heralds' Visitation of Norfolk in 1563; although there is no record of a grant of these arms, to which the diarist Samuel Pepys was also entitled, they look like a sixteenth-century grant rather than a confirmation of a medieval coat. Lord Cottenham was granted supporters in 1836. Lord St Leonards never had a grant in his lifetime, but his daughter applied retrospectively for a grant in 1908 of armorial bearings suitable to be placed on a monument to her father. Lord Cranworth was granted arms and a crest in 1851, and had a subsequent grant of supporters. Sir Frederick Thesiger, later Lord Chelmsford, was granted arms and a crest as Solicitor-General in 1845 and supporters in 1858. Lord Campbell had a confirmation of arms and a crest, and a grant of supporters in a separate patent in 1841. Lord Westbury was granted arms and a crest, and, in a separate patent, supporters in 1861. Lord Cairns had a confirmation of arms stated to be borne by prescription from Ulster King of Arms in 1878. His successor, Lord Selborne, was entitled to the arms of Palmer granted in February 1634/5 at the time of the Heralds' Visitation of Bedfordshire,

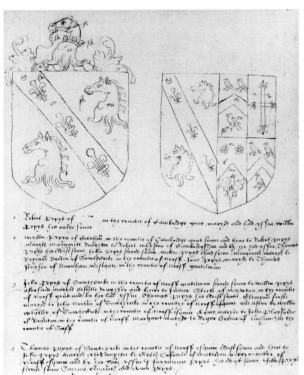

(*left*) Visitation of Norfolk carried out by William Hervy, Clarenceux, in 1563. Narrative pedigree of Pepys with arms and camel's-head crest. Ancestors of Samuel Pepys and Lord Cottenham (Coll. Arms, G 1, fo. 71).

(*right*) Visitation of Devon and Cornwall 1531 carried out by Thomas Benolt, Clarenceux. The arms of Gifford, shown as *Sable three Lozenges or Fusils in fess Ermine*, are filled in on a prepared page (Coll. Arms, G 2, fo. 29v).

and was granted supporters in 1872. Hardinge Stanley (Gifford), Lord Halsbury, was the only nineteenth-century Lord Chancellor entitled to medieval arms; their earliest entry in a College manuscript is in one entitled *Ballard's Book* of about 1480, and they were subsequently confirmed at the Heralds' Visitation of Devonshire in 1531. Farrer Herschell was granted arms and a crest in 1877, nine years before he became Lord Chancellor.

The grantees of the twentieth century are similar to those of the nineteenth. Consequently England in the 1980s has seen new grants to an Archbishop of Canterbury and Bishops of Norwich and Truro (subsequently Bishop of London). There are in addition many more grants today to eminent subjects of other countries of which the Queen is Sovereign, such as Canada⋆, Australia, and New Zealand

⋆ By Letters Patent dated 4 June 1988 The Queen established a separate heraldic authority for Canada with its own Chief Herald. After this date the English Kings of Arms, who had previously operated under the Earl Marshal's imperial jurisdiction, ceased to grant new armorial bearings to subjects of the Canadian Crown.

1. 'Prince Arthur's Book', c.1520: Ordinary of lions showing the similarity of early arms, which would have reduced their efficacy as a means of identification in battle (Coll. Arms, Vincent 152, p. 39).

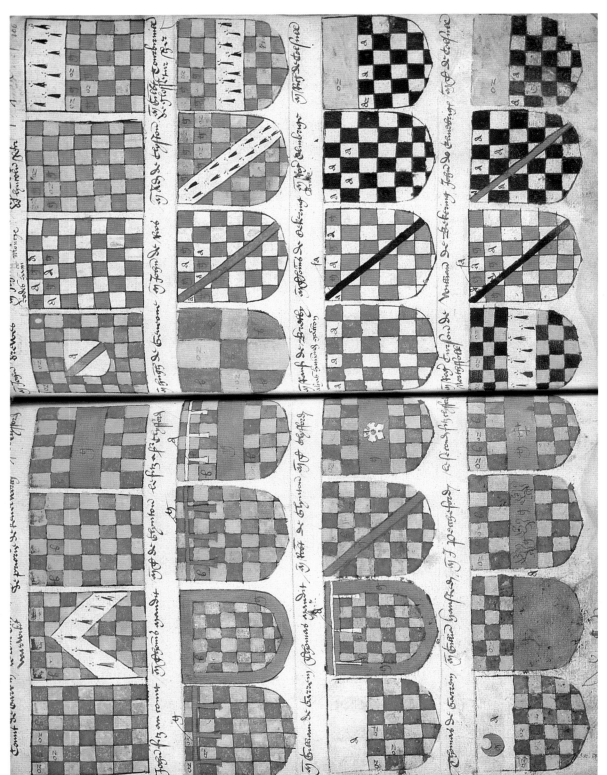

2. 'Flower's Ordinary', c.1520: showing Warenne and other checky coats on banners and shields (Coll. Arms, 2 G 9, fos. 105v–106).

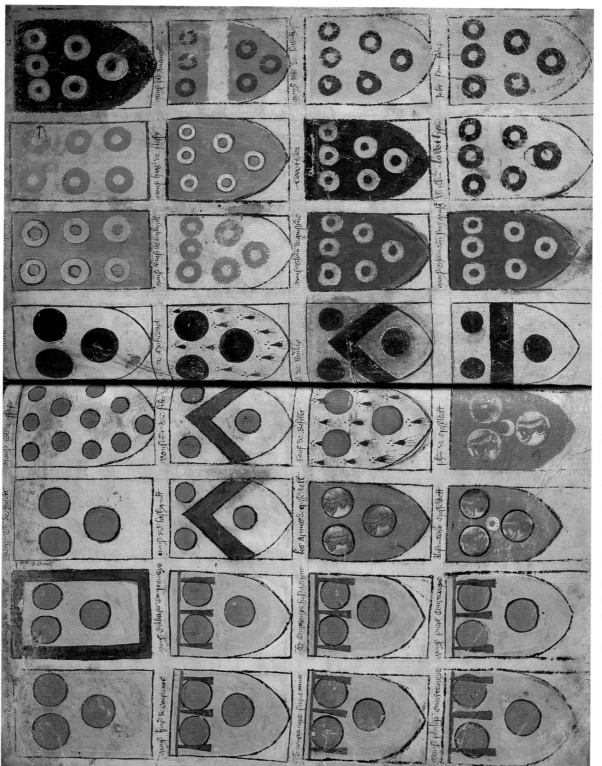

3. 'Jenyns's Ordinary', c. 1380: showing roundels and annulets, the latter including arms of Westmorland families composed of annulets derived from their Vipont overlords, whose arms are shown on a banner rather than a shield (Coll. Arms, Jenyns's Ordinary, fos. 25v–26).

The generall office of Armes: 4

4. 'Lant's Roll' of *c.*1595, prepared by Thomas Lant (*c.*1556–*c.*1601), Windsor Herald: a catalogue recording Officers of Arms from the time of Henry V illustrating the arms of the College of Arms, and the arms of Office of Garter, Clarenceux, Norroy, and Ulster Kings of Arms. In the case of Garter and Clarenceux there is an additional charge in the first quarter which does not appear subsequently (Coll. Arms, Lant's Roll, fo. 2).

To All and Singular to whom these Presents
shall come Sir Isaac Heard Knight Garter
Principal King of Arms sendeth Greeting Whereas

5. The arms of Lord Harris with the citadel of Seringapatam on a chief, an example of Georgian landscape
heraldry shown on his grant of supporters, 12 Sept. 1815 (Coll. Arms, Grants 29, p. 115).

6. German heraldry: the 'Hyghalmen Roll' (late fifteenth century), showing how in Germany the tinctures and charges of the shield are often repeated in the crest. The arms include those of the families of Monnich and Kreys, and the MS has been in the College since the death of its owner, Thomas Benolt, Clarenceux, in 1534 (Coll. Arms, Hyghalmen Roll, I M 5, fos. 18v–19).

7 (*facing*). French heraldry, *c.*1629: seventeenth-century pedigree of the Counts of Artois, showing the ancient royal arms of France, *Azure semy de lis Or* differenced with a label charged with gold towers and the arms of spouses, which include Castille, Navarre, and Brittany (private collection: *Généalogie de la Royale Maison de France*, by C. Soyer, p. 35).

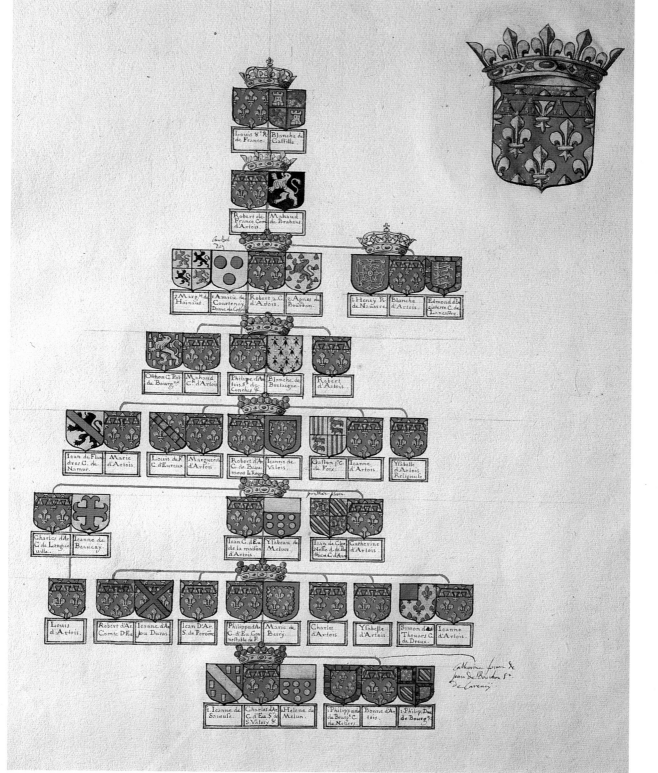

Louis 8.e R. de France. — Blanche de Castille.

Robert de France Comte d'Artois. — Mahaud de Brabant.

2 Marg.te de Hainaut. | 1 Amicie de Courtenay Dame de Cohci. | Robert 2. C. d'Artois. | 2 Agnes de Bourbon.

1 Henry R. de Nauarre. | Blanche d'Artois. | Edmond de Glebere C. de Lancastre.

Otthon G. Pal. de Bourg.ne | Mahaud C.te d'Artois | Philippe d'Artois S. de Conches &. | Blanche de Bretaigne. | Robert d'Artois.

Iean de Flandres C. de Namur. | Marie d'Artois. | Louis de F. C. d'Eureux | Marguerite d'Artois | Robert d'Ar. C. de Beaumont le Roger | Ieanne de Valois. | Gaston J.C. de Foix. | Ieanne d'Artois. | Ysabelle d'Artois Religieuse.

Charles d'Ar. C. de Longueuille. | Ieanne de Beaucay. | Iean C. d'Eu de la maison d'Artois | Ysabeau de Melun. | Iean de Cler Nesle S. de Bouthieu C.d'Au | Catherine d'Artois.

Louis d'Artois | Robert d'Ar. Comte D'Eu | Ieanne d'An. Iou Duras | Iean D'Ar. S. de Perône | Philippe d'Ar. C. d'Eu, Connestable de F. | Marie de Berry. | Charles d'Artois | Ysabelle d'Artois | Simon d.s Thouars C. de Dreux. | Ieanne d'Artois.

Catherine fçme de Iean de Bourbon S.r de Carency.

1 Ieanne de Saueuse. | Charles d'Ar. C. d'Eu S.te S. Valery &. | 2 Helene de Melun | 1 Philippe de Bourg.e C. de Nevers. | Bonne d'Artois. | 1 Philip. Duc de Bourg.e

8. Confirmation of arms and crest by Robert Cooke, Clarenceux, to Henry Stanley of Sutton Bonnington, Nottinghamshire, and his wife Anne, née Bradshaw, dated 18 Mar. 1576/7 (Coll. Arms, Muniment Room 11, no. 22).

9. Grant of arms and crest by Gilbert Dethick, Norroy, to George Toke of Worcester, dated 6 Oct. 1547. The grant contains a portrait of Dethick wearing a tabard of the Royal Arms, and is headed by the Royal badges of a crowned Tudor rose and gold fleur-de-lis. The crest is of an ebeck's (ibex) head (Coll. Arms, Muniment Room 11, No. 9).

10. Grants by William Hervy, Clarenceux, all of c.1560, to Vane, Daper, Seckford, Lynger, Grey, Hornyold, Brideman, The Company of Merchants of Exeter, Wistow, Wilkins, Tyldesley, and Lee (Coll. Arms, L 9, fo. 29).

11. Late fifteenth-century record of British Arms showing simple geometrical divisions such as the chief indented for Butler, saltire for Desmond, compounded arms of John (de Dreux), Earl of Richmond (d. 1333/4), with the checky coat of Dreux, to which has been added a canton of Brittany and bordure of England, various lion coats, and the three garbs of the Earl of Chester. It also illustrates the tinctures Or, Argent, Gules, Sable, Azure, Purpure, and Ermine (Coll. Arms, M 10, fo. 48).

12. 'Segar's Roll': simple medieval coats, including a plain cross and chevron and the canting coat of Corbet with corbies (Coll. Arms, L 14, pt. I, fo. 29v).

13 (*facing*). Roll of grants of arms and crests of *c.*1528 by Sir Thomas Wriothesley, showing complicated early Tudor coats; the shield for Caunton beneath the camel crest illustrates the early sixteenth-century Purpure (private collection).

14 (*above*). Early Tudor crests shown typically multi-coloured, with wreaths and mantling often of different tinctures, including Kebell crest of an elephant's head (Coll. Arms, Vincent 168, fos. 20v–21).

15 (*right*). Alternative crest proposed for Sir Francis Drake, 1581, but not granted (Coll. Arms, Vincent 218, fo. 28).

Non sine numine.

The right honourable Phillipp Lorde Harbert of Sher=land in the County of Kent, Earle of Mount gomery, Knight of the most noble order of the Garter.

16. Full achievement of Philip (Herbert), Earl of Montgomery, KG, 1616, showing Azure, Gules, and Ermine mantling, Argent, Azure, and Gules wreath, a Wyvern crest, and dexter supporter of a Panther incensed and Earl's Coronet (Coll. Arms, E 16, fo. 25v).

The right honourable William Pawlett Marques of Winchester, Earle of Wiltshire, and Lorde St. John of Basinge &c.

AYMES, LOYAVLTE

17. Full achievement of William (Paulet), 4th Marquess of Winchester, 1616, with Pantheon supporters which are surely the product of a herald's imagination. The first quarter of the shield shows the paternal arms of *Paulet Sable three swords in pile points downwards Argent pommels and hilts Or* (Coll. Arms, E 16, fo. 1v).

Grant of arms to the See of Australia, 1836 (Coll. Arms, Grants 41, p. 229).

which now has its own Herald Extraordinary. These were not unknown in the nineteenth century, and a grant to the See of Australia pursuant to a Royal Warrant of William IV was made as early as 1836. The spread of heraldry in the last six decades of the nineteenth century is seen from a sample of Lancashire civic grants: Manchester 1842, Blackburn 1852, Burnley 1862, Rawtenstall 1871, Heywood 1881, and Haslingden 1892. These grants catalogue the desire for arms expanded from the greater out to the lesser centres created by the Industrial Revolution.

The national regulation of arms by confirmation and new grant which existed till the end of the Heralds' Visitations was effectively revived in the second half of the eighteenth century when the grantees ceased to be largely drawn from London. Thus, a system which originally related to medieval knights prospered and developed in England from the late Middle Ages onwards, because the Kings of the House of Lancaster recognized social change and permitted the Kings of Arms to grant new arms to 'eminent men', whereas their counterparts in France, for instance, were restricted to designing arms granted by the Sovereign only. The Tudors developed the Lancastrian system further, by allowing Benolt to undertake the first of the Visitations and giving him powers of enforcement, and by not restricting Wriothesley, despite complaints from Benolt that he granted to 'vile persons'. Henry VIII adapted heraldry to mark both status and social change. The records of grants to men of note from the late fifteenth century onwards are strong evidence of social mobility in England. They support the traditional theory that the upper layers of English society were easily accessible to self-made men, as compared to lesser mobility in the rest of Europe, and would seem to conflict with the anti-meritocratic conclusions drawn by Professor Lawrence Stone in his recent work *An Open Elite? England 1540–1880* (1984). The study of grants of arms is one of the principal unexplored channels for English social history over the last four centuries, and would well repay further research.

IV *The Shield of Arms*

ERALDRY is centred on the shield, though other forms of display have always played their part, and as we saw in the chapter on the Origins of Heraldry, it is probable that proto-heraldic devices were displayed on flags and lance pennants before being transferred to shields. In the twelfth and thirteenth centuries further means for showing arms were provided by the accoutrements of the armed and mounted knight, such as his saddle cloth, or horsetrapper, and the linen surcoat which he wore over his chain mail. Indeed, this latter is the origin of the term 'coat of arms', sometimes wrongly used indiscriminately to denote the whole heraldic achievement of the shield and its adjuncts including the crest, motto, and, where appropriate, supporters. The coat of arms is the shield alone, and without it none of the rest of an achievement can exist; in the case of one or two very ancient coats the shield is the sole achievement. The purpose of this chapter is to explain the nature of the shield of arms which is the vehicle for the display of the basic armorial achievements.

Although the shape and form of shields and other objects on which arms are displayed are of interest in identifying the country of origin or date of a particular representation of arms, they have no additional significance. The shape of shield is a question of artistic licence, and various forms have been favoured in different countries and centuries. It is similarly a matter of taste as to how objects are depicted on a shield. There is no single correct way to paint a lion rampant, although there may be incorrect ways if the rendering ceases to resemble a lion, and there are no standard colours used to depict the various tinctures. Gules means red, and variant shades are acceptable as long as they do not become orange or some other recognized heraldic tincture. The shape of shield, form of lion, and shade of red employed on a family's original grant of arms do not bind them for ever thereafter to that particular representation. The many versions of the Royal Arms seen, for example, in churches, as the Sovereign is Head of the Anglican Church, are instances of acceptable variations. The coat of arms consists of either a pattern formed by geometrical divisions or of beasts, birds, or other animate or inanimate objects arranged in a particular manner in certain colours on a shield. It often contains a combination of geometrical divisions and charges, which is the general term used in heraldry to describe monsters, human beings, and other objects. Arms are a form of property, but as the particular depiction is not important, it is the blazon or written description over which an individual possesses legal rights and a knowledge of which is essential to understand the shield of arms.

An understanding of blazon depends initially on a knowledge of the heraldic tinctures. Tincture is the generic term used in heraldry to encompass metals, colours, and furs. English heraldic textbook writers from the sixteenth century onwards have indulged in the production of obscure tinctures which are seldom if ever found, and are both irrelevant to a general grasp of the subject and muddle the student of heraldry. The earliest English heraldic treatise is the Anglo-Norman *De Heraudie*, dated by Professor Gerard J. Brault to 1341–5, and by Rodney Dennys, Somerset Herald, in *The Heraldic Imagination* (1975) to 1280–1300. It quotes thirty-four coats of arms as examples of the way in which charges are borne and blazoned. It does not distinguish between colours and metals, and lists them as Or, Azure, Argent, Gules, Sable, Vert, and Purpure. The second earliest treatise, stated to have been written at the instance of the lately deceased Anne of Bohemia, Queen of Richard II, and thus dating from shortly after 1394, the year of her death, is the *Tractatus de Armis* written in Latin by Johannes de Bado Aureo, identified by Professor Evan J. Jones as Bishop John Trevor and edited by him in *Medieval Heraldry* (1943). The *Tractatus* similarly does not distinguish between colours and metals; it lists white, black, blue, gold, red, and green in descending order of dignity. In the lack of distinction between colour and metal it follows not only *De Heraudie* but also the earlier European work on heraldry the *Tractatus de Insigniis et Armis* by Bartolo de Sassoferrato of Perugia, published posthumously in 1358, which lists the colours as gold, red or purple, blue, white, and black. A much shorter treatise in English, either by the same author as the English *Tractatus* or someone else named John and of much the same date, states that in arms there are two metals, Gold and Silver, and five colours, Sable, Gules, Azure, Vert, and Purple, with an additional colour borne only in the Empire and France called Tawny. A mid-fifteenth century roll of arms known as *Bradfer-Lawrence's Roll* again fails to distinguish between metals and colours, listing as the ordinary colours in arms Sable, Silver, Gold, Azure, Vert, Gules, and Purple. Gerard Leigh, in *The Accedence of Armory* (1562), acknowledges in the text two metals, gold and silver, and five colours, red, blue, black, green, and purple, and also 'proper', which is the natural colour of any beast, fowl, or herb. He rejects as false Tenné or Tawny and Sanguine or Murrey, the former as non-existent and the latter as a mistake for Purpure. Despite the exclusion of these colours, Leigh includes them in a list of abbreviations at the end of his work to assist the reader in interpreting pen and ink sketches of arms where the tinctures are indicated by a single letter. This system of indicating tincture in uncoloured records by abbreviation is known as tricking arms, and has always been used by heralds in England rather than the system known as hatching, principally used on silver and sometimes on glass, which was developed by several continental writers in the early seventeenth century, whereby vertical lines denote Gules, horizontal lines Azure, and so on. (One of the earliest instances of hatching in England is the engraving of Charles I's death warrant, where the seals of the subscribing parties are hatched.) Leigh's list of abbreviations is as follows:

O	Or	Yellow
A	Argent	White
G	Geules	betweene Red and Tenne
B	Azure	bright Blew
V	Vert	Greene
P	Purpure	Purple
E	Ermine	White powdered with Blacke
Es	Ermines	Black poudred White
T	Tenne	Orenge colour
M	Sanguine	Murrey
Pr	Proper colour	Naturall
BB	Blew	Sad Blew

Certain aspects of the list have always been accepted, while others appear to have neither historical nor subsequent support. The two metals, gold and silver, are interchangeable with and can be shown as yellow and white. On the other hand Geules which is now spelled Gules, is generally accepted as red, and Azure as blue of any shade. The former is probably Arabic in origin, derived either from *gul* a rose or *ghül* a feeder on carcasses. The latter has unfortunately been restricted since the Second World War, when a sky blue termed Bleu Celeste, for which there is neither an abbreviation nor an accepted form of hatching, emerged in response to the wartime requirements of the Royal Air Force. Purpure is interesting, as the colour in which it was painted seems to have changed in the course of the sixteenth century. In the fifteenth century it appears as mauve in a painting of the arms of Lacy in a manuscript numbered M 10 in the College library. A considerable number of grants by Wriothesley contain the colour that would now be blazoned Murrey, but the original grant of 1516 to John Compton preserved in the College of Arms blazons it Purpure. This explains the references to Purpure by the early writers, and the apparent lack of purple in arms of the period. By 1616 the Purpure supporters of the Marquess of Winchester are once more a shade of mauve, and in the 1813 grant of arms to Anne Cranmer

Purpure is shown as dark purple. Wriothesley's Purpure and Azure were the livery colours of the House of York, which may explain their frequency in arms such as those granted to Dame Isabelle Mylbery, natural daughter of Edward IV and wife of John Audley. Similarly, those whose arms contain Azure and Argent may have had a link with the House of Lancaster, and Vert and Argent were Tudor livery colours and sometimes appear on arms in a manner suggestive of a link with that dynasty, such as a green and white bordure. The extraordinary elements in the rest of Leigh's list are T, M, and BB; the first two, now blazoned Tenné and Murrey more often than Sanguine, occur occasionally in the twentieth century but have never been spotted in a Visitation record. No evidence beyond Leigh has been found for the existence of BB, or sad blue, either in the sixteenth century or subsequently.

A common failing of most early English heraldic writers hinted at in de Bado Aureo's descending order of dignity of colours is to attribute particular qualities to different tinctures and charges. This matter is dealt with by the Scottish writer Alexander Nisbet in his *System of Heraldry* (1722) where he writes

some Heraulds will have those tinctures above-mentioned to have mystical significations, and to represent moral, politick, and military virtues, in the bearers of such colours; which fancies I designedly omit as ridiculous: For Arms of whatsoever tinctures they be, are equally noble, if the bearers of them be of equal dignity. . . . most of the English writers, not only insist too tediously on their virtues and qualities which they fancy they represent, but give out for a rule in this science; that Gentlemen's Arms should be blazoned by tinctures, the nobility's by precious stones and Sovereign Princes by planets, to show their supposed eminent virtues.

Joseph Edmondson, in his *Complete Body of Heraldry* (1780), dismisses the practice in much the same manner when he writes 'White, say they, denotes chastity; black constancy; blue loyalty, &c, &c. But as to such ridiculous fancies, the mere mention of them is fully sufficient.'

An early sixteenth-century French manuscript, *Les Règles de Blazon*, lists the two metals, five colours, and two furs which comprise the basic heraldic tinctures. These are listed below with the abbreviations most commonly used in reference books since the eighteenth century, and for the sake of interest the precious stones, planets, and virtues attributed by the sixteenth- and seventeenth-century English writers, together with the form of hatching following the widely adopted scheme devised by Sylvester Petra Sancta in his *Terrerae Gentilitia* (1638) are also given. Those who wish to pursue the supposed symbolism of tincture combinations should consult Leigh's *Accedence of Armory*, and for ten further forms of blazon by flowers, elements, numbers, and metals, the best source is Sir John Ferne's *The Glory of Generositie* (1586). The tinctures are:

Metals	Term of Blazon	Abbrev.	Precious Stones	Planets	Virtues	Hatching
Gold	Or	Or	Topaz	Sun	Faith	Dots
Silver	Argent	Arg	Pearl	Moon	Innocency	Unhatched

Colours	Term of Blazon	Abbrev.	Precious Stones	Planets	Virtues	Hatching
Blue	Azure	Az	Sapphire	Jupiter	Loyalty	Horizontal lines
Red	Gules	Gu	Ruby	Mars	Magnanimity	Vertical lines
Black	Sable	Sa	Diamond	Saturn	Prudence	Cross-hatched vertical & horizontal
Green	Vert Sinople in France	Vert Sin	Emerald	Venus	Love	Diagonal \
Purple	Purpure	Purp	Amethyst	Mercury	Temperance	Diagonal /

Furs	Term of Blazon	Abbrev.	Precious Stones	Planets	Virtues	Hatching
Ermine	Ermine	Erm	—	—	—	—
Vair	Vair	Vair	—	—	—	—

Not all writers attribute the same virtues to the tinctures. De Bado Aureo states that white signifies light, black, the second colour in dignity, darkness, blue is associated with iron and strength, reconciliation and friendship, gold implies obedience and gentility, and red cruelty; while green, considered a later addition as an heraldic colour, has no virtues at all attributed to it. Gold was sometimes blazoned Gold rather than Or in the sixteenth century, and this alternative subsequently occurs sporadically depending on the whim of the Kings of Arms. Ermine is white covered with black spots, which can be stylized in a variety of ways derived from and representing the tail of the stoat in winter. Variations of Ermine are Ermines, white spots on black, Erminois, black spots on gold, and Pean, gold spots on black. Vair is a white and blue pattern created by sewing squirrel skins together. A muddle between Verre (glass) and Vair (the fur) led to the mistranslation of the fairy tale of 'Cinderella', which came to England from France, and transformed her slippers of squirrel fur into glass in England. Had it not been a fairy tale this would presumably have been rectified as a ridiculous mistake some centuries ago. Vair has been drawn in a variety of forms. If it is shown in tinctures other than white and blue it is termed Vairy, and the tinctures must be specified, such as Vairy Or and Sable, which is a pattern of Vair in gold and black.

Every shield is of a tincture or combination of tinctures, and in any English blazon of arms it is the tincture of the surface of the shield or field as it is termed that is given first. *Vert a Lion rampant Argent*, therefore, means a green shield on which is a silver or white rampant

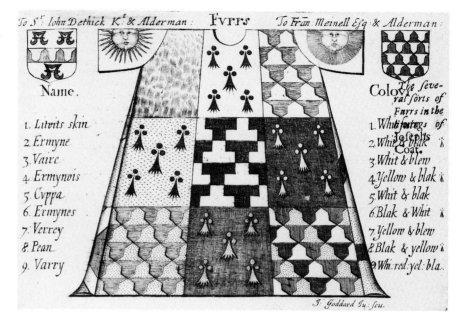

A tabard of furs from Sylvanus Morgan's *Sphere of Gentry* illustrating Ermine, Vair, and variants (Lib. 2, p. 73).

lion. A knowledge of terms used to describe the different parts of the shield can be helpful in understanding blazon. The parts of the shield are illustrated in detail from a manuscript in the hand of Stephen Martin Leake, Garter; the principal point to remember is that all directions are given as if the spectator was behind the shield, dexter is used to denote right, and sinister left. Chief refers to the top part of the shield and base to the bottom part; these are not affected whether one is behind or looking at the shield, but a charge in dexter chief is in the top left-hand corner as you look at the shield as this would be the top right-hand corner if you stood behind it. Plain shields may have been used by the anonymous black, white, or other knights in tournaments in preference to their own arms so that their identity should remain a mystery , but few if any people or families were recognized as bearing a plain coat, the Ermine coat of the Dukes of Brittany being an obvious exception. Shields were either divided geometrically or charged. Leigh lists nine partitions or methods of partition:

1. *Per pale*: a vertical division of the shield as in *Per pale Argent and Gules* of Waldegrave now represented by Earl Waldegrave, KG. The dexter half is blazoned first.

2. *Quarterly*: where the shield is divided into four as if by a cross, as in *Quarterly Or and Gules* of Mandeville, Earl of Essex, extinct in 1227. The quarter in dexter chief is blazoned first and is the first quarter; normally this would be the same as that in sinister base, the fourth quarter. The second quarter is in sinister chief and the third in dexter base.

3. *Per fess*: where the shield is divided horizontally, as in *Per fess Gules and Argent* of Magdeburg impaled by George II. The half in chief is blazoned first.

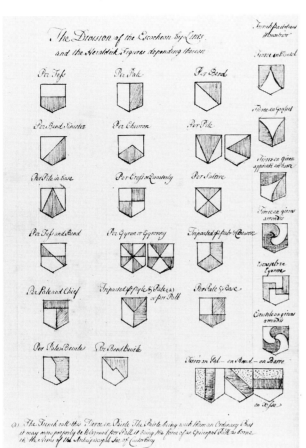

(*above*) Armorial bearings of Campbell, Earls (and subsequently Dukes) of Argyll, illustrating gyronny in the first and fourth quarters of the shield. There is no ermine in the mantling (Coll. Arms, The Arms of Scotch Nobility, The Hamilton Armorial [*c.*1560–64], fo. 33).

(*left*) English and French lines of partition in the hand of Stephen Martin Leake, Garter (Coll. Arms, SML 56).

4. *Per bend*: where the shield is split by a diagonal division from dexter chief to sinister base, of which the most celebrated British example has a modified line of partition, *Per bend embattled Argent and Gules* for Boyle, Earls of Burlington and Cork. The half in chief, i.e. to the sinister, is blazoned first.

5. *Per bend sinister*: the reverse of *Per bend*, and the shield is divided by a diagonal line from sinister chief to dexter base. The half in chief, in this case to the dexter, is blazoned first.

6. *Per chevron*: where the shield is divided by an inverted V, the point usually two-thirds of the way up the shield and the ends towards the foot of the dexter and sinister sides of the shield, as in *Per chevron Sable and Argent* the arms of the Aston family of Cheshire. The half in chief is blazoned first.

7. *Per saltire*: which divides the shield into four as if by an X, as in *Per saltire Sable and Or* attributed to Bartholomew Hottyngdene in about 1520. The quarter in chief is blazoned first.

8. *Per pile.* Subsequent writers have considered that this is meaningless, being no different from a pile. *Per pile* is illustrated by Leigh as formed by diagonal lines commencing in dexter and sinister chief and joining in centre base. Since the sixteenth century the pile has not touched the bottom of the shield, and does not occupy the whole of the top of the shield.

Invected, engrailed, indented, and other lines of partition in the hand of Stephen Martin Leake, Garter, with cadency marks and the parts of the shield (Coll. Arms, SML 56).

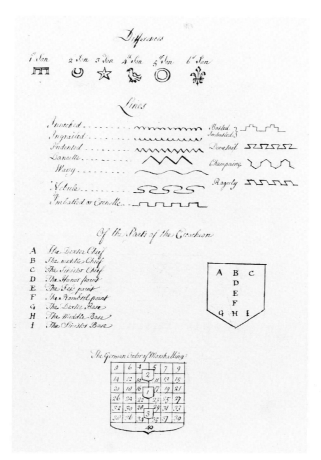

9. *Gyronny*: a division of the shield into eight, produced by halving each quarter of quarterly, or in other words by a combination of quarterly and per saltire as in *Gyronny of eight Or and Sable* of Campbell, whose principal representative is the Duke of Argyll. The tincture in the sinister chief half of the first quarter is blazoned first.

In addition to partitions or methods of partition there are lines of partition. All but one of the instances above have assumed plain or straight lines of partition, but lines of partition may be of a considerable number of different forms, such as embattled in the case of Boyle, Earls of Burlington and Cork as mentioned above. Examples of lines of partition that have been used for some centuries are wavy, engrailed, invected, indented, dancetty, and raguly. A recent addition in England is dentilly, a line of partition resembling the teeth of a ratchet wheel first granted by the English Kings of Arms in 1986. The principal interest in the lines of partition lies in the point that the differences of detail and consequent distinctions are a post-medieval development, and in the fourteenth century wavy, indented, and dancetty, for instance, were not regarded as distinct from one another.

The next stage in complication is the painting of simple geometrical shapes on the shield. Although logically one stage beyond shields with linear divisions alone, they are, together with coats containing lions and eagles, the principal early stages of heraldic design. These shapes are known as Honourable Ordinaries and Sub-Ordinaries, and writers have argued as to which shapes fall into which category and as to their size, earlier writers, such as Leigh, Holme, and Guillim favouring the occupation of one-third of the shield, and later writers such as Edmondson favouring one-fifth, on the grounds that a bend, pale, or chevron occupying one-third of the field makes the coat look clumsy and disagreeable.

The first Honourable Ordinary is the cross, classed first because Christ died on the Cross. There are many forms of cross in addition to the plain cross, such as the cross flory, the extremities of which resemble fleurs-de-lis, and the cross potent, the ends of which resemble the heads of crutches. Chaucer used the word potent to mean a crutch as in, 'So eld she was that she ne went unless it was by a potent'. As this is the first case of a charge or geometrical shape of one tincture which must be placed on a field of another tincture, it is an appropriate moment to mention one of the basic rules in the composition of arms, which is that a colour may not be placed on a colour and a metal may not be placed on a metal. Furs may be placed on either, as may charges blazoned as proper, and fur may be placed on fur. Questions do arise as to whether one part of the shield lies on another or not. Charges, Ordinaries, and Sub-Ordinaries are on the field, but equal divisions of the field do not lie on one another so may both be coloured or of a metal. Occasional exceptions occur but these, like *Or a Cross Argent*, borne by several Kings of Jerusalem, are usually not English, and this coat was criticized in *De Heraudie*.

The second Honourable Ordinary is the chief, created by a straight line dividing the top third or fifth of the shield, depending on taste, from the rest of the field. On a curved shield such a line might appear curved, and consequently the introduction of enarched lines as a means of difference must be approached with caution. A chief is generally regarded as a charge placed on the field, and following this a coloured chief may not be placed on a coloured field. There is a small body of precedent to the contrary, which suggests that a chief should not be regarded as the second Honourable Ordinary (or, if the early writers are to be believed, the first Honourable Ordinary before the Crucifixion elevated the status of the cross), but rather as a division of the field. The precedents are Lloyd, *Sable a Spear Head Argent embrued proper between three scaling Ladders on a chief Gules a triple-towered Castle Argent*; Middlecot, recorded at the Heralds' Visitation of Lincolnshire in 1634, *Azure an Eagle displayed Ermine on a Chief Gules three Escallops Or*; and Lovelace, confirmed in a grant of a Crest by Robert Cooke, Clarenceux, in 1573, *Gules on a Chief indented Sable three Martlets Argent*. The term chief is said to be derived from *chef*, signifying the head or top part of the shield.

The third Honourable Ordinary is the pale, supposedly derived from pales or pallisades of defence. It is a vertical stripe occupying one-third or one-fifth of a shield, and can, like the chief, be plain or modified, as indented, wavy, and so on. If the shield is divided into an even number of vertical stripes it is termed paly of the number of divisions. The diminutive of a pale is a pallet, and this term tends to be used in preference to pale when two or more are shown. If a shield is divided into an odd number of vertical stripes, such as seven gold and black stripes, it would be blazoned *Or three Pallets Sable*, and the tinctures cannot both be colours or metals, whereas a similar pattern of eight stripes would be blazoned *Paly of eight Or and Sable* and could be Or and Argent or Gules and Sable, as in such a case one tincture is not deemed to be the field on which the other is placed. Textbooks state that the pallet is half a pale in width, and half a pallet is an endorse, which may, however, only be borne on either side of a pale.

The fourth Honourable Ordinary is the bend, possibly derived from the shoulder belt, though Guillim derives it from the French *bender*, to stretch forth. It is a diagonal band stretching from dexter chief to sinister base. Leigh makes it occupy one-fifth of the field, with which Guillim agrees if it is uncharged; if charged he makes it occupy one-third. The bend, like its fellow Ordinaries, suffers from the English disease of diminutives. In Europe a blazon of three bends would be acceptable; in England, to complicate matters, there is a bendlet which is half a bend, a garter, which is one-third of a bend (and on which one may only place flowers or foils), a cotise, which is quarter of a bend (and which, like the endorse, may be borne only on either side of the bend), and finally a riband, which is one-eighth of the width of a bend. The most celebrated English coat incorporating a bend is *Azure a Bend Or* round which centred the case of *Scrope* v. *Grosvenor* (1385–90), the former family winning the case and retaining the coat which they bear to this day. *Azure two Bends Or* is the coat of Buonarotti as borne by Michelangelo. A bend running from sinister chief to dexter base is known as a bend sinister. In England its diminutives are a skarpe or skarfe, which is one-half the width, and a baton, which is one-quarter. The latter is one of the charges associated with illegitimacy in England, and it is usually shown couped, that is, not touching the sides of the shield; according to Leigh, 'Every bastard also may have his batune, of which colour he will, but not of mettal. For mettal is for the bastards of Princes'. If a shield is divided into an even number of diagonal bands it is blazoned bendy or bendy sinister, depending on their angle.

The fifth Honourable Ordinary is the fess. This is a horizontal band across the centre of the shield. Like the other Ordinaries it can be modified, and when more than one appears on a shield in England they are termed bars, although there are no rules as to comparative width. When the whole shield is divided into an equal number of horizontal stripes it is blazoned barry of the number. In England a rule emerged that if the number of stripes is of ten or more the term barruly or burely should be used instead of barry. Guillim derives the word fess from a French word meaning the loins of a man, and from there interprets it as a girdle of honour surrounding the middle. The English heralds in search of diminutives produced the barrulet and the closet. The former is half the width of a bar, but if borne in pairs is termed a bar gemel. The latter is an indeterminate width between a bar and barrulet, and seldom found. A cotise, defined as half a barrulet, may be borne with a fess usually on either side.

The sixth Honourable Ordinary is the inescutcheon, which is a shield borne as a charge on the arms. Textbooks suggest that it should be the same shape as the shield on which it is borne. A celebrated example of a coat bearing inescutcheons is that of Hay, *Argent three Inescutcheons Gules* as represented by the Earl of Erroll, Hereditary Lord High Constable of Scotland. If an inescutcheon is voided,

Armorial bearings of Hay, Earl of Errol, recorded mid-seventeenth century, with three inescutcheons on the arms and the badge shown as inanimate supporters. Unlike English peers of the seventeenth century, there is no ermine mantling (Coll. Arms, EDN 17, Scotland's Nobility, fo. 26).

meaning its centre is removed following the shape of the shield showing the field and leaving a narrow border, it is termed an orle.

The seventh Honourable Ordinary is the chevron, derived from a similar French word meaning a rafter. This is formed by two diagonal bands, commencing in dexter and sinister base, meeting in different periods at different heights in the centre of the shield, and resembling the silhouette of a roof or an inverted letter V. *Or a Chevron Gules* was the coat of the Stafford family, sometime Dukes of Buckingham, and *Or three Chevrons Gules* was borne by the distinguished medieval family of Clare, Lords of Clare and Earls of Hertford and Gloucester. In England half a chevron in width is termed a chevronel, although the writers disagree as to whether only three may be borne on a shield or two or three. Under either interpretation Clare would be reduced to chevronels. Half a chevronel is a couple close, and like the endorse and cotise these are borne in pairs on either side of the chevron. A shield divided into an equal number of chevron shapes is termed chevronny. Unlike the bend, where charges follow the angle of the bend unless otherwise specified, charges on a chevron are shown erect, or palewise to use the heraldic term. A chevron is sometimes shown reversed with the point to the base, when it is blazoned a *chevron reversed*.

The eighth Honourable Ordinary is the saltire, better known as St Andrew's Cross. If charged the charges are usually shown erect, and it can be modified, for instance engrailed or invected. Fitzgerald, Duke of Leinster bears *Argent a Saltire Gules*.

The ninth and last Honourable Ordinary according to the English writers is the bar. This has already been discussed under fess. In France the term fasce is used for the fess and all its diminutives, and the term bar in France means a bend sinister. Some writers add the bordure as a further Ordinary. As the name suggests, this is a border round the shield, and those who favour it make the orle discussed under inescutcheons a diminutive and the tressure, best known from its presence as a double tressure flory counter-flory in the Royal Arms of Scotland, a diminutive of the orle. Flory counter-flory means that the tressures are ornamented with the heads of fleurs-de-lis facing outwards from the outer tressure and inwards from the inner one. In the case of the Royal Arms of Scotland the tressures surround a lion rampant.

The other class of geometrical shapes ranking after the Honourable Ordinaries are termed Sub-Ordinaries or plain Ordinaries without the prefix Honourable; with charges such as the bordure and the related forms of inescutcheon, orle, and tressure there is some dispute as to whether they should be classed as Ordinaries or Sub-Ordinaries. Leigh numbers the Sub-Ordinaries as nine, of which the first is the gyron, which is of triangular form created by drawing a straight line from one corner in the chief of the shield to its centre, and joining this to the edge of the shield by a vertical or horizontal line. Leigh's second Sub-Ordinary is the orle, as he does not regard it as a diminutive of the inescutcheon. The third Sub-Ordinary is the pile, which has already been mentioned under lines of partition. It is a wedge shape issuing from the chief unless otherwise blazoned, and ending in a point. The sixteenth-century pile occupied one-third of the chief as compared to Leigh's Per pile, which occupied the whole chief. The modern pile is closer to Per pile unless there are two or more. It is disputed whether three piles should join in one point or not. Piles can be modified, such as engrailed. The fourth Sub-Ordinary is the quarter, always shown in dexter chief, and originally occupying a quarter of the shield although the tendency is to draw it smaller. The fifth is the quarter sinister, which is borne in sinister chief. The sixth is the canton, which is the same square shape as the quarter and originally occupied one-ninth part of the shield in dexter chief, being the same depth as a chief which occupies one-third of the field. The seventh is the canton sinister, which is similar to the canton but borne in sinister chief. The eighth is the flasque, now obsolete, which might be best described as a narrow flaunch, the ninth Sub-Ordinary. The flaunch, like the flasque, must be borne in pairs, and a pair are produced by drawing a line arched towards the centre of the shield from the dexter and sinister chief points of the shield down either side, rejoining the edge of the shield in dexter and sinister base. Flasques occupy less of the shield, as do voiders, another diminutive.

Later writers such as Mark Anthony Porny, French master at Eton College, in *The Elements of Heraldry* (1765) add other Sub-Ordinaries, namely the fret, lozenge, fusil, and mascle. These are related, the lozenge being a diamond shape with four equal sides, best known not as a charge but in place of the shield as a vehicle on which to display the arms of a spinster or widow; the mascle, a voided lozenge; the fret, a mascle interlaced by two lines in saltire of similar width to the sides of the mascle, and crossing in its centre; and the fusil, a tall narrow lozenge. The label, a thin bar with dependent points or lambeaux, although the cadency mark for an eldest son in his father's lifetime when of three points, and used to distinguish the arms of members of the British Royal Family, was used as a charge in medieval heraldry, and could be classed as a plain Ordinary or Sub-Ordinary.

Most shields contain some charges other than mere geometrical divisions of the field. The number of possible charges is never-ending, and can vary from the lion, usually found either rampant or passant in the earliest coats, to a representation of a DNA double helix, as in the arms of Warwick University. Glossaries such as James Parker and Co.'s *A Glossary of Terms used in Heraldry* (1894) provide detailed catalogues of heraldic charges. In a general survey other questions, such as the first date of appearance of certain charges and changes in the composition of new designs of arms are perhaps more interesting. Very broadly, charges can be divided into beasts, birds, other creatures, divine and human beings, monsters, natural objects, inanimate objects, and parts thereof. Except in *De Heraudie*, the obsession with symbolism appears throughout the early treatises, but as the *Tractatus*, the second oldest English treatise of arms, is comparatively late, dating from a year or two before 1400, one hundred and fifty years after the first rolls of arms, its symbolism can have had no effect on the early development of heraldry.

The increase in the variety of charges borne on arms can be seen from an examination of medieval sources such as rolls of arms, seals, and the early treatises. *De Heraudie* mentions the griffin, lion, leopard, eagle, martlet, popinjay, crow, swan, and heron. To this de Bado Aureo adds the pard and panther, stag, boar, horse, bear, dog, dragon, hawk, owl, dove, jackdaw (probably the same as the crow), cock, pike, and crab, attributing particular qualities to each animal. The initial preponderance of lions amongst the beasts can be seen by examining the three earliest English rolls of arms, all of the reign of Henry III. They contain seventy-five different coats with lions, one with a hind for the Count of Tierstein (a punning or canting coat as tier means a hind), one with a bull, one with a horse, and one with three dogs, again a punning coat for Nicholas de Kennet, a kennet being a type of dog. A similar comparison can be made with the birds, which reveals sixteen different coats with eagles and one for each of the following birds—crow, heron, hawk, cock, and martlet. Two of the coats *Or two Corbies Sable* (the crows) and *Azure three Herons Argent* are canting coats for Thomas Corbet of Caus, Shropshire, who died in 1274, and Odinel Heron a younger son of William Heron of Ford, Northumberland. Several further beasts appear before the first foundation of the College of Arms in 1484 and the activity of the Heralds and Kings of Arms of the late fifteenth and early sixteenth centuries. Lambs are seen on templar seals of the late thirteenth century but not normally on a shield; a hare riding a dog, and a squirrel eating a nut both appear on seals of arms in 1323 for Nicholas Acton and Robert de Cressewell; there is a goat on a seal of arms of John de Bowes in 1358 and a wolf on that of Roger Louthe in 1361, a camel was used by John Cammel of Queen Camel in Somerset in 1418, and the seal of the town of Coventry in 1424 shows an elephant and castle. Symkin Eyre, Lord Mayor of London bore a porcupine on his arms in 1445.

If those being granted or assuming arms paid any attention to the supposed symbolism some charges would never have been used. The lion signifies bravery, ferocity, might, gentility, and liberality according

to de Bado Aureo, but his attributions for the other beasts are less
favourable. The leopard is considered to be borne of an adulterous
union between a lioness and a pard, and like the mule is incapable
of reproducing itself. It is suggested as an appropriate charge for
someone born in adultery or someone barred from producing heirs of
his body, such as an abbot. The distinction between the pard and the
panther is slight, being in whiteness of spots, and they both signify an
original bearer of the arms who was not free-born. The stag signifies
poverty in youth and wisdom in war, the boar a valiant, wily, and
envious warrior, the horse form, beauty, prowess, and colour, and the
bear—an irate, intolerant animal—signifies a strong, unwise warrior,
whereas the dog represents a loyal man. The owl, surprisingly,
signifies a lazy man, cowardly in battle, who lives on plunder and
rapine, in contrast to its usual role as a symbol of wisdom sacred to
Athene.

The medieval bestiaries, containing a mixture of natural history and
myth, must have played some role in the expansion of supposedly
natural charges on shields. However, the unicorn, which appears in
bestiaries of the early thirteenth century, is omitted by de Bado Aureo,
and does not occur in arms till the early fifteenth century, so the
influence was not immediate. The whale with two spouts in the arms
of the Soap Boilers of London is an example of literary influence,
being taken from Conrad Gesner's *De Avibus et Piscibus* (1560). But a
search amongst bestiaries is an overcomplication when a reason is
sought for the appearance of one comparatively obscure natural
creature rather than another. Fish in thirteenth-century rolls of arms
include barbels, lucies (pike), and hake, for families of Bar, Lucy, and
Hacket. One need look no further than the surnames of the bearers for
a reason for the charges, and although the traditional qualities of the
lion and eagle must have contributed to their frequent use, the popular
belief that coats of arms must have some meaning has no historical

A whale with two spouts, as
illustrated in Conrad Gesner's
De Avibus et Piscibus (1560),
177.

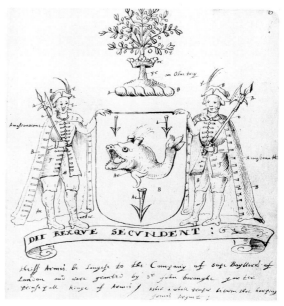

Grant of arms, crest, and supporters (between 1633 and 1643) to the Company of Soap Boilers of London. The arms are based on Conrad Gesner's preceding depiction of a whale (Coll. Arms, Miscellaneous Grants 4, fo.6).

basis. Originally the number of charges used was limited, and fabulous beasts and monsters such as the bonacon, bagwyn, trogodice, tragopan and theow, ypotryll, yale, and pantheon, introduced to English heraldry in the fifteenth and sixteenth centuries, were derived in part from the bestiaries, as was the griffin in the late thirteenth century, and were in part the product of the fertile imagination of heralds such as Sir Thomas Wriothesley who granted the tragopan, a demi-eagle with ram's horns, as a crest to Robert Lord of London.

Flowers and leaves are another familiar charge of heraldry. Fleurs-de-lis and roses are amongst the earliest flowers, the former appearing on the Royal Arms of France first borne in the reign of Louis VII (1137–80) as *Azure semy de lis Or*. Semy means that the field of a shield is scattered or powdered with a charge. The number of fleurs-de-lis was reduced to three by Charles V of France (1364–80) after the assumption of the arms by Edward III of England as part of his claim to the throne of France. Henry IV reduced the number to three in the coat he bore, and they remained in this form, known as France modern, in the English and subsequently British Royal Arms till their removal in 1801. Foils are a group of charges which, depending on the number of lobes or petals, may represent leaves or flowers. A trefoil of three lobes resembles a clover leaf, whereas a cinquefoil of five is closer to a flower, and different names are assigned by Leigh according to the tincture of cinquefoil, a golden one being a ranuncula. The blazon of cinquefoil by tincture has not been followed in England, but the English whim of classification did succeed with the roundel which has a different name according to its tincture, whereas in France there is only one distinction between those that are of a metal termed bezants and those of a colour termed torteaux, the terms used for gold and red roundels alone in England. The roundel Argent or plate produces the canting coat of Standish, *Sable three Plates* representing standing dishes; to blazon them as standing dishes fails to conceal the pun. The classification of charges was an early development in England, as the author of *De Heraudie* mentions besauntz, platz, gasteuls (precursor of the torteau), and pelots (for pellets, black roundels, also known as gunstones and ogresses).

In the Middle Ages importance was attached to the distinctiveness of arms, and this may have influenced the complicated designs and new monsters produced at the end of the period by the early Tudor heralds for the new men of that era. As knowledge of heraldry increased towards the end of the sixteenth century grantees tried to persuade the Kings of Arms to return to the simplicity of medieval design. Complicated designs reappear in the late eighteenth century in the landscape chiefs often depicting a scene from a distinguished soldier or sailor's career, usually granted by Sir Isaac Heard, Garter. Whilst avoiding such excesses, Victorian designs tended to be cluttered; in the present century some heralds show remarkable ingenuity in producing simple designs of a medieval nature which have never been used before, while others continue in the Victorian tradition.

The granting or assigning of complicated new arms distinguished new arms from old, but it did not distinguish the arms of brothers. Various means were adopted so that the arms of younger brothers should be distinct from one another and the paternal arms, but recognizable in origin. Colours were altered or reversed as in *Argent a Saltire Gules* borne by the Nevilles of Hornby in Lancashire, descended from a younger brother in the late thirteenth century, to distinguish their arms from *Gules a Saltire Argent* borne by the senior line. One disadvantage of tincture reversal is the risk of clashing with an unrelated family. Neville of Hornby and Fitzgerald are indistinguishable. Other forms of difference were the transposition or substitution of charges, and the addition of labels and bordures. This is the system that is still followed in Scotland, where no two men bear the same arms. In England a system of charging small marks on the shield was devised; these are known as cadency marks, and the system is said to have been invented by John Writhe, Garter, in about 1500. The English system attributes a label of three points to the eldest son in the lifetime of his father and one of five points to his eldest son, a crescent to the second son, a mullet (a five-pointed star) to the third, a martlet to the fourth, an annulet to the fifth, a fleur-de-lis to the sixth, a rose to the seventh, a cross moline to the eighth, and a double quatrefoil to the ninth. Such cadency marks should be painted smaller than a charge on a shield, and are generally borne in the chief of a shield and are of a

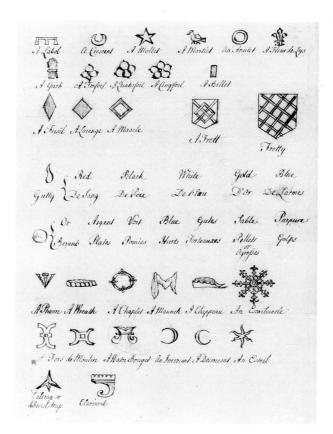

Cadency marks, gouttes, roundels, and some charges in the hand of Stephen Martin Leake, Garter (Coll. Arms, SML 56).

suitable tincture for the arms. If the arms are quartered the cadency mark should be placed in the centre of the shield where the quarters join. The second son of a second son places a crescent on a crescent, and so the system continues, but it does contain a logical flaw as, although a good system for seeing a man's position in his family, it fails to distinguish between an uncle and nephew who are both second sons.

Cadency marks tend to be used as a matter of courtesy today rather than as a rule. There seems to be no more recent statement on the law of arms relating to cadency marks than that of Sir Edward Coke, who wrote in his *Commentary upon Littleton* (1628): 'Gentry and Armes is of the nature of Gavelkind; for they descend to all the sonnes, every sonne being a gentleman alike. Which gentry and armes do not descend to all the brethren alone, but to all their posterity. But yet *jure primogeniturae*, the eldest shall beare as a badge of his birthright, his father's armes without any differences for that as Littleton saith, sectione 5 he is more worthy of blood but all the younger brethren shall give several differences.' This appears to suggest that, whatever the failings of the system, arms should be borne with an appropriate cadency mark. The only case where an argument might be made for not doing so is where a member of a family is entitled to a quartering which distinguishes his coat from that of his cousins.

Arms are also differenced for illegitimacy. Historically an illegitimate child was a stranger in blood to his father, and probably as a matter of custom rather than law an illegitimate child, if acknowledged, might be granted a variation of his father's arms. This is discussed further in the chapter on marshalling of arms. In the seventeenth century in England a plain bordure was often used for non-Royal illegitimacy, as in the two grants in 1664 to Henry Cavendish of Doveridge, Derbyshire, and Anabella, natural daughter of Emanuel, Earl of Sunderland, of the arms of Cavendish and Scrope in plain borders Or and Argent. This changed to wavy bordures in more recent centuries as seen in the seven grants of 30 August 1806 to the seven natural children of Thomas Peter Legh of Lyme Park in Cheshire. The baton sinister also occurs particularly in grants to natural children of the Sovereign, though it is also a general mark of illegitimacy; if Gerard Leigh is followed it should be of a colour rather than a metal for non-Royal illegitimacy.

The appearance of the shield can be altered by additions or augmentations of honour. The traditional view is that these are a mark of honour granted by the Sovereign, some out of mere grace but mostly for merit. The textbooks produce nine additions of honour, namely the bordure, quarter, canton, gyron, pile, flasque, flaunch, voider (diminutive of the flaunch), and escutcheon of pretence. In contrast there are also nine abatements of honour which could be added to arms by the Court of Chivalry for base behaviour. As no examples exist of arms with such abatements, at best they are a theoretical punishment to discourage armigers from dishonourable acts. Abatements must be of a stain, i.e. sanguine or tenné rather than a metal or colour. Leigh gives the following order, but without the stains which later writers add. First, a point dexter parted tenné for one who boasts of some valiant act which he never performed, and second, a point champaine tenné for one who kills his prisoner after quarter demanded. The third is a plain point sanguine for a person who lies to his Sovereign or Commander-in-Chief; the fourth, a point in point sanguine for cowardice; the fifth, a gusset sanguine borne to the dexter by an adulterer and to the sinister by a drunkard—the two gussets can be borne together; the sixth, a gore sinister tenné for cowardice towards an enemy; the seventh, a delf tenné for one who revokes a challenge he has given; the eighth, an inescutcheon reversed sanguine for any man who 'discourteously entreateth eyther maid or widow against her will, or flieth from his Soveraignes banner', and the ninth, the whole coat reversed for treason. If treason implies attainder then the right to arms is forfeited by the attainder, so the question of displaying the arms upside down does not arise. In theory these charges or divisions of the shield, if of a colour or metal, are honourable, but their supposedly dishonourable attributes mean that they seldom if ever appear.

In practice the nine additions of honour are not the only way in which Armorial Bearings can be augmented. An additional crest can be granted as an augmentation, as can a whole coat which, as it is an honour, should be borne in the first quarter before the paternal arms. Examples are the augmentations granted by Henry VIII to his non-Royal wives and still borne by the Seymour family, Dukes of Somerset, and the arms of the City of Westminster granted as an augmentation in 1832 to the first Marquess of Westminster and borne by his descendant the Duke of Westminster. Arms granted as an honour where no arms previously existed are not augmentations as nothing existed before to which they can be added. Although there are isolated documented examples of pre-Tudor augmentations, most of the well-known and supposed English medieval augmentations can be shown to be Tudor inventions. The grant on 3 January 1385/6 by Richard II to Robert de Vere, 9th Earl of Oxford, then Marquess of Dublin and subsequently Duke of Ireland, of arms of *Azure three Crowns Or within a Bordure Argent for Ireland* to be borne in the first and fourth quarters for as long as he held the Lordship of Ireland is genuine and recorded in the Patent Rolls. Other so called augmentations with origins in the fourteenth century are those to Dodge (1306), Legh (1346), Pelham (1356), and Leche (1357–60). These are all spurious. An alleged copy of the 1306 grant to Peter Dodge is written on a blank page of the 1531 Visitation of Surrey. The grant is by an otherwise unknown Guyenne King of Arms, James Hedingley, and the arms granted *Barry of six Or and Sable on a Pale Gules a woman's Dugge or Breast distilling drops of milk Proper* do not appear without the breast in other records, which suggests it is anyway not an augmentation. The text refers to the loyal and valiant service of the grantee, and the whole thing seems to be an early sixteenth-century joke.

In 1575 William Flower granted Sir Peter Legh of Lyme an augmentation of *an Inescutcheon Sable semy of Mullets and charged with an Arm embowed in armour Argent the hand grasping a Pennon of St George.* The grant was an augmentation in token of his descent from Piers Legh, a hero of the battle of Crécy where he took the Count of Tanquervil prisoner. The augmentation does not pretend to be of other than sixteenth-century origin but it is nevertheless a pity that Piers Legh, the so-called hero of Crécy, was not born till fourteen years after the battle, and the feats attributed to him were those of his father-in-law Sir Thomas Danyers. Piers Legh was in fact beheaded in 1399 as a supporter of Richard II. It is questionable whether the

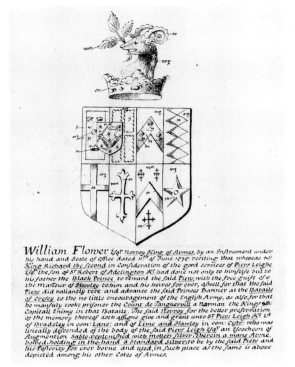

William Flower Esq. Norroy King of Armes, by an Instrument under his hand and Seale of office dated 11th of June 1575: reciting that whereas King Richard the second in Consideration of the good services of Piers Leigbe Esq the son of Sr Robert of Adelington Kt had done not only to himselfe but to his father the Black Prince to reward the said Piers, with the free guift of the Mannour of Hawley to him and his heires for ever, aswell for that the said Piers did valiantly vere and advance the said Princes banner at the Bataile of Cressey to the no little encouragement of the English Army, as also for that he manfully tooke prisoner the Count de Tanguervill a Norman the Kings Capitall Enimy in that Bataile. The said Norroy for the better preservation of the memory thereof doth assigne give and grant unto Sr Piers Leigh Kt Ld of Bradeley in com: Lanc: and of Lime and Hanley in com: Cestr: who was lineally descended of the body of the said Piers Leigh Esq an Escocheon of Augmention sable replenished with mollets silver, therein a mans Arme bowed, holding in the hand a Standard silver, to be by the said Piers and his Posterity for ever borne and used, in such place as the same is above depicted among: his other Cotes of Armes.

augmentation should have been retained in the 1806 grant to the illegitimate children of Thomas Peter Legh (the rights of illegitimate children are discussed in the chapter on marshalling of arms). A Pelham is credited with the capture of King John of France at the battle of Poitiers in 1356. As a result he is said to have been granted a coat of augmentation of *Gules two broken Buckles palewise the Buckles upwards Argent.* This coat, now borne by the Duke of Newcastle and Earls of Chichester and Yarborough, is not borne in the first quarter, as an augmentation should be, but the second, and occurs in no medieval sources, so it would seem to be another Tudor creation. Sometime between 1357 and 1360 a member of the Leche family living in Berkshire is said to have entertained three kings in his house, Edward III and his two prisoners John of France and David II of Scotland: Edward is reputed to have augmented Leche's arms by the addition of three crowns so they became *Ermine on a Chief indented Gules three Crowns Or.* But the arms never appear attributed to Leche without the crowns, and their first occurrence is on the *County Roll*, a lost roll of arms of people living in the reign of Richard II of which a late sixteenth-century copy exists where the coat is stated to be that of Sir Roger Leche of Derbyshire.

A Royal Warrant of King Charles II dated 3 September 1660 (I 25,82) addressed to Sir Edward Walker, Garter, 'in this tyme of generall reward' and 'to avoyd the trouble and importunity of passing such under Our Great Seale', gave him 'full power and authority to give grant and assigne unto any person of eminent quality fidelity and extraordinary merit that shall desire it such augmentation of any of Our Royall badges to be added unto his Armes as you shall judge most proper to testify the same'. The Warrant also refers to one in similar terms given by Charles I to Walker at Oxford on 6 May 1645. Walker made about fifty grants of augmentation under the terms of these general warrants, although the augmentation to the Lane family of Bentley and subsequently King's Bromley in Staffordshire, of the arms of England to be borne on a canton which is most frequently associated with the Civil War, was made not by Walker but by Sir William Dugdale, Garter, and Henry St George, Clarenceux, by Letters Patent dated 5 February 1678/9. The grantee was Thomas, nephew of Jane Lane who helped Charles II to escape after the battle of Worcester, although the patent refers to the service of the grantee's father Colonel John Lane. Examples of augmentations under the 1645 warrant are of the *Bordure Azure charged with Saltires Argent* (eight saltires are in the College records; ten have subsequently been used) granted in September 1645 to the City of Hereford for 'valiantly defending themselves against the Scottish army', and the *Canton Gules charged with a Lion of England* added to the arms of Sir John Walpole in June 1646. Examples of augmentations granted under the 1660 warrant are those to Francis Wolfe of Madesely, Shropshire in 1661, Samuel Isaac of Exeter, and Sir Charles Harbord in 1670, and to Robert Foley, High Sheriff of Worcestershire, in 1671. The Civil War

Augmentations made in 1645 and 1646 to the City of Hereford and others by Sir Edward Walker, Garter, for supporting the Royalist cause in the Civil War (Coll. Arms, Walker 2, pp. 26–7).

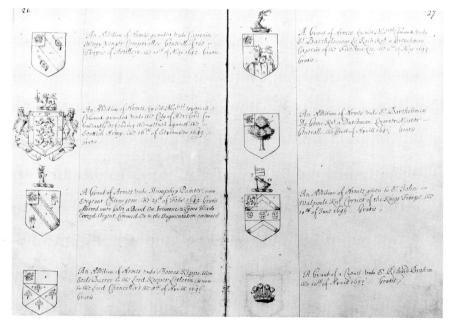

augmentations by Walker are marked 'gratis' so they were a means of rewarding fifty or so Royalists at no expense to the grantees.

Eighteenth-century and later augmentations can be divided into two groups, those that were granted as the result of a Royal Warrant and those that were not. Admiral Sir George Pocock was granted arms and a crest in 1761. His son George was granted an augmentation of *two Flaunches Azure on each a Sea Horse erect respecting each other proper and supporting an Anchor Gold* in 1794 in commemoration of his father's services, and a further augmentation again for his father's services in 1821. On neither occasion was there a Royal Warrant and there was a similar lack of one when Thomas Pakenham, Captain RN and uncle to the Earl of Longford was granted in 1795 by Sir Chichester Fortescue, Ulster King of Arms, an augmentation of *On a Chief the Sea and on the stern of an antique Ship riding thereon Britannia standing: Victory alighting on the Prow and placing a wreath of Laurel on her Head all Proper.* In contrast there was a Royal Warrant pursuant to which Lord Heathfield was granted the arms of Gibraltar to be borne on a chief of his own arms in 1787, and in 1789 a Royal Warrant permitted Lord Malmesbury to add to the arms of his family the black eagle of Prussia, thereby availing himself and his issue of a grant by the King of Prussia. The eagle was added on a chief by Letters Patent of 30 July 1789.

No examples of abatements have been found, but the loss of arms by attainder can be seen in the Royal Warrant addressed by George I to John Anstis, Garter, after Anstis refused to grant supporters to Gilbert (Vane), Lord Barnard, son of Christopher (Vane), 1st Lord Barnard. The relevant part of the Warrant states

that you Our said Officer being apprized that Sir Henry Vane father of the said Christopher was attainted whereby the said ancient arms were forfeited, and not knowing that either the said attainder was reversed or that there was any restitution in blood did according to the trust reposed in you decline to proceed therein without Our special Commands for that purpose, we therefore to whom the said Arms are escheated by virtue of the said attainder, do hereby declare it to be Our Royal will and pleasure, and we hereby direct and command you, forthwith to grant the Arms borne by the said Sir Henry Vane before his said attainder and by his ancestors unto Our said Right Trusty and Wellbeloved Gilbert now Lord Barnard.

The re-grant of the old armorial bearings with supporters is dated 27 February 1724/5.

Arms are intelligible if painted, less so if tricked or hatched, and unintelligible to many when blazoned. A blazon should be a description of what should be or is drawn, not an explanation of its reference. Allusions should be concealed not explained. Unfortunately, there have been periods when the essential point that the blazon is to guide

Re-grant in 1724/5 of arms and quarterings of Vane to Gilbert (Vane), Lord Barnard, lost through his grandfather's attainder. Vane quarters (2) De La Dene (3) De La Lake (4) St Owen (5) FitzElles (6) Persalt, and is impaling (1) Randell (2) Shelley (3) Harding (4) Morgan (Coll. Arms, Grants 7, p. 261).

the artist has been lost sight of, and the blazon has contained symbolic or canting references for the supposed benefit of the grantee. The wider a blazon is the greater is the scope for artistic variation. English styles of blazon have altered but the principle has remained unaltered of first stating the tincture or tinctures of the field, and then giving the principal charge such as an Ordinary, followed by the next most significant charges such as those on either side of the Ordinary, then any charges on the Ordinary, and finally any cadency marks. The form remains the same whatever the language of the grant. Grants of the first part of the reign of Henry VIII and earlier tend to be in French, and that to John Rympyngden of Leatherhead in 1516 is blazoned *gueules a une bende engrelee dor entre trois cornes et les laces dargent sur la bende trois hurtes.* This might be blazoned today *Gules on a Bend engrailed Or between three Bugle Horns stringed Argent three Roundels Azure* or *three Hurts* if the alternative blazoning of roundels by tincture is followed. In both cases the field Gules is mentioned first, then the principal charge, the bend, and then the charges on either side of the bend which are of greater linear importance than the charges on the bend, which come last. Common sense dictates that when a bend is between three objects two occupy the larger space above it and one the smaller space below. A grant by Christopher Barker, Garter, to Henry Parker of Fryth Hall, Essex in 1537/8 is blazoned *Gold three enschochens Sable upon eche schochen a brode arow hedde of the felde.* This might now be blazoned *Or on three Inescutcheons Sable three Pheons Or.* There are some who would replace the final Or with gold, and others, to avoid repeating tinctures, would copy Barker and say 'of the field' or 'of the first' meaning the first tincture mentioned in the blazon. Pheon is the term now used for a broad arrow head.

A mode of blazon has developed at the College of Arms which has been used since the last century in Letters Patent and College records. Capital letters are given to all tinctures, proper names, and principal charges, and punctuation is omitted in blazon. The omission of punctuation follows the form of other legal documents which omit it so that punctuation cannot change the sense. There is less logic in the particular use of capital letters which are given, for instance, to furs but not the term proper. In the examples above, bend, bugle horns, roundels, or hurts all receive capitals, as do inescutcheons and pheons, and all the tinctures.

V *Crests*

Full achievement of armorial bearings consists of arms on the shield, crest on the helmet, around the top of which is usually wound the crest wreath or torse, mantling, and possibly supporters and a badge or badges with a motto or mottoes. Although it is only one part of the whole achievement the crest, which is usually displayed on the crest wreath, an object resembling a ribbed rolling-pin, has long enjoyed the greatest popular appeal. Spoons, forks, and signet rings have spread the knowledge of the family crest to the exclusion of all else. In 1778 William Sharpe, a herald painter, issued a series of fourteen plates of crests of the nobility and gentry at the price of 2s. a plate. This was a forerunner to books of crests which devoted whole volumes to illustrations, such as Alexander Deuchar's *British Crests* (1817), Fairbairn's *Book of Crests* (1859), which ran to four editions by 1905, and the *Royal Book of Crests* (1883). Jewellers, engravers, and stationers used these as a key to stamp crests on innumerable objects, often irrespective of entitlement: this has led people to declare that whilst they possess a crest they have no arms, something that is generally speaking impossible, although arms can exist without a crest. It has also resulted in the indiscriminate use of the word 'crest' to describe armorial bearings when anything but the crest is intended. It is nonsense to say that one's crest consists of various charges on a shield surrounded by leaves, meaning mantling, of a particular form, with a helmet above the shield. The crest is only the part of the design on top of the helmet, but despite the logic of a crest like that of a bird being worn on the head people remain muddled.

As the crest is borne on the helmet it is only used by the male members of the family. Unmarried daughters and widows use their father's arms or their late husband's and father's arms on a lozenge. Married women bear their husband's arms or their husband's and father's arms on a shield. As badges were originally intended for feudal retainers and associated people they may be used equally by sons or daughters if wished. Women who are sovereign princes are an exception to the rule, as are clergymen who, despite sixteenth-century exceptions such as the grant of a crest to John Whitgift, Archbishop of Canterbury, place above their arms a mitre or ecclesiastical hat appropriate to their status. It has, however, been the practice to allow Anglican churchmen below the rank of bishop crests if wished. The rule that crests should not be used by women was stated at a Chapter of the College (R 21, 139) held in Broyderers' Hall in 1561, when it was resolved:

That no inheritrix mayde wife or widdow shall neyther beare nor cause to be borne any creast or cognisance of her anchester but as heere followeth. If she be unmaried to beare in her ring cognisance or otherwise the first cote of her anchesters in a lozenge and during her widdowhood to use the first cote of her aunchesters, and if she be maried with one yt [that] is no gentilman then she to be exempted clearly of this conclusion.

There is always a problem with a precedent or authority such as this where there is a desire to use half as evidence for a particular statement and to disregard the other half, in this case the statement that women may not use their father's quarterings. Sixteenth- and seventeenth-century funeral certificates show that women did not only bear their father's paternal arms but his quarterings as well, so that quite apart from their ability to transmit quarterings, which is not necessarily disputed, heraldic practice has consistently shown a use of quarterings by daughters. The initial statement that no inheritrix should bear any crest has not been disregarded in the same way by sixteenth-century and subsequent practice. An heiress or coheir may not bear a crest, and equally she may not transmit a right to a crest to her issue. Unless there has been a specific grant of an additional crest or crests, a man is only entitled to his paternal crest however many arms he is entitled to quarter. This position has not gone unchallenged, as is evidenced by a Warrant of the Deputy Earl Marshal dated 5 June 1817 which forbade the transmission or use of crests by women, as certain officers of arms had suggested that this was possible. The complete text of the Warrant is given in Appendix 1 at the end of the chapter.

The immediate history of the Warrant was a motion put to Chapter by Sir Isaac Heard, Garter, on 22 April 1817 (C.B. 8,82) 'That no person entitled to quarter the Arms of an Heiress or Coheiress from whom he is descended can of right bear the crest appertaining to the family of such heiress or coheiress without a regular authority for that purpose by Royal Sign Manual, Act of Parliament or other regular Authority.' The motion was defeated, Somerset, Lancaster, Chester, Norroy, and Clarenceux voting against it, and only George Nayler, York (subsequently Garter) supported the 86-year-old Garter. Garter returned to the question a week later when he put to Chapter (C.B. 8,90) a list of six inconveniences (see Appendix 2 at end of the chapter) that resulted from the decision that any person entitled to quarter arms of an heiress or coheir might of right bear the crest of her family without any regular authority. These principally related to the lack of order that resulted from such a decision, with families without a crest adopting one of another family whose heiress they had married, entitlement to the Royal Crest arising, and the pointlessness of previous Royal Licences to permit the use of certain crests.

The matter was put to the vote again on 5 May, when Clarenceux joined Garter and York, and Somerset was absent, resulting in a tie with two Kings of Arms and one Herald on the one side and one King of Arms and three Heralds on the other. On 6 May Somerset's opinion was sought and he voted against Garter, resulting in the need for the Earl Marshal's Warrant.

The surprising aspect of the matter is that so many Officers of Arms should have opposed the traditional view. Lord Pembroke's remark to the younger Anstis as reported by Horace Walpole, 'Thou silly fellow, thou dost not know thy own silly business', might have been directed at them with some justification. It is remarkable that in a profession of only thirteen people there has often been a contrasting mixture of notable scholars and fools, with the latter often in the majority. It is unlikely that personal animosity affected the voting, as relations between Nayler and Heard, who voted together, can hardly have been good. Nayler, as Genealogist of the Order of the Bath, sued Heard in 1814 for soliciting business from Knights of the Bath, and received £1,000 damages subject to the award of Serjeant Bosanquet who reduced the damages to one shilling in 1815. The two Heralds probably of the greatest ability with the exception of Nayler, namely Joseph Hawker, Richmond, and Francis Townsend, Windsor, were both absent. It was Townsend who, in March 1817, had reported to Chapter on the pedigree recorded in 1810 by William Radclyffe, appointed Rouge Croix in 1803, of which 'the three upper generations are utterly destitute of truth', which led to Radclyffe's conviction for forgery at York Assizes in 1820 when he received a £50 fine and three-month prison sentence, and which resulted in his expulsion from the College. The proceedings reflected on the judgement of Edmund Lodge, Lancaster, the other Herald of some note, who had accepted the pedigree in 1801, and who had introduced Radclyffe to the College. Those who disagreed with Garter in 1817 went against the precedents, and received little support from textbook writers such as Joseph Edmondson, who wrote in his *Complete Body of Heraldry* (1780):

Occasionally we meet with persons bearing two crests on their carriages but this practice is to be condemned, since by the strict rules of armory, whenever any man assumes a crest which belonged to another family, he should lay aside that which is borne by his own, except for the purpose of a badge or device. The Germans indeed have long been accustomed to bear, in a row over their shields of arms, the crests of all the families whose arms they quarter: but in this they are not followed by any other nation; and in truth the absurdity and impropriety of such a practice is remarkably striking, the instant we recollect the purpose for which crests were originally designed. Heraldic writers universally agree that a woman cannot bear a crest.

The suggestion that one should stop using one's own crest on assumption of another could imply some degree of choice which would only have been appropriate in a description of practice prior to the regularization of the sixteenth century. Edmondson may simply be disapproving of the practice of a grant of a second crest rather than a grant of one crest in substitution of another. However the Heralds interpreted Edmondson, they only had to consult *An Introduction to Heraldry* (1810) by William Berry, fifteen years Clerk to the Registrar of the College of Arms, to read

In Germany and other foreign countries, it is the custom to bear the crest belonging to every quartering the family is entitled to; but in England it is otherways, and but one crest is usually borne, except in cases where an additional name is taken upon the inheritance of property, or for the particular alliance with the representative of some ancient family whose possessions are inherited by it.

The Earl Marshal's Warrant of June 1817 referred to two crests placed over the lozenge containing the arms and quarterings of a female. This has not been identified, but a Painter's work book in the College library covering the years 1813–26 shows crests with lozenges, although not directly above them, for the funerals in February 1816 of Mrs Bernard, widow (where on the lozenge Bernard impales Codrington with the wrong tinctures or an unregistered coat of the same linear appearance as Codrington), in April 1816 of Mrs Leigh née Brown, and in March 1817 of Mrs White née Chamberlayne.

In England the crest did not have the same significance as arms. Of the ninety-eight rolls listed chronologically in Sir Anthony Wagner's *Catalogue of English Medieval Rolls of Arms* (1950) only seven contain crests, and of these the earliest dates from the mid-fifteenth century and is the sixty-fourth roll to be listed. In contrast, most of the eighty rolls in the equivalent catalogue of German medieval rolls of arms before 1500 (E. Frh. v. Berchem, D. L. Galbreath, and O. Hupp, *Die Wappenbucher des deutschen Mittelatters*, 1939) show crests, and they appear in the illustrated German roll of the early fifteenth century known as 'Povey's Roll'. The two twelfth-century German heraldic manuscripts, the *Aeneid* of Heinrich von Veldeke (1174) and the *Carmen de bello siculo* of Peter de Ebulo (1195–6), which are the first two entries in the catalogue, both show devices on the helmets. Two of the greatest European rolls, the 'Zurich Roll' of about 1340 and the '*Armorial de Gelre*' produced by the Herald of the Duke of Gelderland between 1369 and 1396, which contains over 1,800 entries of Sovereigns and Noblemen from western Europe, show crests as well as

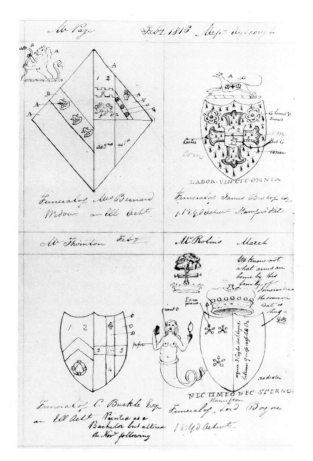

Herald painter's work book, with an order for Mrs Bernard's funeral of an ell (45-inch) achievement with a crest (Coll. Arms, PWB 1813–26, fo. 62v).

arms. In the twelfth-century German rolls some figures have a painting of the arms on their helmets, others show a small flag attached to the helmet with a device painted on it, and there are also cut-out models on the helmet.

The forerunners of crests were fan-shaped plates attached to the top of the helmet to deflect the blow of a sword. These were originally undecorated but were soon painted with the arms on a design based on part of the arms. These plates are visible on the equestrian seals of Humphrey de Bohun, Earl of Hereford, and Richard Fitzalan, Earl of Arundel, both attached to the Barons' Letter to the Pope of 1301. Its modern survival is in crests shown on wings such as that of the City of London *On a helm with a wreath Argent and Gules a Dragon's sinister Wing Argent charged on the underside with a Cross Gules*, where the origin of the crest as a plate on which all or part of the arms has been painted is forgotten. This may also account for its lack of registration at the College of Arms till 1957, as it could be argued that it is not a genuine crest, although there is an example as early as 1478 of the arms on a plate again blazoned as a dragon's wing granted as a crest to John and

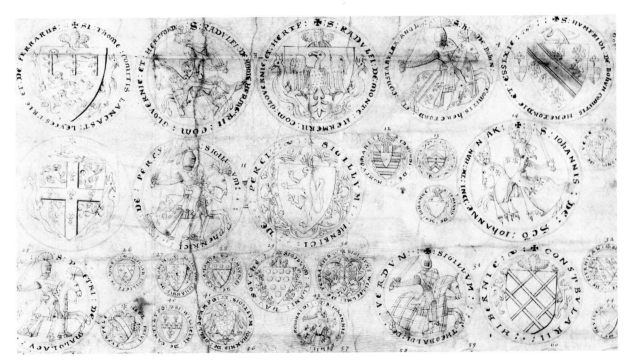

Late sixteenth-century facsimile of the seals attached to the Barons' Letter to the Pope, 1301, showing fan-shaped plates on the equestrian seals of the Earl of Hereford (in the first row), Henry de Percy (in the second row), and Peter de Mauley (third row), with wyvern and lion precursors of supporters on either side of some shields (Coll. Arms, Vincent 104).

Armorial bearings of the City of London, where the crest originates as a plate, later developing into a dragon's wing charged with a cross as in the arms. The London Armory was printed for Richard Wallis, citizen and arms painter of London in 1677, to be sold in his shop in the Royal Exchange (*Armory of London*, pl. I).

James Tadlow of London, so the Kings of Arms were prepared to make a formal grant of such an object as a crest in the fifteenth century. The painted fan was followed by one showing a silhouette, and this was succeeded by an arrangement of feathers often rising in several tiers and known as a panache. Examples of panaches which appear on seals before the first English roll of arms to show crests are those of Ingram de Coucy, Earl of Bedford (1357), William Latimer (1374), Sir Richard Waldegrave (1389), Richard Le Scrope (1399), Sir Thomas La Warre (1414), and John Montgomery (1433). Many families used what was sometimes termed a bush of feathers on their helmets in the fourteenth century, just as they had earlier used a fan-shaped plate, and when in the late fifteenth and early sixteenth centuries codification began, some adopted them as crests in the modern sense, and to this day those that survive, such as Waldegrave and Scrope, have feathers as a crest. Whatever their origin, the ostrich feathers of the Prince of Wales are an example of such a panache.

As there was an opportunity to display a visually striking three-dimensional model on the helmet in tournaments, beasts, birds, monsters, human beings, objects, and parts of objects were adopted with as much frequency in the fourteenth century as the plain panaches of feathers. Early in the century the German rolls show that such crests were mostly derived from the arms. In the *Wappenfolge von Erstfelden* of 1309, the design on the arms of von Belmont reappears on a mitre as the crest, and the buckle on the shields of Weissenburg and Wadiswil also appear on the helmets. An early fifteenth-century English example is the seal used in 1401 by Oliver Mauleverer of Lincolnshire, where the three greyhounds in the arms are represented as a crest by *on a Chapeau*

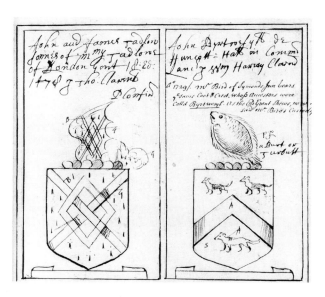

Crest of the arms on a dragon's wing granted to John and James Tadlow in 1478. The adjacent trick shows the canting grant by Hervy, Clarenceux, of a burt (turbot) and weasels for Birtwistle (Coll. Arms, EDN 56, fo. 88).

turned up Ermine a Greyhound collared lined and ringed. A variety of beasts appear, and fourteenth-century seals show a fox for Oddyngescles (1350), a dead fox for Walter de Mounci (1307), a goat passant for John Sacheverell of Hopwell, Derbyshire (1385), a ram for Sir William Frank (1383), a squirrel for John Pecche (1323), a stag's head for Adam Babington (1384), a bull's head for John Neville of Raby (1371), while examples from the '*Armorial de Gelre*' are the *Bat Argent winged Sable on a Chapeau Azure* for Sir Miles Stapleton, and the boar of the Vere family, Earls of Oxford. Canting crests are the coney sejant of Sir William Cunningham (1398), the bear on a chapeau of Sir Baldwin Bereford (1389), the talbot statant of John Talbot (1352), and the cat collared on a chapeau of Thomas Catesby (1385). Cats as canting crests appear in *Ballard's Book* of *c.*1480 as a cat (pussy) statant guardant proper for Pudsey, and a cat couchant guardant proper for Cathrall. More unusual natural animals can be seen in the fifteenth-century seal device of William, Viscount Beaumont, of an elephant and castle, and the camel statant Sable attributed to the King of Crawcow in 'Shirley's Roll' of *c.*1450. Birds are represented by the peacock crest on the seal of William de Harcourt (1339), the cock's head of Sir Adam de Louches (1373) and Sir John Cockayne (1421), and the swan's head and neck originally between wings for John Beauchamp of Holt (1371) and subsequently issuing from a coronet for Richard Beauchamp, Earl of Warwick (1406). Human beings are seen in the woman's head with long hair in a plait of Sir John Dipres (1382), and the crowned negro's head of Sir Matthew de Gurney (1393). Only simple monsters occur in early crests, such as the griffin's head and wings within a crown of Sir John Montagu (1389), the griffin sejant with wings outstretched of Thomas Hoo (1480) and the dragon's head and wings issuing from a crown of John Goldington (1401). Inanimate crests include the upwright millstone on a chapeau of Sir Robert de Lisle (1368), the palm tree between wings of Laurence Greyndor (1351), and the cup and ball of John de Ramsbury (1388).

The question as to whether crests mean anything is no different to whether any part of the armorial bearings have a meaning. For instance, do saracens' heads signify that a family went on the Crusades? The answer is that some families with a saracen's head crest, such as Lygon, Stapleton, Warburton, and Willoughby, did go on Crusades, and to commemorate this may, in the fourteenth or fifteenth centuries, have adopted the head to replace the panache or dragon's wing. Like the sixteenth-century augmentation or additions to arms such as Legh of Lyme and Pelham given or adopted for medieval feats, their assumption probably took place some centuries after the attendance on a Crusade. It seems probable that other families bearing saracens' heads in the sixteenth century, such as Prideaux and

Penhellick, Shirley, Irby, and Marbury may have been on a Crusade. Different reasons must be sought for later grants incorporating turks or saracens, such as that to John Tivitoe of London, merchant, granted in 1761 *a demy Turk guardant habited proper holding in his dexter hand a Scimitar Argent pomel and hilt Or*. The quest for reasons or origins of charges must be approached with care, as the very similar moors' heads are no more than canting crests when used by families of Moore and Mordaunt.

The late development of crests and their use initially more as an ornament on the helmet than a means of identification is probably responsible for their comparative insignificance in Scotland where, although no two men may bear the same arms, and younger brothers must matriculate a variation of the paternal arms, different families use the same comparatively simple crest, and there were many grants of arms without a crest. In England the influence of the late fifteenth- and early sixteenth-century Kings of Arms resulted in a different evolution. It has been suggested that crests were originally a mark of special dignity associated with those of sufficient standing to take part in tournaments. Cennino Cennini writing in *The Craftsman's Handbook* (1437) on how to model crests refers to making them for a tourney or for rulers who have to march in state, which lends some support to this. But by the late fifteenth century in England manuscripts such as *Ballard's Book* record crests for the county families who appear in the Visitations of the 1530s, and crests were granted irrespective of rank. The complicated striped and charged beasts granted as crests by Sir Thomas Wriothesley were individually distinctive, and there is no doubt from the texts of the Letters Patent granting them that they were to be borne in perpetuity in the same way as the arms. Wriothesley's predecessors granted much simpler crests and if the practice had continued it would have been difficult to avoid duplication of crests such as *a demi Bear Sable muzzled and chained Or* granted in 1450 by John Smert, Garter, to Edmond Mille or the *Elephant's head proper* granted in 1492 by Wriothesley's father John Writhe, Garter, to the brothers Thomas and John Elyott. Not all simple crests, were prone to repetition, and it is unlikely that many people would wish to have *ung orynall dedens son case en leurs propres coleurs* as granted by Writhe to Louis Caerlion in 1491; this is usually translated as *a Urinal in a Basket proper*. Caerlion was a doctor of medicine, and perhaps as such had no intention of participating in a tournament with a urinal on his head, but should he have wished to there would have been no difficulty in making a model of one out of gessoed leather.

The need for a crest to be a three-dimensional object capable of being worn on a helmet was sometimes forgotten, and as early as 1581 Sir Francis Drake was granted a crest which might be termed as bad heraldry. It is blazoned *A globe terrestriall upon the height whereof in a shyppe under sayle trayned aboute the same with golden haulsers by the direction of a hand appeerings owte of the cloudes, all yn proper colour a read dragon volant sheweth it self regardinge the said direction with these words Auxilio divino.* Sketches for alternative crests for Drake which are equally impractical also exist. The worst cases are those where part of the crest is detached and hovering above the rest of it, but there are many crests, particularly of the late eighteenth and early nineteenth century, which would be difficult to model and are too complicated. An example is *Issuant from the Waves a Demi Neptune proper crowned Gold mantled Vert the dexter Arm elevated the hand grasping a Trident Or in the attitude of striking, the sinister supporting a Shield Argent repelling a Shark in the act of seizing its Prey also proper.* This was granted to Brook Watson in 1803 in allusion to an awful event in his life when, as a 14-year old boy in the Navy, he was attacked by a shark when bathing near Havana and lost his right leg below the knee. As a result he left the Navy, became Commissary General to the Forces Serving in Great Britain, and was Lord Mayor and a Member of Parliament for the City of London, being created a Baronet shortly after the grant in 1803.

(*right*) Grant of arms with an impractical crest, as it is incapable of being worn on a helmet, to Sir Francis Drake in 1581 (Coll. Arms, Miscellaneous Grants I, fo. 57v).

(*below*) Alternative proposal for a crest for Sir Francis Drake (Coll. Arms, Vincent 218, fo. 27v).

The family of Buckworth is cited by Fox-Davies as the only example known to him of a crest existing without arms. There is no evidence of the arms being respited as suggested, but the first and fourth quarters are shown blank in the 1619 and 1684 Visitations of Cambridgeshire. In the sixteenth and seventeenth centuries there were many grants of crests to be borne with existing arms but the Kings of Arms always confirmed the arms in the Patent granting the crest, thereby avoiding the risk of granting a crest where there were no arms. When, in the 1577 grant to William Webbe of Motcombe, Dorset, Robert Cooke stated 'And forasmuch as I fynd no creast to the said Armes and name of Webbe belonginge as comonly to all auncient Armes there belongeth none, I the said Clarencieux King of Armes have given unto him by way of encrease for his creast. . .', he followed a standard formula which might support an argument that without arms there can be no crest, as crests only exist as an addition to arms. But as the power to grant armorial bearings is vested in the Sovereign and delegated to the Kings of Arms this would restrict the power of the Sovereign if a grant of a crest to non-existent arms was automatically invalid. Its validity must turn on the text of the Patent. Grants of crests in a Patent without arms have been made as honourable augmentations, as in that of 1814 to Sir Philip Bowes Vere Broke, Bt., Commander of HM ship *Shannon* for his distinguished zeal, courage, and intrepidity displayed in his brilliant engagement with the United States frigate *Chesapeake* of superior force off Boston. A right to arms is assumed, and if there were none they could not be augmented. Where there are two crests the crest of augmentation takes the senior position to the dexter. When there are three crests the principal one is in the centre, the second to the dexter, and the third to the sinister. The first crest normally relates to the arms in the first quarter, which should relate to the last surname if the surname is double or more barrelled. Where two or more crests are shown above a shield they should all face to the dexter if on crest wreaths, and if on helmets they should similarly either all face to the dexter or the helmets may face one another, in which case the crests as attached to the helmets face one another. In England cadency marks, if borne on the arms, should also appear on the crest.

A crest can be altered by endorsement of the Patent as long as the granting Kings of Arms are still in office. Thereafter it can be changed by a subsequent Patent such as the alteration and augmentation of the crest granted to Sir Moses Montefiore in 1831 in lieu of the original grant to him in 1819. If the grant of the crest of another family is sought, one of the considerations is whether anyone's rights are prejudiced. In 1663 Sir Robert Cann of Bristol, 1st Bt., was granted *Out of a mural Crown Gules a Plume of six feathers Argent and Azure alternately*. In 1776 the same crest was granted to Henry Lippincott, who had married the niece and heir of the 6th and last Baronet, and who was 'desirous out of affection and respect to his memory of bearing the crest of Cann'. The Chapter Book of the College (C.B. 6,197) contains a report that the male issue of the 1663 grantee was extinct, and the Kings of Arms accordingly were prepared to make the grant. Henry Lippincott was himself created a baronet in 1778, but the title and right to the crest failed again on the death without legitimate issue of his son Sir Henry Cann Lippincott in 1829. The latter's illegitimate son Robert Cann Lippincott was granted the same crest debruised by a bendlet sinister wavy Erminois in 1831. Although John (Holles), Earl of Clare (subsequently Duke of Newcastle), obtained a Warrant from the Earl Marshal to Garter dated 25 January 1691/2 stating that he desired that he might bear and use the same crest that is used by the Earl of Oxford with proper differences on account of his descent from Elizabeth, eldest daughter and one of the coheirs of Horace (Vere), Lord Vere of Tilbury, and in the Warrant the Earl Marshal required that the same be allowed, there is no subsequent grant by Garter. Clare's nephew Thomas (Pelham-Holles), Duke of Newcastle, obtained a Royal Licence to use the same crest, and the Royal Warrant to the Deputy Earl Marshal commanding that the concession and declaration be registered at the College is dated 14 April 1718. The extinction of the Earldom of Oxford in 1702 between the two Warrants is probably coincidental. There can be little doubt as to the efficacy of the second Warrant, as there is no clause requiring exemplification of the crest, but the first would appear to be of no effect, as whereas grants can be made by the Sovereign, Kings of Arms, or Act of Parliament, there is no power to grant vested in the Earl Marshal.

The crest developed as an ornament on the helmet, and in the period when helmets were used crests are shown on closed tilting helms irrespective of rank. It was not till the early seventeenth century that different helmets began to be used according to rank. The present practice in England is that helmets of the Sovereign and royal princes are gold, barred and affronty, those of peers are silver with gold bars and in profile, those of honorary knights, knights, and baronets are steel with a raised visor and affronty, and those of esquires and gentlemen are of steel with a closed visor and in profile. In the late eighteenth century Edmondson subdivided the peers, and affronty steel rather than silver helms with five gold bars are attributed to dukes and marquesses, and similar helms in profile are attributed to earls, viscounts, and barons. Although there was no distinction between different types of helm before the early seventeenth century in England this was not the case in Germany and France. In Germany the only forms of helm were the barred helm and the helm with a closed visor; the former belonged to the old nobility entitled by birth to participate in tournaments and the latter to the newly ennobled. By the late fifteenth century the newly ennobled were using barred helms, and the closed helm could only be used by third-generation noblemen or those of longer standing. The practice in Europe probably led Gerard Leigh to suggest in *The Accedence of Armory* (1562) the use of different forms of helm in England according to rank. He assigned the helm in profile to knights, and it was John Guillim in his *Display of Heraldry* (1610) who put forward the open full-faced or affronty helm for knights. In 1950 a committee consisting of A. R. Wagner, Richmond, and M. R. Trappes-Lomax, Rouge Dragon, was appointed by Chapter to report on the helmet rank suitable to be displayed by an honorary knight. The committee concluded that since helmets of rank are not covered by the Laws of Arms there is no rule of law that can be applied, and consequently that permission to use the open full-faced helmet would better accord with the intention of the bestower of the knighthood. On a vote the majority concurred with this recommendation (C.B. 22,136). The possible flexibility with regard to helmets can be seen in the Royal Warrant dated 8 April 1957 (I 82,103) confirming the armorial bearings used unofficially by the Colony of Jamaica since the reign of Charles II. The crest is shown on a Royal helm, and in 1956 Garter gave notice to Chapter that he did not intend to oppose the inclusion of the Royal helm as it had been used unofficially since the seventeenth century (C.B. 24,103).

The stall plates of the Knights of the Order of the Garter provide some of the best early examples of crests in England. In many cases these show the crest continuing down over the helmet forming a short mantle protecting the back of the head and shoulders. This seems to be the earliest form of the mantling or lambrequin, a piece of usually slashed cloth often attached to the helmet by a chapeau, coronet, or by the heraldic wreath or torse normally depicted two-dimensionally in England as six twists of cloth alternately of a metal and colour. These precursors of mantling are seen in the blackamoor's head with ass's ears crest of Sir John de Grailly KG, who died 1377, which terminates in black cloth with slashed ends and gold edges, and in the crests of Sir William Arundel, KG 1395–1400, and those of Sir Thomas Beauchamp, Earl of Warwick, KG 1373–1401 and his son Sir Richard Beauchamp, Earl of Warwick, KG 1403–39, the latter being father-in-law of Warwick the Kingmaker. In the crest of Sir William Arundel, the feathering of the wyvern's head continues down to form the mantle, which has a red lining with gold decoration and is attached to the helmet by a coronet. The Beauchamp crest of a swan's head descends into a mantling of feathers, with a red lining in the case of the

Garter stall plate of Sir John de Grailly KG (d. 1377), with crest continuing to form mantling (*The Stall Plates of the Knights of the Order of the Garter (1348–1485)*, by W. H. St John Hope, pl. 2).

Garter stall plate of Sir Thomas Beauchamp, Earl of Warwick, KG 1373–1401, where the swan crest continues into mantling (*The Stall Plates of the Knights of the Order of the Garter (1348–1485)*, by W. H. St John Hope, pl. 41).

father and a purple one in that of the son. The crest and mantling are again secured to the helmet by means of a coronet. In all these cases the chapeau, coronet, torse, and plain untwisted wreaths or fillets of one tincture appear to be a means of attaching the mantling to the helmet. From the sixteenth century onwards those families using a chapeau or coronet incorporate it as part of the crest; the fillet seen, for instance, in the early fifteenth-century stall plate of Sir Reginald Cobham, Lord Cobham of Sterborough, KG 1352–61 disappears, not to re-emerge untill the present century when a plain circlet occurs as an alternative to a wreath, probably for reasons of differencing new crests. Since the sixteenth century the wreath occurs with much greater frequency than the chapeau or coronet, and it comes to be shown not as a means of securing the mantling to the helmet but often without the helmet and mantling, as a base on which the crest stands.

Whereas the extension of the crest to form mantling continued on the continent, it did not survive the increasing regulation of heraldry in England of the late fifteenth and early sixteenth century. Although no rules or directions seem to exist prior to a Warrant of the Deputy Earl Marshal of 1682, a pattern emerges in the sixteenth century where more than eighty per cent of English mantling is red with a white lining. This combination of Gules and Argent is not necessarily followed in the wreath, in contrast to the practice of later centuries where it is unusual for the tinctures of mantling and wreath to differ. Mantling was soon established as of a colour lined with a metal or fur (which was invariably Ermine), and the wreath was of six alternate twists of a metal and a colour but not a fur, of which the first twist was metal. There are occasional instances of two colours and a metal on a wreath and of the coloured sections on mantling showing more than one colour. The exact form that mantling takes, although alluded to in 1682, is a question of artistic licence. Most textbooks repeat the idea that it developed with the Crusades and should, therefore, be shown as if slashed by swords; it is consequently shown in shreds, often stylized to resemble acanthus leaves and sometimes terminating in tassels. Unslashed mantling occurs very seldom in England, and scarcely at all after the seventeenth century; it must be distinguished from peers' robes of estate on which the arms of peers were depicted on coach panels after 1760 following a suggestion by Joseph Edmondson to which he refers in his *Complete Body of Heraldry* (1780).

The Warrant of 1682 referred to specified irregularities that were to be speedily rectified. There were three complaints relating to some persons under the degree of nobility of the realm, namely, that they caused Ermine to be depicted on the lining of their mantling, that their mantling was 'painted like ostrich feathers as though they were of some superior and peculiar degree of honor', and that some of those whose crests issue out of ducal coronets do not use them upon a wreath of their colours. The mention of an Ermine lining in mantling implies that peers might have such a lining. An official record in the College number E.16 and dating from 1616, contains paintings of the full achievements of sixty-two peers. All those of the rank of Earl and above, with the exception of the Earl of Buckingham who is the last earl to be listed, have Ermine linings. Thirteen of these are *Gules lined Ermine*, nine *Azure lined Ermine*, four *Sable lined Ermine*, and one (the Earl of Montgomery) *Azure and Gules lined Ermine*. Where there are wreaths rather than chapeaux or coronets they are all of two tinctures, except Montgomery and his brother, the Earl of Pembroke, who have a wreath of *Argent, Azure and Gules*, although the latter's mantling is *Gules and Ermine*. A fifteenth-century example of a wreath of three tinctures is that of Sir John Grey, Earl of Tankerville, KG 1419–21 whose stall plate shows a wreath of *Vert, Gules and Argent*. In E.16 the viscounts and barons, including Lord Audley who was Earl of Castlehaven in Ireland, have linings of both *Argent and Or*. Gules is again the principal colour, followed by Sable and Azure, and there is a single instance of Vert in the *Vert and Or* of Lord Dudley which follows the *Or and Vert* of his arms. Both the lack of any rules and of clear evidence make deduction difficult. Helmet and mantling are almost invariably omitted from most College records, and only appear in the earliest Heralds' Visitations. The fifth (1679) and sixth (1724) editions of Guillim's *Heraldry* contain plates of the full achievements of all peers; in both cases most dukes, marquesses, and earls have Ermine linings to their mantles, whereas only some viscounts and barons do, so that if there was any distinction in mantling between the ranks of peer in England at the beginning of the seventeenth century it was becoming forgotten by the end. In the second edition of Collins's *Peerage of England* of 1741 no English peers are shown with Ermine-lined mantling, and this has remained the custom to the present day.

In Scotland the practice has been the reverse of that in England. George Seton's *The Law and Practice of Heraldry in Scotland* (1863) states that in Scotland the mantlings of the nobility have long been red doubled with Ermine. The available evidence does not support this contention, as there is not one case of an Ermine-lined mantling in two early seventeenth-century manuscript records of the full achievements of peers of Scotland in the College of Arms. Similarly, Crawfurd's *Peerage of Scotland* (1764) shows no Ermine-lined mantling, and since according to Seton it is only in volume iii of 'The Lord Lyon's Register', covering the years 1822–35, that mantling first appears, it would seem that the peers of Scotland adopted the sixteenth- and seventeenth-century English practice in the early nineteenth century.

A. C. Fox-Davies's *Complete Guide to Heraldry*, revised by J. P. Brooke-Little (1969), states that in Scotland the mantling of peers whose arms were matriculated before 1890 are red lined with Ermine, or Gules doubled Ermine, as it is more usually described, and that other arms matriculated before 1890 have Gules and Argent mantling. This also seems to copy the sixteenth-century English practice. Since 1890, peers' mantling in Scotland is either of the principal colour of the arms lined with Ermine or of Gules doubled Ermine, and all other mantling is of the livery colours unless otherwise specified. The livery colours are interpreted as the first colour and first metal blazoned in the arms. If the arms contain a fur, the metal with which that fur is associated is used. In England, the mantling of the Sovereign and Prince of Wales is of cloth of gold lined with Ermine, and that of other members of the Royal Family is of cloth of gold lined Argent. Since the end of use of Ermine lining by English peers, all other mantling in England, unless otherwise specified, has been of the colours, and this is confirmed by a ruling entered in the Chapter Book of the College of Arms for 7 February 1957 (C.B. 24, 171) which states that:

1. Unless specially described a wreath should consist of the first metal and first colour mentioned in the blazon of the shield (proper and furs are neither metal nor colour) and should be described as a wreath of the colours.

2. Unless specially described the mantle should follow the wreath and if the wreath is of three tinctures the mantle should be and there is no need to describe it.

3. Only when the mantle differs from the wreath should the mantle be described.

4. When there is no wreath the mantle should be described.

The two other complaints of 1682 relating to non-noble armorial bearings, that unsuitable mantling was used, as were coronets without wreaths, in crests, do not seem to have been acted on. Innumerable different forms of mantling are used, and although grants in the 1680s, such as that to Henry Loades, Chamberlain of the City of London, in 1687, show a coronet on a wreath, others of the same date, such as that to James Rothwell, Assistant Surveyor of His Majesty's Ordnance, in 1687, and to Lawrence Halsted, Deputy Keeper of His Majesty's Records in the Tower, in 1688, contain a coronet without a wreath. The practice of using crest coronets without wreaths, irrespective of a grantee's non-noble rank, has continued in England to the present day.

A ruling of the three Kings of Arms in 1953 (C.B. 23, 55) stated that:

1. No unauthorized charge or charges shall be depicted on mantling in Letters Patent of arms or in official paintings of arms.

2. Badges provided they are of authority may be so displayed but such badges will not when depicted on mantling in Letters Patent be blazoned.

3. Diapered mantling may be used as hitherto.

The second of these rules is the most interesting, as badges on mantling can be found at an early period, as in the Garter stall plate of Sir John Bourchier, Lord Berners, KG 1459–74, where the red of the mantling is scattered with gold billets for Lovain, and the silver lining is powdered with black water-bougets and Bourchier knots. Lord Berners's grandmother was a daughter and heiress of John de Lovain, and both water-bougets and Bourchier knots were badges of his family. Although the Kings of Arms ruled that badges should not be blazoned if shown on the mantling, modern instances do occur where the badge is blazoned. This emphasizes that a Patent is the document of the Kings of Arms who sign it, and changes will occur under different Kings of Arms in England.

APPENDIX 1. *The Deputy Earl Marshal's Warrant of 5 June 1817 (I 41,337)*

Whereas I have been informed that certain of the Officers of Arms have recently ascribed to persons entitled to quarter the Arms of noble and other families in virtue of their descent from heiresses or coheiresses the crest appertaining to the Arms of such Families respectively, and that they have caused the same to be set forth with the Armorial Achievements annexed to the Record of the Pedigrees of such persons: And whereas the introduction of such a practice is in contravention of the general usage observed in the Marshalling of Armorial Achievements in this Realm; a manifest infringement upon the Earl Marshal's Authority long established and exercised in respect to the allowance and assignment of crests;★ and calculated to create great doubts and confusion in the Heraldic system as to the bearing of crests: And whereas I have also been informed that in a particular instance two crests have even been placed over a lozenge containing the Arms and Quarterings of a female although the setting forth of any crest over the achievement of a female be contrary to the laws and practice of Arms: I Henry Thomas Howard-Molyneux, Deputy (with the Royal Approbation) to my brother the Most Noble Bernard Edward, Duke of Norfolk Earl Marshal and Hereditary Marshal of England, having taken the premises into my consideration do by these presents, in virtue of the Authority vested in the office of Earl Marshal, order and direct you Garter and Clarenceux and Norroy Kings of Arms, to examine all such entries of crests so ascribed as aforesaid and in the discharge of your duties respectively to make such corrections therein as may appear to you to be proper: And to prevent a recurrence of such errors I do hereby further order that no Officer of Arms shall ascribe to any person whatsoever entitled to quarter the Arms of any Heiress or Coheiress the crest appertaining to the Arms of the Family of such Heiress or Coheiress or set forth such crest in any pedigrees of such person or otherwise; or advise or sanction the assumption or use of the same without an especial authority for that purpose from the Earl Marshal for the time being or his Deputy: Provided always and it is hereby declared that this order is not intended to

★ This must refer to the fact that the Earl Marshal must sanction every grant; he has no power to grant, allow or assign crests; this is vested in the Kings of Arms.

supersede or invalidate the right of any person to any crest or crests which may have been anciently allowed or set forth by the Kings of Arms respectively at their Visitations or by or under any other due authority and I do direct that this present Warrant be by the Register of the College of Arms forthwith duly recorded to the end that you and all others may upon occasion take full notice and have knowledge thereof. And hereof you are not to fail. Given under my hand and Seal this fifth day of June 1817

H. HOWARD-MOLYNEUX D. E. M.

APPENDIX 2. *The six inconveniences listed on 29 April 1817 by Sir Isaac Heard resulting from Chapter's acceptance that a right to a crest could be acquired through an heraldic heiress (C.B. 8,90)*

1. Any person to whom Arms had been allowed without a crest (as to Pole, Gillibrand, and many others who bear ancient coats without crests) might by adopting the crest of any family whose coat he may be entitled to quarter appear to transfer such crest to his own surname and thereby create great confusion in armorial bearings.

2. Any person entitled (as Lord Hastings and many others) to quarter the Royal Arms of Plantagenet, might adopt the Royal Crest: Whereas Thomas Mowbray Duke of Norfolk who was entitled by descent to quarter the Arms of Plantagenet had a grant from Richard II of the Royal Crest with a distinction as a mark of special favour which grant would not have been necessary if the right to bear the crest had existed.

3. The grants of crests of Godolphin to the Marquis of Carmarthen, of Jeffreys to Earl Camden, of the ancient Earls of Warwick to Lord Warwick, of Hovell to Thurlow and many others, under the Earl Marshal's authority, were for the same reason wholly unnecessary.

4. In any case where a person is directed to apply for a Royal Licence to take the name and Arms of an heiress or coheiress from whom he may be descended, to be borne in the second quarter with his paternal Arms, it would be only necessary to apply for leave to take the surname as the coat and crest would have descended as of right to the applicant.

5. If the principle of Garter's Resolution be not admitted it must appear upon a retrospection of the past that whenever grants of crests under the circumstances above mentioned have been issued, the parties have been put to unnecessary expense.

6. The Earl Marshal's authority would be manifestly abridged by rendering the usual applications to him in such cases wholly unnecessary—a step which certainly cannot be taken without his consent.

Supporters, Badges, and Mottoes

UPPORTERS are the beasts, birds, monsters, human, or other figures that stand either side of and support the shield of arms. On the Continent a distinction tends to be drawn between animal, human, and inanimate supporters; in Italy, for instance, the term *tenenti* is used only for those of anthropomorphic appearance such as angels, giants, sirens and human beings; animals and monsters are termed *sopporti*. There is a similar distinction between the French *tenants* and *supports*, and in France inanimate supporters are called *soutiens*.

The particular interest of supporters in England is that their use has become restricted to the highest rank of those entitled to arms. The surprising aspect of this development is the apparent lack of documentation relating to the assumption and change of status of supporters in the sixteenth century. William Berry wrote in *An Introduction to Heraldry* (1810), 'None but peers of the Realm, knights of the several orders, and proxies of the Blood Royal at installations, are entitled to bear supporters to their arms, unless, (as in many cases) for some particular cause His Majesty by Royal Warrant especially grants the use thereof.' The current position in England is much the same, and personal grants of hereditary supporters may be made to hereditary peers, and supporters for life may be granted to life peers and to Knights of the Garter and the Thistle, and those who are Knights Grand Cross or Knights Grand Commanders of the various Orders of Chivalry. The textbooks suggest that in the eighteenth and nineteenth centuries the impersonal bodies eligible for a grant of supporters were counties, cities, and corporate bodies which had received a Royal Charter, but not towns. Liverpool, granted supporters as a town in 1797, is quoted as an exception, and there are sixteenth-century precedents such as the 1561 grant to Newark-upon-Trent. In the present century towns have been granted supporters, as have certain large corporate bodies at the discretion of the Kings of Arms. There is no reason to believe that grants would not still be made to proxies of the Blood Royal at installations, and anyone may be granted supporters pursuant to a Royal Warrant. Many Knights of the Garter and the

Thistle are peers already entitled to supporters, so they do not have a second grant.

There are various theories as to the origins of supporters. One is that they derived from servants in fancy dress disguised as savages, wild animals, or monsters, who held the shields of knights participating in tournaments. Another is that they are connected with heraldic badges. They first appear in any number as often identical decoration on late thirteenth-century heraldic seals, and it seems most probable that they originate as a decorative addition invented by seal engravers to occupy a blank space on either side of triangular shields on circular seals. Although seal decoration appears to be their origin, badges or retainers disguised as badges seem to have influenced the transformation from mere decoration to a distinctive part of the armorial bearings.

One of the best sources for early English heraldic seals is the Barons' Letter to the Pope of 1301 sent in answer to the Pope's letter to Edward I in 1299 claiming feudal superiority over Scotland (edited and published in facsimile as *Some Feudal Lords and Their Seals MDCCI* by The De Walden Library, 1904). The heraldic seals of ninety-six signatories survive. About one-third show shields supported by two wyverns, if wyverns placed on either side of a shield can be termed supporters. That of John de Hastings has a third wyvern occupying the space above the shield. Guy de Beauchamp, Earl of Warwick, Theobald de Verdon, Roger Mortimer of Chirk, and John de Mohun each have two lions, and Eustace de Hacche, Walter de Beauchamp, Steward of the King's Household, and Peter de Mauley have three lions arranged in a manner similar to John de Hastings's wyverns. There can be no question of identification by supporters or exclusive property which could give rise to a case in the High Court of Chivalry when so many are similar to one another. Although English Royal heraldry is a distinct subject with its own rules, the frequency with which the Royal supporters were changed prior to the reign of James I would support a theory that they were originally regarded as a decorative addition and not a part of the armorial bearings over which there might be any legally enforceable rights. Evidence of use and traditional attribution of supporters to English sovereigns produce two different lists, though both demonstrate the regular changes. In the sixteenth century the first English king to use supporters was considered to be Edward III, who came to the throne in 1327. He is shown with dexter *a Lion guardant with a small imperial crown Or* sinister *a Hawk proper belled Or*. His grandson and successor Richard II bore the same dexter supporter and sinister *a Hart Argent attired Or*. There is no contemporary evidence on the other hand that Edward III used supporters, and the privy seal of Richard II shows *two Lions couchant guardant each holding an ostrich Feather charged with a scroll* as supporters. Henry IV was thought to have used dexter *an heraldic Antelope Argent ducally gorged chained maned and armed Or* and sinister *a Swan Argent similarly gorged and chained Or*. These were badges, and there is no evidence that he used supporters, or that his son Henry V did, although dexter *a Lion guardant imperially crowned Or* and sinister *an heraldic Antelope attired Or* are attributed to him.

Henry VI is given a similar dexter supporter to his grandfather Henry IV, that is *an heraldic Antelope Argent ducally gorged chained maned and armed Or* with, according to Edmondson in his *Complete Body of Heraldry*, sinister *a Leopard Argent spotted with various colours and issuing from his mouth and ears flames of fire proper* (this sounds indistinguishable from a panther incensed) but, both at Eton College which he founded and in St George's Chapel, Windsor, they are shown as *two heraldic Antelopes Argent armed and tufted Or*. Edward IV, as Henry VIII's maternal grandfather, was almost within living memory of Tudor writers, and it is agreed that he changed his supporters several times. They appear as dexter *a Bull Sable crowned horned unguled and membered Or* sinister *a Lion guardant Argent*, and, as the same combination reversed, as *two Lions guardant Argent* and dexter *a Lion guardant Argent* sinister *a Hart Argent*. The lion and hart used by his father are attributed to Edward V, the elder prince in the Tower who reigned for two months. The hart is sometimes called a hind. Richard III used both dexter *a Lion guardant Argent imperially crowned Or* sinister *a Boar Argent armed and bristled Or* and *two Boars Argent armed and bristled Or*. Henry VII's dexter supporter was *a Dragon Gules* and the sinister supporter was *a Greyhound Argent collared Gules*. His eldest son Prince Arthur's arms are supported on his tomb by *two heraldic Antelopes*. Initially Henry VIII bore the same supporters as his father but later changed to dexter *a Lion guardant and imperially crowned Or* sinister *a Dragon Gules*. Edward VI and Queen Mary used the same supporters, but the latter changed them on her marriage, moving the lion to the sinister and placing an *Eagle wings elevated Sable armed and crowned Or* to the dexter. Elizabeth I bore the same supporters as her brother Edward VI. Her successor James I retained the dexter supporter but replaced the dragon with one of the two unicorns used by him as King of Scotland and blazoned *a Unicorn Argent armed tufted and maned Or gorged with a coronet composed of crosses pattee and fleurs de lis thereto a chain affixed also Or*. These supporters have been retained to the present day. In Scotland the first king to use supporters seems to have been James I who used *two Lions rampant guardant* on his Privy Seal of 1429. These were copied by James II. A single unicorn appears on the gold coinage of James III seated behind and holding a shield of the arms, and the two unicorns associated with Scotland first appear in a stone carving at

Seal showing supporters of
Henry Algernon (Percy), Earl
of Northumberland. Both the
5th (d. 1527) and 6th (d. 1537)
Earls of Northumberland were
named Henry Algernon (PRO
E329/405).

Melrose Abbey dated 1505 for James IV, and were used by his
successors.

Many of these Royal supporters are known as badges, emerging as
the King's and Queen's Beasts of the sixteenth and later centuries.
They adorned the pavilion at the Field of the Cloth of Gold in 1513, are
seen at St George's Chapel, Windsor, and Hampton Court Palace, and
were put upon Rochester Bridge in the 1530s and on the landing stage
at Greenwich Palace in 1588. More recently, ten of the Queen's Beasts
lined the entrance to Westminster Abbey for the Coronation on 2 June
1953. H. S. London, in *Royal Beasts* (1956), refers to the decorative use
of heraldic beasts on the gable-ends of buildings and elsewhere from at
least the thirteenth century. In 1237 the 'Pipe Roll' records a payment
for making a stone lion and setting it on the gable of the King's Hall in
Windsor Castle. He suggests that these beasts were a form of personal
badge as compared to the smaller badges of simple shapes, such as the
Percy crescent or Beaufort portcullis, which could be powdered on
flags or worn by retainers. Although supporters developed out of the
decoration on seals, these distinctive beasts which also appear on the
houses of the nobility and others must have had some influence in the
transition from amorphous creatures which might have decorated the
border of a medieval manuscript to recognizable beasts and monsters
borne hereditarily as supporters. The profusion of Royal beasts
explains the change of Royal supporters as contrasted with those of
commoners.

When peers adopted distinctive supporters in the fifteenth and
sixteenth centuries they tended to retain them. From 1537 onwards
the stall plates of the Knights of the Garter in St George's Chapel,
Windsor consistently show supporters, but there are only three
instances before the reign of Henry VIII: these are John (Beaufort),
Duke of Somerset elected, *c.*1442, John (Dynham), Lord Dynham
(*c.*1487), and Henry Algernon (Percy), Earl of Northumberland
(*c.*1495), and they appear on a Northumberland seal of 1528. Thirty-
four Knights were elected in Henry VIII's reign before 1537, and of
these the stall plates of only five, Thomas Howard (1510), Thomas
Boleyn (1523), Robert Radcliffe (1524), and William Fitzwilliam
(1526), subsequently Duke of Norfolk and Earls of Wiltshire, Sussex,
and Southampton respectively, and that of James V of Scotland (1534/
5) show supporters.

Although supporters had their origins in the embellishment of
thirteenth- and fourteenth-century seals, and became distinctive in the
fifteenth century, their regular use by the nobility dates from the reign
of Henry VIII and that of Sir Thomas Wriothesley and his immediate
successors as Garter Kings of Arms. The question which is as yet
unanswered is how these supporters were assumed, since, although

there are sixteenth-century grants of supporters to a knight in 1508, and to corporate bodies, such as the undated grant by Thomas Benolt, Clarenceux (died 1534) to the Grocers Company and that of 1568 by Sir Gilbert Dethick, Garter and Robert Cooke, Clarenceux to the Corporation of Mines Royal, there appear with one exception to be no sixteenth-century grants to peers. The exception is the grant of 1542/3 made by special command of the King by Sir Christopher Barker, Garter, to Gregory (Cromwell), Lord Cromwell, of arms, crest, and beasts when he was restored in blood. This is a grant of armorial bearings forfeited by the attainder of his father, similar to the 1724/5 grant to Lord Barnard, and is therefore exceptional. The shield is *supported between two Pegasus Gules horned winged membered Gold.*

A brief look at the hybrid, mythical, and monstrous creatures adopted without a grant by other peers suggests that the Heralds must have played some part in their assumption. The pantheons of the Paulets, borne to this day by their descendant the Marquess of Winchester, the bagwyn of William, Earl of Arundel, theow of Sir

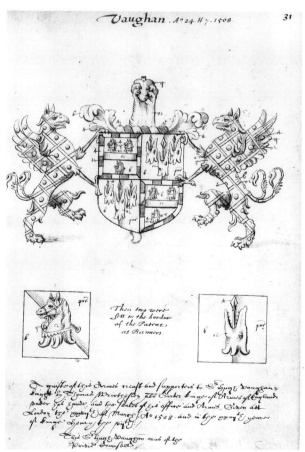

(*right*) Grant of arms and crest with supporters to Sir Hugh Vaughan, made on 27 Mar. 1508. One of the earliest recorded grants of supporters to an individual (Coll. Arms, Vincent 169, p. 31).

(*below*) Grant of supporters with arms and a crest in 1568 by Garter, Clarenceux, and Norroy to the Company of Miners Royal. The supporters are blazoned as two men, one called the hammer man with a hammer over his shoulder, and the other the smelter with a fork in his hand (Coll. Arms, Vincent 162, p. 80).

Thomas Cheney KG, and yale of Henry (Carey), Lord Hunsdon could scarcely have been conceived by their bearers.

The Barony of Hunsdon conferred by Elizabeth I on her first cousin, Henry Carey, was one of the first creations of her reign. Subsequent barons created by Elizabeth include St John of Bletso; Sackville, Lord Buckhurst; West, Lord De La Warr; Cecil, Lord Burghley; Compton and Cheney of Toddington. A search of the records of the College of Arms for grants of supporters to these men and their peers produces nothing beyond an unusual Patent of 1580 by Robert Cooke, Clarenceux, setting forth the full achievement including supporters of Philip Howard, Earl of Arundel. It is unusual in that it omits the arms of Howard in the first quarter. The position changes in the seventeenth century, and in 1628, for example, Sir William Segar granted supporters to Lords Botiler of Bramfield, Mohun, Dunsmore, and Pierrepont. Sir Edward Walker, Garter, made thirty-one grants of supporters to new peers and three to new peeresses in their own right between 1644 and 1663, and from the seventeenth century to the present day grants of supporters in England have been regularly recorded. In Scotland the granting of supporters according to George Seton in *The Law and Practice of Heraldry in Scotland* (1863) dates only from the mid-eighteenth century. Seton wrote: 'Probably one of the most delicate and touchy points in Scottish heraldry is involved in the question relative to the right to bear supporters. The practice of granting these armorial appendages appears to have commenced about the middle of the last century, and to have become very frequent during the time of Mr James Home who held the office of Lyon Depute from 1796 to 1819.'

Two questions which arise when examining the development of supporters are the extent to which families of gentry originally used or were recognized as entitled to supporters, and whether it is possible to be entitled to more or less than two supporters. Single beasts and monsters appear supporting banners of arms in a manuscript in the College of Arms principally of the first half of the sixteenth century, entitled 'Prince Arthur's Book'. It is generally alleged that they are not single supporters or badges but one of two supporters. Nine banners and single supporters are shown per page; those on page 107 appear to be a theow for Sir Thomas Cheney KG 1539, black goat for Sir John Wallop KG 1543, cockatrice for Sir William Kingston KG 1539, silver ram for Sir John Gage KG 1541, bull for Sir Anthony Wingfield KG 1541, unidentifiable monster for Thomas (Audley), Lord Audley, KG 1540, unicorn and bull supporting two banners for Edward (Seymour), Duke of Somerset, KG 1540/1, and griffin for Sir Anthony St Leger KG 1544. On the facing page, 108, there are two banners for Carey supported by a yale and male griffin, a lion supporting the arms of the Duke of Holstein for Adolphus, Duke of Holstein, KG 1560, two lions supporting two banners for Dudley, a lion supporting a banner for Savoy for Emmanuel Philibert, Duke of Savoy, KG 1554, a lion and a porcupine supporting two Sidney banners, and a panther supporting a banner for Sackville (see Plate 19). It is comparatively simple to demonstrate that these paintings show either one or both the beasts or monsters used then or subsequently as supporters. Modern peerages show that two black wild goats support the arms of Wallop, Earls of Portsmouth, a unicorn and bull those of the Duke of Somerset, and a porcupine and lion those of Sidney, Viscount De L'Isle. Henry (Carey), Lord Hunsdon bore a yale and male griffin as supporters, the Dudley family, as Dukes of Northumberland and Earls of Leicester and Warwick, all bore two lions as supporters, and Thomas (Audley), Lord Audley, Lord Chancellor from 1532 till his death in 1544, bore two of the unidentifiable monsters. The generally held view would, therefore, seem to be correct with regard to these particular illustrations, even if occasional anomalies occur such as the Gage ram, now borne statant Argent as the crest of Sir John Gage's descendant Viscount Gage, whose supporters are two greyhounds. The explanation seems to be that the family was only elevated to the peerage in 1720, so had probably not used supporters for almost two centuries. There is, therefore, evidence that these beasts are often one of a pair and not a single supporter. This does not mean that they may not have started as personal badges, and where appropriate emerged as supporters, in other cases, such as that of Gage, becoming the crest. It would account for single figures which occur on seals with arms as badges, and consequently mean that the single supporter is a bogus concept, only given any weight many centuries later by acts such as the matriculation of a single supporter for Falkirk in the Lyon Office in 1906.

'Prince Arthur's Book' is not the only source of supposed single supporters. The arms of the Littleton family of Frankley in Worcestershire are shown supported by a single triton in the record of the Heralds' Visitation of that county of 1634. However, the record of the 1623 Visitation of Shropshire gives the source, which is a seal used in 1481. Does such a record confer a right? An argument could be put forward that the 1623 entry is no more than a record of past use in copying a seal attached to a deed, a form of laudable antiquarianism that was increasingly common in the seventeenth century as standards of genealogical scholarship improved. The 1634 entry is a different matter, as there is no suggestion that it relates to past use, and as an official record it could confer a right. But the development of the Law of Arms in England, which does not now allow supporters to commoners except by Royal Warrant, probably negates any rights confirmed in 1634. 1694 is the year that marks the erosion if not the destruction of these rights, when the Earl Marshal asked for the observations of the Chapter of the College of Arms on several matters relating to the peerage (C.B. 1,307). One question was as to supporters, and the answer he received on 21 November 1694 was that 'They of right belong to Peers of the realm and their heirs male succeeding in their Honours and to Knights of the Garter and Bannerets during their lives only. But there are some families of the Gentry who have anciently borne supporters, but by what right is not known'. This ruling questions the right of gentry to supporters, if it does not destroy it. The bannerets referred to are Knights Banneret, those knighted by the Sovereign or his proxy on the field of battle, not baronets. The family of Stawell of Somerset are shown with a single

(*top left*) Single triton supporter of Littleton recorded at the Visitation of Worcestershire 1634 (Coll. Arms, C 30, fo. 31).

(*bottom left*) Copy of Littleton seal of 1481, entered at Visitation of Shropshire 1623, showing origin of single supporter (Coll. Arms, C 20 [2], p. 17).

(*right*) Supporters of a commoner: St Leger entered at the Visitation of Devon and Cornwall 1531. The sinister supporter is a male griffin (Coll. Arms, G 2, fo. 24v).

supporter at the Somerset Visitation of 1531. Two supporters are also recorded for families of gentry, such as the two St Leger supporters in Cornwall in 1531, one of which is the wingless male griffin, and the two lions rampant Azure shown for Hilton of Hilton in County Durham in 1666; further historical use in the fifteenth century is shown in the Popham seals recorded in Somerset in 1623. A manuscript in the library of the College of Arms in the hand of John Wingfield, York Herald (1663–74), has a section entitled 'Concerning Supporters used in England by noblemen and some other degree called the lesser nobility'. Joseph Edmondson lifted some of his section on supporters from Wingfield for his *Complete Body of Heraldry* (1780), and he is quoting Wingfield when he writes:

Supporters were likewise anciently used by divers persons in private life as appears by their seals who held office of high dignity in the state and more especially by those whose employments had the title of Lord prefixed to their style; as Lord Deputy of Ireland, Lord Warden of the Cinque Ports, Lord President of the Council, Lord of the Marches of Wales, Lord Warden of the Stannaries.

Examples are the families of Cheney and Guildford, both of whom were Lord Wardens of the Cinque Ports, Sir Thomas Moyle, Chancellor of the Court of Augmentations under Henry VIII, and Richard Curson, Captain of Honfleur, Normandy in 1446. Wingfield also produced a list of 'diverse whose ancestors used supporters and were never called to parliament whose descendants have still continued the same'. The list, which is stated to have been collected by John Philipot, Somerset Herald (1624–45), includes Heveningham of Suffolk, Stawell and Lutterell of Somerset, Tichborne, Wallop, and Popham of Hampshire, Paston of Norfolk, Sherard of Leicestershire, Savage of Cheshire, and St Leger of Kent. Peter Le Neve, Norroy (1704–29), subsequent owner of the manuscript, has added Shirborn and Houghton (now de Hoghton) of Lancashire, Hilton of Northumberland and Durham, and Foljambe of Derbyshire.

Three, four, or more supporters would seem to be as false a concept in England as the single supporter. In the very rare instances in which they occur, such as in the trick in a sixteenth-century collection in the College of Arms, where a shield of the arms of Sir Henry Neville, Lord Bergavenny, is shown supported on poles by three monsters, they would be better classified as badges.

The use of supporters by eldest sons and wives of peers are subjects that give rise to questions. In England an eldest son of a peer may only use his father's supporters differenced by a label with the consent of Garter if he is summoned to Parliament as a peer in the lifetime of his parent. The case of Charles (North), Lord Grey of Rolleston, who was

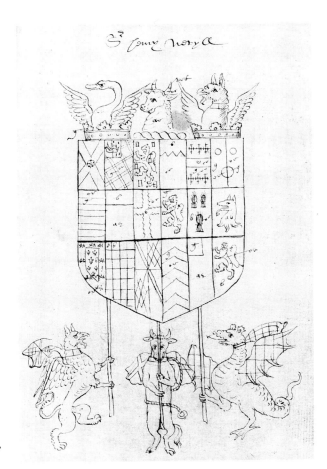

Three monsters (a griffin, winged bull, and wyvern) supporting arms and three crests of Henry Neville, Lord Bergavenny, recorded late sixteenth century (Coll. Arms, Vincent 184, p. 416).

summoned to Parliament in 1673 in the lifetime of his father is an example of it (I 25,33). On this occasion Lord Grey of Rolleston alleged that 'he and all other the sons and heirs apparent of the former Lords North had in the lifetime of their respective fathers successively used and borne their father's supporters'. Those who adopted this practice aped the use of the Royal Supporters differenced by a label by the Prince of Wales without grasping the point that the Prince of Wales is a peer. An example of unauthorized use of this type appears on a funeral certificate dated 1634 for Henry, Lord Stanhope, eldest son and heir of Lord Chesterfield, where supporters are shown, of which the dexter is differenced by a label.

The wives and widows of peers may bear their husband's supporters, and peeresses in their own right may bear their own supporters either by descent, if the supporters were created by Patent and devolve with the title, or in England by grant from Garter. There is an early seventeenth-century precedent which suggests that the wife of a peer not being a peeress in her own right may be granted different supporters from those of her husband. This is a grant in 1602 to

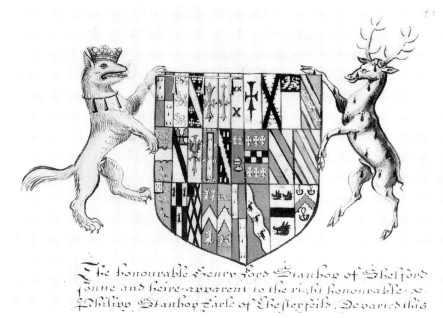

The honourable Henry Lord Stanhop of Shelford sonne and heire apparent to the right honourable Philip Stanhop Earle of Chesterfeild, Departed this

Funeral certificate of Henry (Stanhope), Lord Stanhope by courtesy (d. 24 Nov. 1634), showing the eldest son of a peer using supporters with a label contrary to accepted English practice (Coll. Arms, I 8, fo. 44).

Cicely, wife of Thomas (Sackville), Lord Buckhurst, of supporters of *two Greyhounds Sable collared Vair the rings and terrets gold*. The Vair of the collars is taken from the arms of Sackville. This precedent has not been followed, and only has a slight parallel in the combination of supporters that occurred in the eighteenth century when a peer married the daughter of another peer. Edmondson writes that it was the peers themselves who retained their own dexter supporter and marshalled it with one of their father-in-law's supporters as a sinister supporter. But the current practice whereby wives of the Sovereign and of some other members of the Royal Family are assigned by Royal Warrant their husband's dexter supporter with a different sinister supporter, suggests that it was not the peers but their wives who altered the supporters in this way to distinguish their armorial bearings from those of their husbands. A Royal Warrant of 2 February 1937 assigns Queen Elizabeth the Royal dexter supporter *a Lion guardant Or imperially crowned* with, as a sinister supporter, her father the Earl of Strathmore and Kinghorne's sinister supporter *a Lion per fess Or and Gules*. The grant by Royal Warrant of 30 July 1981 of supporters to the Princess of Wales includes her husband's dexter supporter and a sinister supporter derived from her father Earl Spencer's dexter supporter. The sinister supporter granted is blazoned *a Griffin Ermine winged Erminois beaked and legged Or gorged with a Prince's coronet thereto a chain reflected behind the back and ending in a ring all of Gold*. The Duchess of York, whose father has no supporters, was granted as a dexter supporter that of her husband with a sinister supporter of *a Pegasus Argent winged and unguled Or and gorged with a*

Prince's coronet Gold by Royal Warrant dated 14 April 1987. The introduction of gorging with a Prince's coronet is perhaps more permanently appropriate in the case of the Duchess of York than that of the Princess of Wales. Although Edmondson considered the eighteenth-century combinations unauthorized, a case in 1715 of which he was probably unaware goes some way towards sanctioning the practice for peeresses who are the daughters of peers. In 1715 part of an opinion given by Chapter to the Earl of Suffolk and Bindon about his wife's funeral achievement was that it should show his dexter supporter to the dexter and her father the Duke of Beaufort's dexter supporter to the sinister (C.B. 3,88).

In Scotland supporters were granted to many people to whom they would not be granted in England. This aggravated the arrangement whereby grants by Lord Lyon could be registered in England. In 1812 Garter proposed that: 'in all future cases where arms certified by Lord Lyon were accompanied with supporters, the arms only be recorded unless the party be according to the Laws of Arms of England entitled to use such a distinction' (C.B. 7,266). The matter came to the Chapter of the College again in 1815, when an attempt was made to register supporters granted by Lord Lyon to an English baronet, Sir Edmund Antrobus. The Chapter Book records: 'That it is a rule in England not to allow the use of supporters to any persons under the rank of Peerage except Knights of the Garter and Bath and such persons whom His Majesty shall be graciously pleased especially to distinguish with that mark of his Royal favour' (C.B. 8,2). Statements such as this would seem to negate any prescriptive rights that commoners might have to supporters borne from time immemorial. The 1812 resolution was reversed in 1832 on the grounds that Lord Lyon's right to grant supporters according to the law and practice of Scotland was admitted and undoubted (C.B. 10,30). This means that supporters granted to commoners domiciled in Scotland, such as James Tennant, who was granted supporters in 1813, can be registered in England. It does not mean that any recognition is given to supporters granted to those such as English baronets outside Lord Lyon's jurisdiction.

The evidence relating to grants of impersonal supporters in England seems to show that between 1806 and 1823 they were granted pursuant to a Royal Warrant, and before and after that date they have been granted by the Kings of Arms without a Royal Warrant. Royal Warrants were directed to the Deputy Earl Marshal in 1806 and 1823 for a grant of supporters to the Board of Ordnance. Although the Deputy Earl Marshal issued warrants to the Kings of Arms in both cases, for some unexplained reason only the second was acted on, and a grant of supporters was made by Garter to the Board of Ordnance in

1823. Between 1806 and 1823 supporters were granted pursuant to a Royal Warrant to East India College (1807), the London Institution (1807), Artillery Company (1821), and College of Surgeons (1822). Supporters granted without a Royal Licence include the Coachmakers and East India Companies in 1677 and 1698, and the South Sea Company and Royal Exchange Assurance in 1711 and 1723. At some time between the grant to the Foundling Hospital by Garter and Clarenceux in 1747 and the grant to Liverpool by Garter alone in 1797, the rule that Garter makes grants of supporters alone, whether to individuals or corporate bodies, must have evolved. Garter's exclusive right to grant supporters was acknowledged by Serjeant Bosanquet in his award following the case of *Nayler* v. *Heard* (1814), although Garter's claim to an exclusive right to act as agent in such cases was not allowed. Grants of supporters without a Royal Licence just before 1806 are those to the Linnean Society (1802) and Kingston, Jamaica (1803). After 1823 the grants to the Canada Company (1825) and American Land Company (1834) were made without Royal Licences.

There are few examples of supporters for Royal proxies, but one is the grant in 1772 to Sir George Osborne, Bt., of supporters for life. He was proxy to Prince Frederick, Bishop of Osnaburgh, and did 'represent our dearly beloved son in the procession to the Chapel and in the return from thence'. A baronet granted hereditary supporters in 1814 pursuant to a Royal Licence was Sir John Thomas Duckworth; as a Knight Companion of the Most Honourable Military Order of the Bath he had been granted supporters for life in 1803, following a grant of arms in the same year. In 1808 the arms were augmented and the sinister supporter was altered; the grant in 1814 altered the dexter supporter. Someone below the degree of baronet granted supporters pursuant to a Royal Warrant was Major-General Vere Warner Hussey. He had petitioned that he might bear some particular mark of distinction in his armorial ensigns allusive to the Imperial Patent he had received from the Emperor of Hindostan, Shah Allum, creating him a noble or Omrah of the Mogul Empire. He was consequently granted, in two patents of 1807, an augmentation of a plate in the centre chief point charged with a turban of an Omrah of the Mogul Empire, and as a further privilege supporters of *dexter a Soldier of the East India Company's Artillery habited proper the exterior hand supporting a Flag flying to the sinister Azure and sinister a Soldier of the Native Artillery of Bengal also habited proper and holding a Flag flying to the dexter Gules both inscribed with the word HINDOSTAN in letters of Gold.*

Those interested in the possibility of supporters without arms should pursue the case of Sir Benjamin Keene, Ambassador at Madrid, granted supporters in 1754. The grant shows the supporters

(*left*) Armorial bearings of Sir John Thomas Duckworth in 1803, with supporters for life (Coll. Arms, Order of the Bath, Knights Pedigrees, vol. 5, p. 20).

(*right*) Armorial bearings of Sir John Thomas Duckworth, Bt., in 1814, with altered arms as augmented in 1808 with the words *St Domingo* within a wreath of laurel and oak on a wavy chief, and naval crown and estoiles moved from the chief into the base and on to the chevron, the badge of the baronetage, the red hand of Ulster, on an escutcheon on the shield, and altered supporters, including a halo of estoiles round the dexter supporter, and the word *Minorca* on the flag of a Rear-Admiral of the White held by the sinister supporter (Coll. Arms, Order of the Bath, Knights Pedigrees, vol. 5, p. 22).

holding the arms of the Keene family of Filby and Brooke in Norfolk, as registered at the 1664 Norfolk Visitation, but no common ancestry is shown in the records of the College of Arms. Printed pedigrees of the Ruck Keene family descended from Sir Benjamin's brother Edmund, Bishop of Ely, commence with Sir Benjamin's grandfather Benjamin Keene born in 1631, subsequently Mayor of King's Lynn. The validity of such a grant must turn on the wording of the patent, which in this case refers to the Royal Will that certain knights should bear supporters to their arms. There is also the question as to whether the depiction of the arms of another family on the patent confers any rights over them.

Supporters sometimes stand on an elaborate motto scroll. On other occasions they stand on a grassy mount or other solid base. This is known as a compartment. In the past these seldom formed part of a grant but were added by artists as a decorative addition. The requirements for distinctiveness in England have increasingly led to the compartment forming part of the grant; the two lions in the 1963 grant to Kenya stand on a compartment representing Mount Kenya, and the lion and penguin in the grant to the British Antarctic Territory of the same year stand on a compartment divided per pale representing dexter a grassy mount and sinister an ice floe.

Whereas in sixteenth-century England supporters emerged as the subject of grants, badges largely disappeared, not to re-emerge until

1906. Although heraldry, as the hereditary use of certain charges, developed on the shield, and crests and supporters were a later occurrence, the shield or the design on it was not of practical use in warfare as it was too complicated. Symbols on flags have been used in warfare since long before heraldry. When, after the emergence of heraldry, these symbols are used by individuals or several generations of a family together with arms, they can be termed heraldic badges. It was badges, not arms, that had a practical use in the Wars of the Roses, named after the red and white rose badges of the Houses of Lancaster and York, and the confusion between the Yorkist white rose *en soleil* and the silver star of de Vere lost the Lancastrians the battle of Barnet in 1471. Although the nature of badges seems to differ from livery badges worn by retainers and placed on property, and from personal badges, the military use to which they could be put ensured their downfall under the Tudors, whose reign saw the end of the private armies and the badges that went with them, before the English heralds were able to apply rules to them.

As a simple charge that could be used to mark property or retainers the heraldic badge may have no similarity to the arms or crest. On the other hand often nothing more than the crest or a charge from the arms is used, as seen in the badges of Yorkshire and Lancashire families illustrated with the arms and crest in 'Ballard's Book' of about 1480. Torbock, Farrington, and Ireland took charges from the arms, whereas Talbot, Pudsey, and Urswick used their crests as badges.

The profusion of Royal supporters in the fifteenth century is similarly reflected in the number of badges used by each Sovereign, some of which are allied to their supporters. Edward IV used the white rose en soleil, a hawk and fetterlock, sunburst, white lion, and black

(*left*) Arms and supporters of Kenya 1963, with a compartment of Mount Kenya (Coll. Arms, I 83, p. 2).

(*right*) Arms, crest, and supporters, with a compartment representing a grassy mount and ice floe, for the British Antarctic Territory 1963 (Coll. Arms, I 83, p. 4).

bull, of which the last two also appear as supporters. In 1895 a lidded copper jug approximately sixteen inches high was found in the palace of King Prempeh at Kumasi in Ghana. It is inscribed '*He that wyl not spare when he may He shal not spend when he would*' and '*Deme the best in every dowt Til the trowthe be tryid owte*'. On it are the English Royal Arms incorporating France ancient as borne from 1340 to 1405, and badges of falcons on roundels, lions facing to the sinister, and a stag or hart couchant. The lions seem to be taken from the arms, and the hart associated with Richard II dates the jug to his reign, and probably between 1390 and 1399 as, although he came to the throne in 1377, he was then only aged 11. How the jug, which is now in the British Museum, ever got to Ghana is a mystery, but it is a good illustration of the evolution of badges, some of which were taken from the arms or crest and others of which were distinct. Several badges are equally associated with families such as the Nevilles, some being linked to lordships or titles such as Raby and Bergavenny, and others, such as the Dun Cow and interlaced staples, being more general. Beast badges of other families, such as the griffin of the Spencers, reappear as one of the supporters.

It has been suggested that the medieval badge only related to the head of the family. This is a matter of speculation, although the head

(*right*) Copper jug *c.*1390 with arms, supporters, and badges of Richard II, found in Ghana in 1895 (British Museum).

(*below*) Early seventeenth-century record of badges of Edward IV (Coll. Arms, L 14 [pt. 2], fo. 380v).

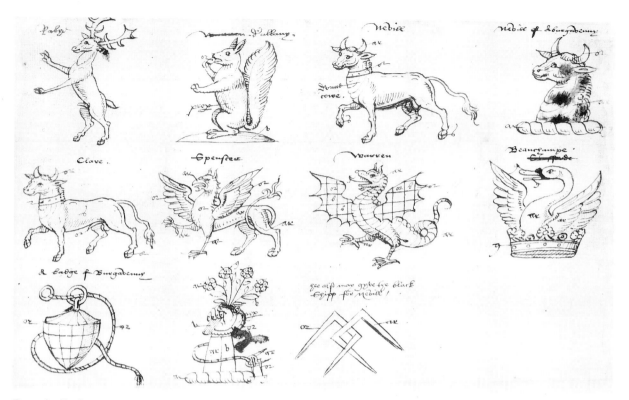

Record of badges c.1600 principally connected with the Neville family, in the hand of Richard Scarlett, herald painter and genealogist (d. 1607) (Coll. Arms, Vincent 172, fo. 42v).

of any family would be the man with the greatest potential use of a simple symbol. One of the fullest records of English badges is in an early sixteenth-century collection of standards in the College of Arms numbered I 2, where the cross of St George is shown next to the pole to indicate that the person to whom it related was an Englishman, and the rest of the standard, a tapering flag with a rounded and split end, shows a badge or badges, sometimes a crest, and the motto. As this record relates to individuals rather than families it lends weight to the concept of a badge being personal. The appearance of the standards, which tend to show single beasts on a background scattered with smaller charges, tends to support H. S. London's distinction between the personal and retainer's badge.

The revival of granting badges in England dates from an Earl Marshal's Warrant of 18 June 1906, which states that 'from and after the date of these presents the Kings of Arms shall grant badges'. This followed a report to the Earl Marshal by Sir Alfred Scott-Gatty, Garter, on badges and ancient flags. The principal ancient flags were the banner, standard, guidon, and pennon. The banner was square, and showed the arms with a fringe of the livery colours. None below the rank of a knight banneret might have a banner, and the standard was restricted to knights bachelor and those of higher rank. As noted above, it showed the cross of St George, the motto, badge, and sometimes the crest, with a slit end cut like two round tongues. The authorities differ as to certain details regarding ancient flags, in particular as to their dimensions, although the King's standard in battle seems to have been eleven yards long, his standard for use not in battle eight or nine yards long, with the following decreasing lengths in yards for those of lesser rank: duke seven and a half, marquess six and a half, earl six, viscount five and a half, baron five, knight banneret four and a half, and knight bachelor four. The guidon was the same shape as the standard but with a rounded rather than a split end. It was two-thirds the size of a standard, and might be borne by all armigers. It showed the arms next to the pole, and then a pattern similar to diaper on the tapering body. The pennon was half the size of the guidon and of similar design. If someone was advanced to the degree of knight banneret on the field of battle, the tapering end of his pennon or guidon would be torn off, leaving a banner. Some sources make the guidon a small standard in design rather than a large pennon, though if one tore its end off all that would be left, if this is to be believed, would be a banner of St George. It appears as a 'guyd home' in the grant to Sir John Care, and this is its probable derivation, as a guide to the men (*hommes*) rather than a guide home.

The solitary precedent used by Scott-Gatty to revive badges through grants was a Patent of 1516 by Sir Thomas Wriothesley, Garter, and John Yonge, Norroy, granting a standard with a badge to Sir John Care. It was probably not the only such grant; there is, for instance, evidence of a grant of arms, crest, and a guidon to Hugh Vaughan in 1490 and 1491, and a grant of a new crest and standard to

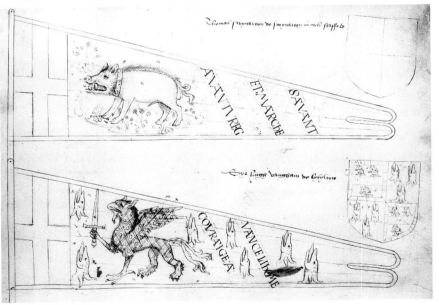

Standards of Sir Hugh Vaughan and Thomas Swynnarton, *c.*1520, showing a *single Griffin Gules fretty Or and semy of Roundels Argent (platey) and grasping in its dexter foreclaw a Sword* for Vaughan, and *Boar Argent plain gorged Azure bezanty on a Mount Vert sprinkled with tufts of daisies* for Swynnarton, with smaller badges of *Fishes heads erased Or with the blade of a fish Spear emerging from the mouth Argent* for Vaughan, and *tufts of Daisies* for Swynnarton (Coll. Arms, I 2, p. 61).

Sir Hugh Vaughan (presumably the same man) in 1514. He was also granted supporters in 1508. Under the post–1906 scheme the Cross of St George was removed from the standard, and replaced by the arms. The reason for this was that, as an English domestic flag, there was no need for the Cross of St George to show the nationality of its bearer. The rest of the standard normally shows either three representations of the badge or two of the badge and one of the crest divided by two diagonal bars, resembling bends on a shield, on which the motto is placed, commencing on the stripe nearest the pole. In cases where there is no motto these are omitted. Standards are no longer restricted to knights and those of superior rank but may be used by esquires and gentlemen, and painted on their Letters Patent. In such cases they have a rounded end, the split end being reserved for those of higher rank. The field of the standard need not necessarily be of the livery colours. There are those who argue that the English practice of granting what was the medieval livery or retainer's badge and showing it on a standard is inappropriate for individuals with no retainers, and should be restricted to corporate bodies. There seems to be no reason why the law of arms and heraldic practice should be petrified at one stage in their development, and whilst the badge is useful to corporate bodies, in that they can license its use to subsidiary or allied bodies and employees, in the personal field the Kings of Arms have sanctioned its use by a married daughter of an armiger whose husband is not armigerous (C.B. 21,43).

All flags flown at sea come under the jurisdiction of the Admiralty, which has laid down that their sides should have a 2:1 ratio. The Earl Marshal is the controlling authority over flags flown on land, and although the heraldic banner showing the arms with a fringe of the livery colours was traditionally square, when the Earl Marshal laid down by a Warrant dated 9 February 1938 that flags flown on churches in the provinces of Canterbury and York should show the Cross of St George with the arms of the diocese on a shield in the first quarter, the opportunity was taken by means of a letter to the Press from Sir Gerald Wollaston, Garter and principal heraldic officer under the Earl Marshal, to state that flags on land should be of the approximate relative dimensions of '5 × 3'. Such a shape flies better than a square flag, whilst reducing the visual distortion caused by a flag of dimensions '2 × 1'. The dimensions of '5 × 3' for flags flown on land were entered in the Chapter Book of the College of Arms for 16 June 1947 (C.B. 21,96) as the officially accepted dimensions of all flags flown on land within the jurisdiction of the Earl Marshal.

The standards of the late fifteenth and early sixteenth centuries contain beasts, smaller badges, sometimes a crest, and usually a word or group of words. These words developed in England into the motto, which is now normally shown on a scroll beneath the shield. Just as there is an argument that badges were originally personal or at least, in the case of livery badges, appropriate only for use by those associated as retainers with the head of a family, it is also argued that mottoes are personal. The reasoning is in part rather different, and in the case of English mottoes controls the current practice. In England it is considered that the Kings of Arms do not have power granted in their patents of appointment to grant legal property over a group of words. It follows that mottoes are very seldom mentioned in the text of a patent, although they may be shown beneath the shield. Consequently, individual members of a family may change their motto at will, as it does not form part of a grant, and two or more families may have the same motto. The motto may be in any language, and control is exercised by the Kings of Arms as they can refuse to issue a patent on which there is a motto of which they disapprove, even though it does not form part of their grant.

Mottoes seem to have had several different origins. They appear very occasionally on medieval seals, such as that of Sir John de Byron attached to a deed of 1293. The motto *Crede Beronti* is still used in the variant *Crede Byron* (Trust Byron) seven hundred years later. Is this a war-cry or simply a sentiment? The English Royal motto *Dieu et Mon Droit* is thought to have originated as a war-cry, as did the French *Montjoye St Denis*, formerly displayed above the Royal Arms of France. Irish mottoes ending with the phrase *A boo*, such as *Crom a boo* of the Fitzgeralds, Earls and subsequently Dukes of Leinster, *Shanet a boo* of the Fitzgeralds, Earls of Desmond, and *Butler a boo* of the Butlers were war-cries. It is in Scotland, however, that there is the strongest tradition of the war-cry or *cri de guerre*, called by heraldic writers a slughorne or slogan (from the Gaelic for war-cry, *sluagh-ghairm*). This is usually displayed above the crest, though a second motto sometimes appears beneath the shield. Some Scottish families shouted their own names, such as *A Home! A Home!* of the Homes, others their place of rendezvous, such as *Craigelachie*, a wooded rock near Aviemore and *Clare Innis*, an island in Loch Lomond, of the Grants and Buchanans, and a third group incorporated a patron saint such as *St Bennet and Set On* of the Setons. In Scottish cases such as Grant, where both a battle-cry, *Craigelachie*, and another motto, *Standfast*, exist, the former is shown on a scroll above the crest and the latter on a scroll beneath the shield. This does not mean that everything shown above the crest in Scotland is a battle- or war-cry. In Scotland the motto is mentioned in the text of the Patent, but as no two men may bear the same armorial bearings it is effectively personal. A grant by Sir James Balfour, Lyon in 1631 to Sir Archibald Acheson, where one word of the motto appears on a scroll above the crest and the other two on a scroll beneath the arms, with the text stating 'over al and below an escrole with this motto *Vigilantibus iura Subveniunt*' suggests that there was little distinction between the two positions. However, sixteenth-century paintings of Scottish arms such as those illustrated of the Earls of Errol and Argyll show a single motto above, and this is the place in which it is customary to show a first motto in Scotland, whatever its status.

Mottoes in the early Tudor period in England were principally in French, with a few in Latin and English. As they largely appeared on standards, records only exist of the mottoes of those entitled to standards, that is, knights and those of higher status. The military uses of badges meant that they did not flourish under the Tudors, and private war-cries were forbidden by a Statute of 1495. Sir Christopher Barker, Garter, was interested in mottoes to the extent that two lists, each of about eighty mottoes, exist in his hand, one written when he was Suffolk Herald (2 M 6, fo. 105v), a post which he held from 1517 to 1522, and the other as Richmond Herald (M 4, fo. 2), which he was from 1522 until 1536. In one list only the mottoes appear, without any names, and in the other only a few are identified, so that the purpose of the lists is not apparent. In most sixteenth- and seventeenth-century grants there are no mottoes, and where they do appear they are nearly all in Latin and express uplifting sentiments. An exception to the Latin and to the custom as to position is *Dieu Veulant Je Feray* which is above the crest in the grant in 1552/3 to William Bromefeyld, Lieutenant of the Ordnance. Thereafter *Honor Virtutis Premium*, *In Ardua Virtus*, *Sapientia Donum Dei*, *Bene Dictus Qui Beat*, and *Per Dura Requiem* are examples of 1571, 1604, 1610, 1612, and 1626, painted on scrolls beneath the shield on grants to John Mabb, John Wolstenholme, Gayus Newman, Benjamin Brond, and Thomas Ivat. Mottoes both above and below the achievement do occur in England, as in the 1600 grant to the East India Merchants. A decreasing percentage of patents were painted without mottoes in England, until the late nineteenth century when nearly all show mottoes, although a few do not, as is the case today.

The ability to change a motto has favoured those that are a pun on or allude to the surname, and the nineteenth century saw them replacing the pious sentiments of earlier generations. Some mottoes of this type, such as *Cavendo Tutus* (Safe by Caution) of Cavendish, Dukes of Devonshire, and *Pie Repone Te* (In Pious Confidence) of Pierrepont, sometimes Dukes of Kingston, can be traced back to the seventeenth century or earlier. Others, like *Festina Lente* (On Slow! or Hasten Cautiously) of the Onslows, Earls of Onslow, can be traced back to the 1820s when it replaced *Semper Fidelis* in printed sources. Similarly between the eighth (1894) and ninth (1898) editions of *Burke's Landed Gentry* the Holden family of Holden in Lancashire changed their motto from *Nec Temere Nec Timide* (Neither Timidly nor Rashly) to *Teneo et Teneor* (I hold and I am Holden). This was perhaps rash, as within forty years they ceased to hold the property which *The Gentleman's Magazine* of 1792 stated had been theirs since the Norman Conquest. Mottoes can allude to the design of the arms or the crest, and some, such as *Recreat et Alit* (usually translated as 'it refreshes and cherishes'), whilst they appear to do so, are not readily explicable. This, the motto of the Duddingston family of Sandford in Fife, is hardly a battle-cry, and one would not expect a comparatively minor family living south of the Highland line to have one, but what is it that refreshes and cherishes? The only suggestions link it to the greyhound's head in the crest as a possible reference to coursing. *Every bullet has its billet*, which appears on the 1809 grant to Catherina, widow of Lieutenant-Colonel Spencer Thomas Vassall, mortally wounded at the storming of Montevideo, is in contrast easily interpreted if somewhat unusual.

In Ireland, Ulster Kings of Arms sometimes mentioned mottoes in the texts of their patents, and always showed them in the English fashion on a scroll beneath the shield, the tinctures of which would not be specified. After 1798 all patents which contain mottoes mention them in the text. In a grant of 1576 by Nicholas Narboon, Ulster King of Arms, the motto is referred to as the grantee's 'word or ponse'.

A.E.I.O.U., the five letters placed by Frederick III, Holy Roman Emperor from 1440 till 1493 on the covers of his books and on his furniture, is usually interpreted as *Austriae est imperare orbi universo* (the whole world is subject to Austria). His successors, Ferdinand I and Rudolph II, had symbols or riddle mottoes of A.I.P.Q.N.S.I.A. and A.D.S.I.T. As a form of motto they are associated with Germany, although F.E.R.T. (rendered by Favine in *The Theater of Honour and Knighthood* (1623) as *Frappez, Entrez, Rompez, Tout*) was associated with the House of Savoy from the early thirteenth century, and after the defence of Rhodes in 1315 by Amadeus IV, Count of Savoy, is rendered as *Fortitudo ejus Rhodium tenuit*. The general use of war-cries does not occur in Germany or the rest of Europe, and it is a British and French phenomenon. This may explain Edmondson's bald statement in the *Complete Body of Heraldry* (1780) that 'By the rules of Heraldry women are not permitted to use mottos [*sic*].' If, like the crest, the motto has warlike connections, it would be considered inappropriate. This rule has been somewhat relaxed in England, and even before Edmondson *The Peerage of Ireland* (1768) illustrates mottoes for Viscountess Langford and Baroness Le Poer.

Supporters, badges, and mottoes generally emerged as heraldic extras in the late Middle Ages. It is not clear how they were controlled, if at all. Some, such as beast badges, metamorphosed into supporters, only retaining any real status as single beasts if counted amongst the King's or Queen's Beasts. A few medieval badges survived, although the crest usurped the role of the badge on objects such as livery buttons. Private English war-cries, to the extent that they existed, were as unacceptable to the Tudors as private armies, and when mottoes began to reappear on late Tudor patents they are harmless expressions of honour, wisdom, and virtue, clothed in Latin. In the post-medieval period heraldry had to suit the requirements of the Sovereign. The coat of arms was available to new men, and the steady if varying stream of grants since 1500 is evidence of the social mobility that has always existed in England. Crests, augmentations of honour, supporters, helmets, and coronets of rank became successively available, and finally the badge re-emerged in 1906.

VII   *Marshalling of Arms*

THE MARSHALLING of arms is the proper arrangement of armorial bearings to denote rank and condition, connection by marriage, or representation of families. Most marshalling is the combination of two or more coats of arms, and for practical modern purposes the relevant forms are impaling, bearing arms on an escutcheon of pretence, and quartering. The principal obsolete forms of combination are compounding and dimidiating.

Bachelors and spinsters do not marshal their arms with another coat unless they are office-holders or entitled to quarterings. A bachelor may use arms, crest, helmet, and mantling. A spinster bears arms alone on a lozenge without crest, helmet, or mantling, and if she wears a signet ring it should show her arms alone and not her father's crest. All women bear any cadency marks borne by their father, but cadency marks are not used between sisters as they rank equally. Marriage is denoted by impaling or escutcheons of pretence. In the former the shield is divided vertically, and the husband's arms are placed to the dexter and the wife's to the sinister, and in the latter the wife's arms are placed in a separate shield in the centre of the husband's arms. As the Law of Arms developed at a time when husband and wife were legally one person, the custom is to show a married woman's arms on a shield either impaled or in pretence, whichever is appropriate, but without crest, helmet, or mantling. A widow reverts to a lozenge of her husband's arms with her own either in pretence or impaled. A recent practice allows a divorced woman her paternal arms with a mascle for difference. A peer is entitled to supporters, as are certain knights, and a married peer or knight may impale or place his wife's arms in pretence on a shield held by his supporters. The widow of a peer bears the same achievement on a lozenge surmounted by a coronet of rank, but without her husband's crest, helmet, or mantling. A married peeress in her own right bears her arms on a lozenge between her own supporters as if unmarried, and her coat of arms can only be combined with that of her husband on a separate shield, where her arms would appear on an escutcheon of pretence surmounted by a coronet of her rank. This would be shown to the dexter of her own achievement if the two were borne together. A peeress married to a peer would retain her own achievement, and to the dexter would be her husband's with her arms in pretence surmounted by a coronet of rank. The eldest son of a peer who uses one of his father's lesser titles by courtesy does not

Armorial bearings of a peer (the 4th Earl of Yarborough), married to a peeress in her own right (Baroness Conyers), recorded in 1893. His arms show the so-called augmentation of the Pelham buckle in an impartible Grand Quarter, and his wife's arms in pretence ensigned with a coronet of her rank (Coll. Arms, Norfolk 16, p. 85).

use supporters. Knights of Orders of Chivalry and Commanders of the Royal Victorian Order may encircle their arms with the ribbon or collar of that Order. In such cases they cannot impale their wives' arms on the same shield unless the wife is personally entitled to encircle her arms with the ribbon or collar of the same Order. Instead, they must impale their wives' arms on another shield placed to the sinister, and if the knight is entitled to supporters one may hold each shield.

The rules relating to the marshalling of arms are similar to much of the English Law of Arms, in that they developed by custom from the thirteenth to the fifteenth century, and were written down in books of precedents by heralds in the sixteenth century. One of the principal precedent books in the College of Arms relating to marshalling of arms is a manuscript numbered L.15 which belonged to Robert Cooke, Clarenceux, entitled *Rules for the dewe quartering of Armes*. This states that any man entitled to arms may impale in times of peace his wife's arms during the lifetime of his father-in-law. The reason for the restriction is that it is inappropriate to display one's wife's arms in battle, as her family is represented then by her father or brother. The husband's arms are placed in the dexter half of the shield and the wife's in the sinister. If a man's wife has a brother or brothers he continues to impale her arms after the death of his father-in-law.

Compounding occurs where charges from or parts of two coats of arms are mingled together to form one new coat. As new arms were created by taking elements from existing coats, the principal purpose of compounding arms was not to denote the arms of a husband and wife, but to create a differenced version of existing arms for use by a younger brother. When Pierre de Dreux (died 1250), who was a younger son, married Alice, daughter and coheir of the Duke of Brittany, he differenced his paternal arms of *Checky Or and Azure a Bordure Gules* with a *a Canton Ermine*. His grandson John de Dreux, Duke of Brittany and Earl of Richmond (died 1305) married a daughter of Henry III, King of England, and the younger son of this marriage, John de Bretagne or de Dreux, Earl of Richmond (died 1333/4), took the gold lions passant guardant from his mother's arms and added them to the bordure of his arms. This compounded coat is illustrated in a manuscript in the college of arms numbered M 10, of the late fifteenth century. In England compounding was an occasional medieval phenomenon which may explain the origin of certain coats, but it was not, unlike dimidiation, a means of showing the arms of a husband and wife.

Dimidiation was the precursor of modern impalement, whereby the husband's and wife's arms were each divided vertically, and the dexter half of the husband's coat was conjoined to the sinister half of the wife's, rather than redrawing the entire coat of husband and wife in each half of the shield. Francis Sandford, Lancaster Herald, in his *Genealogical History of the Kings of England* (1677) illustrates the seal of Margaret de Clare, wife of Edmond, Earl of Cornwall (died 1300), where the arms are dimidiated. This appears to be one of the earliest instances of the practice. Margaret, second wife of Edward I and sister of Philip IV of France, had England and France dimidiated on her seal in 1299, and Isabel, Queen of Edward II, similarly dimidiated her arms. Dimidiation ceased as early as the third year of the reign of Edward III, as shown by the entire impalement on the seal of Thomas de Kingston of 1330. Its demise was justifiable, for many coats cut in half vertically and joined to another treated in the same fashion were unrecognizable. As Joseph Edmondson pointed out in his *Complete Body of Heraldry* (1780), a coat such as Waldegrave *Per pale Argent and Gules* would be plain *Argent* when dimidiated for male members of the family and plain *Gules* for female members. The only survival from dimidiation is the rule that, where either husband or wife's impaled arms contain a tressure or bordure, this should not continue down the palar line but only round the three other sides of the husband or wife's impalement. William Berry in his *Introduction to Heraldry* (1810) extends the rule to the orle, but A. C. Fox-Davies in his *Complete Guide to Heraldry* (1909) excludes the orle, and J. P. Brooke-Little, now Norroy, editor of the 1969 edition of Fox-Davies, comments that although he has come across examples of an impaled orle discontinued down the palar line, possibly the reason why it has been treated differently from the bordure and tressure is that it is frequently depicted as a voided escutcheon, so that when impaled or placed on a banner it retains its shield shape rather than following the line of the edge of the field. A bordure with a specified number of charges on it, such as in the arms of Molyneux-Carter *Azure two Lions combatant on a Bordure Or four Crescents and four Estoiles alternately Azure*, would seem to be an exception to the rule. If the arms are impaled without a bordure down the palar line, how many crescents and estoiles should be retained? Any depiction of armorial bearings must be capable of being blazoned accurately; without the entire bordure these arms could not be blazoned with certainty.

A husband and a wife who is not an heraldic heiress impale their arms, as do certain office-holders with the arms of their office. In these cases the arms of office are placed in the dexter impalement and the personal arms in the sinister half of the shield. Archbishops and bishops, abbots, Kings of Arms, and Regius Professors at Cambridge are the principal classes who impale their arms of office.

Bishops began to impale their personal arms with the arms of their Sees in the early fifteenth century, and on a seal affixed to a Deed of 1411 the arms of Thomas Arundel, Archbishop of Canterbury, are impaled with those of the See. If a married office-holder wishes to impale the arms of his wife he must do so on a separate shield. The arms of Office of the Kings of Arms are of early sixteenth-century origin, and until the mid-sixteenth century the Kings of Arms sealed patents with their personal arms. Christopher Barker, Garter, and William and Gilbert Dethick and William Hervy as Norroy and Clarenceux, used two seals, one of personal arms and the other of arms of Office. At the end of the century the use of personal arms to seal a patent was discontinued, and Cooke, Camden, Segar, and Richard St George, Norroy, all used arms of Office alone. Although Segar did not seal with impaled arms, the third edition of Guillim's *Display of Heraldry*, published in 1638, illustrates his arms impaled with those of his Office. The regular use of impaled arms by the Kings of Arms dates from the Restoration. In 1651, when Sir Edward Bysshe, the Commonwealth Garter, granted arms to William Rowe, Secretary to the Commissioners of the Parliament of England employed to make the Solemn League and Covenant with Scotland, he sealed with the arms of his Office alone. Twelve years later, as Clarenceux, he was using impaled arms to seal a patent, as was Sir Edward Walker, Garter in 1666, and William Dugdale, Norroy in 1668. Stephen Martin Leake, Garter, states that Thomas Tonge used impaled arms as Norroy, an office which he held from 1522 to 1534; if this is the case it is an exception.

Custom and usage often based on suggestions of the textbook

writers do eventually appear to change the rules relating to the bearing of arms. There was a rule stated by Martin Leake that a man only impales the arms of his living wife. On a hatchment or monument the arms of a man's last wife should be impaled and 'the arms of his other wives should be in separate escocheons about the great one'. Sixteenth-century textbooks such as Gerard Leigh's *The Accedence of Armory* (1562) make no mention of such a rule, but contains complicated schemes for impaling the arms of more than one wife, and although initially it is puzzling that Martin Leake, writing two centuries later, should contradict Leigh and other writers, an examination of the precedents supports him. In 1568 Cooke, Clarenceux, undertook a Visitation of London. In an illuminated copy of the Visitation in the College of Arms, now numbered G 10, showing impaled arms and prepared in about 1590, Sir William Harper, Lord Mayor in 1561, Sir Roger Martin, Lord Mayor in 1567, Aldermen James Bacon and Henry Becher, and Thomas Rivett, a citizen and mercer of London are all shown with two armigerous wives. In every instance the arms are impaled separately. Funeral certificates for those who died in 1599 make no attempt to impale the arms of more than one wife on a single shield. James Quarles, Clerk of the Green Cloth, Thomas Maltby, Sir William Webb, William Hewett of London, and Sir Charles Morison of Cassiobury, Hertfordshire, all had one wife, and impaled arms are shown. William Cockayne, a citizen and skinner of London, George Rotherham of Someryes, Bedfordshire, Sir William Spring of Pakenham, Suffolk, and Robert White of Aldershot, Hampshire, had each been married twice, and in every instance both wives' arms are shown on a separate shield, not impaled with those of their husband. Sir Edmund Verney of Pendley, Hertford-

Entry of Thomas Rivett, of Chippenham, Cambridgeshire, citizen and mercer of London, in 1568 Visitation of London, showing the arms of his wives impaled separately (Coll. Arms, G 10, fo. 31v).

shire, had three wives and their arms are shown on three separate shields, not impaled. Twenty-one years later the practice continued, as is seen in the funeral certificate with rhinoceros crest of Sir Robert Gardiner and three impaled shields for his three wives.

Gerard Leigh put forward alternative schemes for showing the arms of two wives in the sinister impalement, dividing it either per fess, in which case the first wife is in chief and the second in base, or per pale when the first wife is next to the husband. If there are three wives the first two are in chief, the first being next to the husband, and the third is in base. For four wives the sinister impalement should be quartered. This is clearly unsatisfactory, as it is indistinguishable from a single wife with quartered arms. Guillim's *Display of Heraldry* (1611) notes

Funeral certificate (1620) of Sir Robert Gardiner of Breckles, Norfolk (d. 12 Feb. 1619/20), showing the arms of his three wives impaled separately (Coll. Arms, I 22, fo. 31v).

The Right wor[shipful] S[i]r Robert Gardiner knight of Breckles in y[e] County of Norff[olk] deceased the 12 day of ffebruarie 1619 at his house at Breckles & was buried at Elmeswell in an Isle there on y[e] South syde of y[e] Churche as yet without any monument. He had 3 wiues.

His first wife was Anne da[ughter] of John Cordall of Enfeild by whome he had issue S[i]r William & Rachell who dyed both vnmaried.

His 2 wife was Thomazine da[ughter] of John Barker of Ipswiche gent by whome he had issue Thomazine dyed vnmaried.

His 3 wife was Anne da[ughter] of S[i]r   Ireland knight sister of S[i]r Jonathan Ireland lately deceased & widow of John Springe of Pakenham in Com[itatu] Suff[olk] Esq[uire] by whome he had no issue.

She had 4 sisters & heires vizt Anne Elizabeth Alice and Mary. Anne y[e] eldest maried to Richard Well of Fivermere magna in Com[itatu] Suff[olk] gent by whome he had issue S[i]r Will[ia]m Well of Elmeswell in the said County gent who maried Thomazine da[ughter] of Jo[hn] Duffeild gent by whome he hath issue John sonne & heire, Robert 2 sonne, Will[ia]m 3 sonne, Anthony 4 sonne & Gardiner 5 sonne.

Elizabeth 2 sister of S[i]r Robert Gardiner maried to   Smyth and dyed without issue.

Alice 3 sister maried to John Wormeley & dyed without issue.

Mary 4 sister maried to John Mott of Braintree gent by whome she had issue Mary who maried Jo[hn] Clenche gent sonne & heire of Tho[mas] Clenche of Holbroke in y[e] County of Suff[olk] Esq[uire].

This worthy knight lived in very great reputacon all his life, he was a Sergeant at lawe, & Lo[rd] cheife Justice of Ireland by y[e] space of 17 yeares in w[hi]ch tyme he was two whole yeares Lo[rd] Justice of Ireland & was often in y[e] warres of Kinsale in person with & then Lo[rd] Deputy the Lo[rd] Montioy & did muche good service during y[e] whole tyme of the warres there.

He made 5 Executors of his last will & testament, viz[t] the sayd Lady Anne his wife, S[i]r Will[ia]m Spring knight her sonne and Jo[hn] Duffeild gent who have renounced the execution of his sayd will & Jo[hn] Clenche aforesayd & Jo[hn] Well sonne & heire to y[e] foresayd Will[ia]m Well do vndertake the execution & performance of the sayd last will & testament.

This Certificat is testified to be true by the sayd John Well who hath subscribed his name, taken by me Henry Chitting Chester Herald the last day of September 1620.

Leigh's schemes without any remarks other than as to the impracticality of the suggestion for four wives. The fifth edition of Guillim, published in 1679, places as an alternative a husband between his two wives in a shield divided paly, the first to the dexter and the second to the sinister. This edition also illustrates the arms of Sir Gervase Clifton impaling those of his seven wives, the first four to the dexter divided barry of four, the first in chief and the fourth in base, and the last three to the sinister similarly divided. Whilst the textbooks refined their schemes the College continued to follow its precedents. The funeral certificate for Mrs Elizabeth Muschampe, widow of Thomas Collingwood and Ralph Muschampe and daughter of Clement Strother of Newton, Northumberland, who died in 1672, shows her arms impaled by those of each husband on separate lozenges. The funeral certificate of Peter Venables of Kinderton, Cheshire, who died in 1669, shows two shields, one impaling Wilbraham and the other Cholmondeley for each of his wives. Similarly two shields, one impaling More and the other Hales, are shown for George Sheldon who died at his house Dan-John alias Dungeon in the suburbs of Canterbury on 8 May 1678, and separate shields, one impaling Beaumont and the other Hasilrig, are shown on the funeral certificate of Sir Wolstan Dixie who died on 8 February 1682/3.

The Visitation records of the 1680s contain very few impaled coats, but an indication of heraldic practice in the late seventeenth and early eighteenth centuries can be found in herald painters' work books which contain rough notes of artwork commissioned, usually with a trick of the armorial bearings. Much of the work relates to funerals, and in a book numbered H 8 there is an order dated 26 February 1708/9 for the funeral of Sir William Halford, Bt., whose first wife was Lady Frances Cecil, daughter of James, 3rd Earl of Salisbury, and whose second wife seems to have been a Zouche, although printed sources state that she was a daughter of a coachman named Lewis. The trick shows the husband's arms on one shield between those of his two wives, as recommended in the 1679 edition of Guillim. The same work book contains an entry dated 20 April 1713 for the funeral of Catherine, widow of Robert Dorell of Merton, Surrey, whose first husband was Richard Garth of Morden, Surrey. Her paternal arms of Stone are shown between Garth to the dexter and Dorell to the sinister, all on a lozenge. After 1710, impalements showing two wives or husbands on one shield or lozenge occur frequently in the Painters' work books, always following the Guillim pattern, and the custom finds its way into the College records in 'Peers' Pedigrees' in the second half of the eighteenth century. Anthony (Ashley-Cooper), 4th Earl of Shaftesbury, is shown impaling Noel to the dexter and Bouverie to the sinister in a pedigree registered in 1768, and in one of

Herald painter's work book of 1708/9, with order for the funeral of Sir William Halford, showing arms of two wives, née Cecil and Lewis, the latter using a variation of Zouche, impaled on one shield (Coll. Arms, PWB H no. 8, fo. 58).

the previous year John (Perceval), 2nd Earl of Egmont, is shown impaling Cecil to the dexter for his first wife Lady Catherine Cecil, daughter of James, 5th Earl of Salisbury, and Compton to the sinister for his second wife, also Catherine, sister of the 7th and 8th Earls of Northampton. It could be argued that heraldic displays at funerals and pedigrees are matters of record, and do not affect the way in which a man would bear arms in his lifetime. Some weight can be attached to this, but it cannot be denied that in the earlier records the arms of wives are impaled separately and the later appear to follow the textbook writers.

An armigerous man impales the arms of his wife as long as her father is alive. On the father's death he may, if she has no surviving brothers or deceased brothers who left issue, place her arms on a shield in the centre of his own arms. This is termed an escutcheon of pretence because he pretends to represent her family, and as there are no immediate male members of that family it is not inappropriate to bear such a coat in battle or times of war. College manuscript L 15 states that there must be issue of the marriage before a husband may bear his wife's arms in pretence. Prior to the formulation of the present rules there are cases in the early fifteenth century where a husband quartered his wife's arms; for instance, in 1409 Sir John Oldcastle quartered the arms of his wife Joan, Lady Cobham, and John Smert (Garter 1450–78) quartered the arms of his wife Katherine, who was the daughter of his predecessor as Garter, William Bruges. Elias Ashmole, Windsor Herald, in his *Institution, Laws, and Ceremonies of the Most Noble Order of the Garter* (1672) gives instances of Knights of the Garter who quartered their wives' arms, placing the latter in the first quarter, and there are twenty cases of escutcheons of pretence on shields surrounded by the Garter in contradiction to the rule which developed that a military Order may not be placed round the arms of a husband and wife. There are arguments that an Order is more acceptable with an escutcheon of pretence than an impaled coat, as the Order does not touch the wife's arms and the husband has pretended rights over the wife's coat. Joseph Edmondson, Mowbray Herald Extraordinary, did not see any impropriety in a Knight of the Garter either impaling or bearing his wife's arms in pretence within the Garter, and considered that to show the arms on two shields gave the impression of two partners in trade when painted on the side of a coach. Edmondson, a coach painter by occupation, could at least speak with authority as to the appearance of coaches. Fifteen of the twenty escutcheons of pretence borne by Knights of the Garter and referred to by Ashmole were arms of wives; the remaining five were feudal arms, that is, arms relating to feudal fees such as earldoms, and borne in imitation of arms of Dominion borne by Sovereigns. Such escutcheons of pretence did not survive as a rule into the sixteenth century in English heraldry, although a later example is that borne since 1734 by the Dukes of Richmond for the Dukedom of Aubigny in France. When the 3rd Duke of Richmond asked Stephen Martin Leake, Garter, how he should bear his coat in pretence with the arms of Bruce, also in pretence, for his wife, Garter suggested quartering Aubigny but this was rejected, and it was agreed that Bruce should be in pretence with Aubigny above it in the chief point of the escutcheon. The Duke and Duchess had no issue, so that the sixteenth-century rule as to the need for issue before use of an escutcheon of pretence was not being followed by the mid-eighteenth century. Ashmole quotes only one case of a Knight of the Garter, Sir Charles Somerset, subsequently 1st Earl of Worcester (died 1526), who impaled the arms of his wife within the Garter, so there is some evidence that an escutcheon of pretence surrounded by an Order of Chivalry was more acceptable than an impaled coat. The rules rejecting the impalement of more than one coat at once apply equally to arms in pretence, and by the eighteenth century were similarly disregarded in the College records. Examples occur with one coat in pretence and another impaled, and when the pedigree of Brownlow Cust of Belton, who was created Baron Brownlow in 1776, was registered in 1777, two escutcheons of pretence were shown as both his wives were heraldic heiresses.

A question of increasing relevance when there are more grants of arms to women is, whether the arms of a woman who is granted arms

College of Arms record (1777) of Sir John (Cust), Bt., Baron Brownlow, with the arms of Drury and Banks in pretence for his two wives (Coll. Arms, Peers I, p. 102).

should be placed in pretence on her husband's shield or not. The logical answer would appear to be yes, were it not for an entry made in a series entitled 'Miscellaneous Enrolments' in 1968 by Garter and Norroy, Clarenceux being vacant. The preamble states, 'Whereas it hath been represented unto Us that there is doubt as to the right to quarter arms granted to a woman, who was not her father's heir or coheir in blood and that a ruling by us was therefore needed'. The entry continues,

If arms be granted to such a woman to be borne by herself and her descendants according to the Laws of Arms and if she by her husband has issue; then such issue upon the death of the grantee, shall quarter with their paternal arms a quartering of such paternal arms impaling the arms granted to the grantee all within a bordure of distinguishing tincture and shall transmit such quartering to their posterity according to the Laws of Arms.

As escutcheons of pretence and quartering signify marriage to and descent from an heraldic heiress, if the one is inappropriate it would seem that the other should be too. But the reasoning behind the entry is odd as, although the quarterings signify the representation in blood by an ancestress of her armigerous father, arms are in themselves a form of honour, and where the daughter is the first to bear arms which have nothing to do with her father, quartering the arms must surely indicate representation of no one other than the grantee of those arms. If this was not the case, an illegitimate daughter granted arms who historically was a stranger in blood to her natural father would be at an advantage over a legitimate daughter of a non-armiger, as the Law would regard the former as the first of her line. If a man was able to place the arms of his wife who was granted arms on an escutcheon of pretence it would solve the question posed in the 1969 edition of Fox-Davies's *Complete Guide to Heraldry* where the editor, in discussing peers married to peeresses in their own right, asks, 'supposing that the peeress were a peeress by creation and were not an heiress, how would her arms be displayed? Apparently it would not be permissible to place them on an escutcheon of pretence.' Royal Heraldry is a matter for decision by the Sovereign in each individual case, so that normal rules do not apply. However, the present Duchess of York, although she is not a peeress in her own right, does otherwise illustrate the case considered by the Kings of Arms in 1968 of a female grantee with a brother.

The quartering of arms refers to the procedure where a shield is divided into four or more quarters of the same size. In England an even number of quarters is normally shown, and if necessary the paternal arms which are in the first quarter are repeated after the last quartering, and the arms in the second and subsequent quarters can be repeated thereafter if this balances the scheme. Where only two coats are quartered the paternal arms are placed in the first and fourth quarters, that is, in dexter chief and sinister base, and the arms which there is a right to quarter are placed in the second and third quarters. Arms cannot be quartered by someone not entitled to either paternal arms by descent or by grant. A shield with a blank in the first quarter is unacceptable, and an armigerous woman may neither impale a blank nor place an escutcheon of pretence on an empty shield. Fortunately, Gerard Leigh's suggestion that the issue of a gentlewoman married to a man not entitled to arms may bear her arms for life differenced by a cinquefoil never found its way into accepted practice. If a family is entitled to arms, quarterings are acquired by the marriage of an ancestor in an unbroken male line with an heraldic heiress and may be borne by the issue of that marriage. If a man entitled to arms but no quarterings marries an heraldic heiress, whose father quartered ten other coats with his paternal arms, the issue of the marriage may bear all their mother's quarterings, and consequently use a coat that is quarterly of twelve. Quarterings need not, therefore, signify centuries of carefully planned or fortunate alliances by one family but simply one recent judicious match by a father or grandfather. The requirement of descent in an unbroken male line means that descent from the heraldic heiress must be proven. Quarterings are a mark of representation in blood, and the marriage of the brother of an ancestor does not entitle one to quarter the arms of the wife, even if they have been borne for some generations by the issue of the marriage to whom one has become heir on their extinction.

A line can be broken for lack of proof of descent and also by illegitimacy. At a Chapter of the College of Arms held on 25 January 1717/8 (C.B. 3, 128) it was noted that 'by the laws and practice of arms bastards so acknowledged have not only been allowed to be of their father's blood but also to bear the arms and quarterings of their said fathers with due distinctions of bastardy'. An illegitimate child may not bear his or her father's arms and quarterings undifferenced but may have a grant of arms with some mark of distinction. Some grants have included quarterings, and the most obvious extant examples of such quarterings are in the grants of the quartered Royal Arms, three with a baton sinister overall and one within a bordure, made to Charles II's natural sons, now represented by the Dukes of Buccleuch and Queensberry, Grafton, St Albans, and Richmond and Gordon. An earlier quartered Royal Coat within a bordure and borne on a fess can be seen in the arms of the Duke of Beaufort, who is descended from Edward III through John of Gaunt, and a version of the more recent quartered Royal Arms with a baton sinister overall is seen in the arms of the Earls of Munster, descended from William IV. Seven

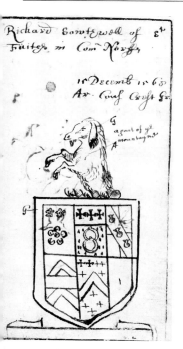

Note of a grant to Richard Southwell on 15 Dec. 1568, which allowed his father's quarterings, although he was illegitimate (Coll. Arms, EDN 56, fo. 77).

instances of illegitimate children bearing their father's quartered arms with some mark of distinction were noted in the Chapter Book in 1717/18. These were Richard and Walter de Cornwall, natural sons of Richard, Earl of Cornwall, the children of John of Gaunt by Catherine Swinford, Edward IV's son Arthur Plantagenet, Viscount Lisle, Sir Charles Brandon, son of Charles, Duke of Suffolk, the natural issue of John Bourchier, Lord Berners, who bore Bourchier, Loveyne, and Berners quarterly with a baton sinister Gules overall, Richard Southwell of St Faiths, Norfolk, natural son of Sir Richard Southwell who was granted the arms and quarterings of his father all within a bordure Gules by Letters Patent of Garter, Clarenceux, and Norroy in 1568, and Sir Thomas Sackville, Gentleman Usher and Daily Waiter to the King, and natural son of Thomas, Earl of Dorset, who was granted his father's arms and quarterings within a bordure engrailed Sable by Garter and Norroy in 1622. Stephen Martin Leake, Garter, disagreed with the 1717/18 opinion, and considered that it was not the Law of Arms but custom arising from legitimation of bastards that allowed them variations of their fathers' arms. Despite the 1568 and 1622 precedents of Southwell and Sackville, which he regarded as bad, he held that there was no basis under the Law of Arms for an illegitimate child to bear his father's quarterings. The various Royal examples need not conflict with Martin Leake, as the Royal Arms can be regarded as an impartible coat. The opinion of Martin Leake, who was described by Young, Garter in 1841, as 'a most able and well informed man upon most subjects but especially upon the science of heraldry', must be preferred to that of a Chapter presided over by Sir John Vanbrugh, Clarenceux, who knew nothing of the subject.

The effects of illegitimacy on a family's right to quarter arms can be illustrated by the case of the Ingilby family of Ripley Castle, thrice baronets. Sir John Ingleby of Ripley bore quartered arms, and died in 1772 leaving two illegitimate sons, John and Henry Wright. From 1772 till 1780 neither had any right to arms. In 1780 the elder son, John, obtained a private Act of Parliament confirming the right to use the surname Ingilby and authorizing him and the heirs male of his body to use and bear the arms of Sir John Ingleby. There is no requirement in the Act, as there normally is in a Royal Licence, that the arms should be exemplified in the College of Arms, and as the Law of Arms cannot be above an Act of Parliament the son John, who was created a baronet in 1781, must as a result have been entitled to his father's arms and quarterings without any marks of illegitimacy. This may not have pleased the College, and it is interesting that a blank shield surmounts his entry in the series of Baronets' Pedigrees, though this may only indicate a reluctance to pay a fee to have the arms painted. This second baronetcy also became extinct, and a third baronetcy was created in 1866 for Henry John Ingilby, son of the first Sir John's younger illegitimate son Henry. Henry, who like his brother John changed his name from Wright to Ingilby, was not within the terms of the 1780 Act of Parliament; he became a clergyman, and died without ever establishing a right to arms. His son Henry John Ingilby had a grant in 1854 of his grandfather's paternal arms in a bordure engrailed gobony Or and Gules. No quarterings were included, so there is no right to the earlier quarterings of the family, and under Martin Leake's view of the Law of Arms it would not have been appropriate to include differenced quarterings either then or in a subsequent grant.

A right to a quartering requires both descent in an unbroken male line and an heraldic heiress at the head of the line. An heraldic heiress is a woman entitled to arms and without a brother or brothers. In England, sisters rank equally as heraldic coheirs, so that it does not matter if a woman has several sisters as long as she has no brother. It is possible to become an heraldic heiress some decades or centuries after one's death on the death without issue of one's brother or the extinction of his issue, but there is no basis for the suggestion advanced occasionally that a woman becomes an heraldic heiress on the extinction of her brother's male issue. Rights of inheritance of armorial bearings are governed by the Law of Arms, and, as we saw in the chapter on grantees, Coke and Littleton regarded it as of the nature of gavelkind, the law which controlled the devolution of certain customary property, principally in Kent. Under the law of gavelkind a man's sons share his land equally. If there are no sons, the daughters share the land equally, and if a man dies leaving daughters and sisters, his sisters do not share with his daughters. The Chapter of the College of Arms in November 1692 (C.B. 1,329) was of unanimous opinion 'that the issue of the ant [aunt] has no pretension to quarter the arms of the nephew, so long as there is issue of the [nephew's] sisters in being'. This rule is accepted by the textbook writers Guillim, Dallaway, Boutell, and Fox-Davies from the seventeenth to the present century. Ironically, although the Law of Arms is based on that of gavelkind as far as inheritance is concerned, gavelkind in land led to the decay of families. Sir John Ferne in *The Glorie of Generositie* (1586) calls it 'that incesate custome of gavelkind because it tendeth, to the destruction of auncient and gentle houses, and so by consequent, to the infeebling of the realme'. Silas Taylor in his *History of Gavelkind* (1663), one of the few law books in the College of Arms library, holds it responsible for the overthrow of the ancient nobility in Wales through the inheritance being continually divided, and suggests it is only beneficial in a large country not inhabited, recommending its use in Virginia. Henry VIII, alarmed by the lack of gentlemen in Kent as gavelkind reduced armigers to husbandmen unable to assist in the defence of the realm, was responsible for the Acts of Parliament which disgavelled parts of Kent in his reign.

The identity of heraldic heiresses can be seen in practice by examining the pedigree of Tatton of Wythenshawe, Cheshire. On the death in 1968 of Thomas Arthur Tatton, the male issue of his grandfather Thomas William Tatton of Wythenshawe became extinct. His daughters became heraldic heiresses, as did those of his cousin Robert Henry Grenville Tatton on their father's death in 1962, but the sisters of Thomas William Tatton, of whom the eldest, Emma, married Sir Harry Mainwaring of Peover, Cheshire, did not become coheirs in their issue in 1968, and would only have done so if their brothers' entire issue was extinct.

The order in which quarterings have been marshalled since the sixteenth century is best illustrated by examining a scheme of quarterings such as that registered for Trevor Tempest Parker in 1932. The coat is as follows:

(1) Parker; (2) Redmayne; (3) Parker; (4) Tempest; (5) Waddington; (6) Hertford; (7) Clitherow; (8) LeGras; (9) Hebden; (10) Rye; (11) Hebden; (12) Gillott; (13) Thorp; (14) Arthur; (15) Mauleverer; (16) Barlow; (17) Colville; (18) Conyers; (19) Wilberfoss; (20) Kyme.

Quarterings of Trevor Tempest Parker, registered at the College of Arms in 1932 (Coll. Arms, Norfolk 34, p. 117).

The first quarter is occupied by the paternal arms. When Edward Parker of Browsholme claimed arms at the 1665 Heralds' Visitation of Yorkshire, a note was made in the record 'respite given for proofe of these Armes'. Beneath this is entered, 'An old embroydered cusheon afterwards produced whereon these Arms were.' By this means the arms were apparently allowed; but of which family of Parker are they the arms? Edward Parker of Browsholme's great-grandfather, Edmund Parker, was a son of Parker of Horrocksford, and married Jennet Redmayne, an heiress whose mother was a daughter and heiress of Robert Parker of Browsholme. The heraldic evidence with identical first and third quarters suggests that the families are the same, and modern printed pedigrees show a link. The second quarter is derived from the earliest ancestress in the direct male line who was an heraldic heiress, in this case Jennet Redmayne, and she brings in any quarterings to which she is entitled, in this case one shown in the third quarter for Parker of Browsholme. The next heraldic heiress married by the family was Bridget Tempest, and by this marriage quarters four to thirteen were acquired. The fact that her grandfather was a younger son of Tempest of Broughton, and the senior male line of Tempest continued, is irrelevant to the right to quarter, although a cadency mark·would not be amiss on the fourth quarter. It is a question which heralds have considered, and in the late sixteenth century Cooke, Clarenceux; Glover, Somerset, the outstanding heraldic scholar of his day; and four other heralds resolved that if a mean gentleman married the daughter of a younger brother of a peer it was not fitting that the issue should quarter all the arms. The resolution implies general unease, emphasized by its vague nature in referring to all the arms, as though a few quarterings might be acceptable. However much a herald may dislike such quartering, it is not against the Law of Arms, and in a case such as this there is nothing inappropriate.

When considering the quarterings brought in by the Tempest marriage the same principles regarding their numbering apply. The pedigree must be examined as far back as possible in the male line, and then, working forwards from the first known ancestor, the scheme of quarterings to which the heiress of the family was entitled can be assembled. The first Tempest marriage to an heraldic heiress was that of Sir Roger Tempest and Alice Waddington, which accounts for the fifth quarter. The sixth quarter for Hertford comes from the marriage of Sir Richard Tempest and Joanna Hertford. In working down the pedigree, the next person to marry an heraldic heiress was the son of this marriage, also Sir Richard Tempest, who married Isabel, daughter and coheir of Sir Hugh Clitherow by his wife Isabel, daughter and heiress of John le Gras. Sir Piers Tempest in the next generation also married an heraldic heiress whose mother and grandmother were similarly heiresses, accounting for quarters nine, ten and eleven. The series of heraldic heiresses ends with the next generation, where the twelfth and thirteenth quarters are brought in.

This accounts for all the quarterings to which Bridget Tempest was entitled, so the progress continues down the Parker pedigree, and none of the wives in the succeeding generations, with the exception of Alice Blakey whose right to arms is doubtful, was an heir or coheir of her father till Hester Worsop, whose father's original name was Arthur. This accounts for the fourteenth quarter, but as no earlier generations of the Arthur family, who recorded a pedigree and arms at the Visitation of Essex in 1634, married an heiress, except Hester's father John Arthur, subsequently Worsop, attention is next concentrated on her mother Sarah Mauleverer, who is responsible for the final six quarters, of which Mauleverer is the first. The Mauleverer pedigree is treated in a similar manner to that of Tempest, and, by working down, the first heiress Elizabeth Barlow produces the sixteenth quarter. The son of that marriage married Joan Colville, who became a coheir of her father on the death of her nephew, and was responsible for the sixteenth and seventeenth quarters. No further heraldic heiresses were married till Sarah Pawson Wilberfoss who provides the last two quarters, one for Wilberfoss and the last quarter for Kyme, referring to the heraldic heiress married by the Wilberfoss family in the late thirteenth century.

This shows the principle upon which quarterings are marshalled and it also leads on to the question of inaccurate pedigrees. The most recent printed pedigree of the Tempest family, in *Burke's Landed Gentry* (1972), makes the descent come through Sir John Tempest, who is shown as an elder brother of Sir Richard Tempest, who married Joanna Hertford in 1342. Roger Tempest of Broughton is shown as a brother of Sir Piers Tempest, and their mother was either Isabel Crassus, widow, or Margaret Stainforth, not Isabel Clitherow. This raises a doubt as to the right to quarters six to eleven. But once accepted, can such a right be removed? The answer is yes, although no such clear response can be given to another matter, unfortunately never answered, which York Herald (G. A. de L. Lee, subsequently Clarenceux 1926–7) raised at a meeting of the Chapter of the College in March 1914 (C.B. 18, 60). He gave notice that he should move at the next Chapter that quarterings, if nominated and allowed at any Visitation, may be allowed at the present time, even though the corresponding marriages be not established and recorded. This is a separate point, as the motion only refers to the marriage being not established and recorded rather than disproved, and is referring, therefore, to quarterings for which there is no apparent justification and which are possibly unidentifiable. The answer must be that such

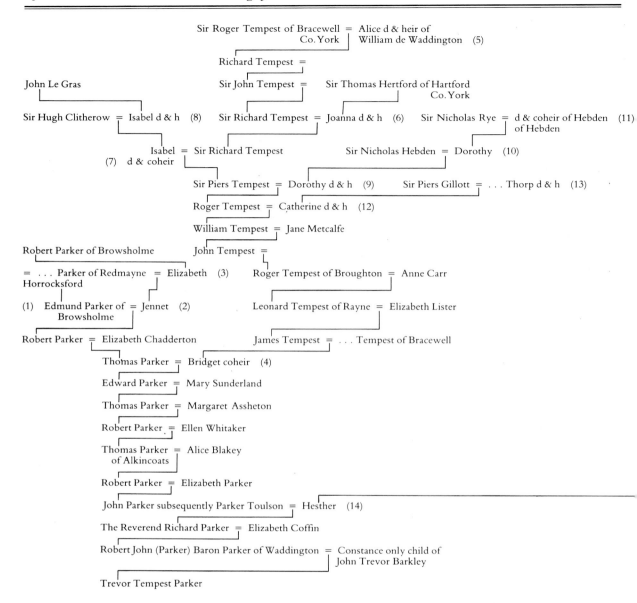

Pedigree of Trevor Tempest Parker

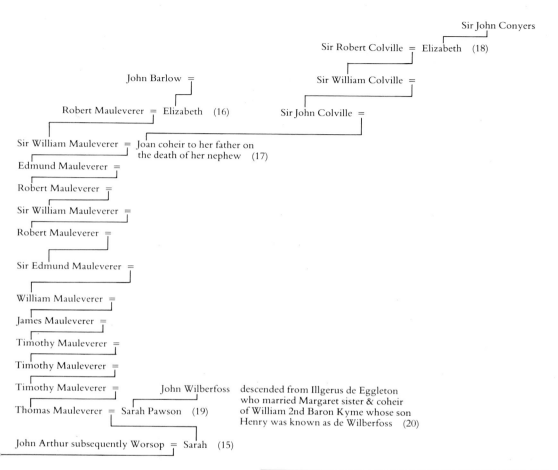

Sir John Conyers

Sir Robert Colville = Elizabeth   (18)

Sir William Colville =

John Barlow =

Robert Mauleverer = Elizabeth   (16)   Sir John Colville =

Sir William Mauleverer = Joan coheir to her father on
the death of her nephew   (17)

Edmund Mauleverer =

Robert Mauleverer =

Sir William Mauleverer =

Robert Mauleverer =

Sir Edmund Mauleverer =

William Mauleverer =

James Mauleverer =

Timothy Mauleverer =

Timothy Mauleverer =

Timothy Mauleverer =   John Wilberfoss   descended from Illgerus de Eggleton
who married Margaret sister & coheir
Thomas Mauleverer = Sarah Pawson   (19)   of William 2nd Baron Kyme whose son
Henry was known as de Wilberfoss   (20)

John Arthur subsequently Worsop = Sarah   (15)

Parker 1	Redmayne 2	Parker 3	Tempest 4	Waddington 5
Hertford 6	Clitherow 7	Le Gras 8	Hebden 9	Rye 10
Hebden 11	Gillott 12	Thorp 13	Arthur 14	Mauleverer 15
Barlow 16	Colville 17	Conyers 18	Wilberfoss 19	Kyme 20

quarterings may be allowed, however unsatisfactory, as long as this is not interpreted to mean that a Visitation entry in itself confers a right even where it can be proved to be incorrect.

Since the sixteenth century, quartering in England has signified representation in blood, and if it is subsequently established that a pedigree is incorrect then the right to quarter the arms is lost and does not continue on the basis of an earlier confirmation. This is illustrated by the case of William Beckford, who recorded a scheme of thirty quarterings in 1808, ten of which were disallowed in 1879. Beckford's paternal descent, though it produced spectacular wealth from the West Indies, was not the source of any quarterings, but his mother was the heir of a younger son of an Earl of Abercorn through whom he possessed many interesting descents. Beckford's claim to and subsequent loss of quarterings was, contrary to popular belief, neither fraudulent nor improbable, but based on a genealogical error in the Scottish Royal Lineage which appears in *Burke's Peerage* to this day. The question was whether Helena, wife of Roger de Quinci, from whom Beckford descended, was a daughter and coheir of both Alan, Lord of Galloway and of his wife Margaret of Scotland. G. E. Cockayne and Edward Bellasis, then Lancaster and Bluemantle, reported that

It is an historical fact that Devorgilda (wife of John Baliol) daughter and coheir of Alan Lord of Galloway, was though the youngest of the two daughters, eventually *sole* heir of her mother Margaret of Scotland—such fact being clearly established by the proceedings in connection with the succession to the Crown of Scotland. It is also clear that Helena wife of Roger de Quinci was another daughter and coheir of the said Alan, Lord of Galloway, and that she as such representative of her father, brought to her said husband the Lordship of Galloway and the Office of Constable, she therefore, though a coheir of her father by another (and former) wife her descendants are in no way entitled to the arms and quarterings of the said Margaret of Scotland. It consequently follows that the quarterings of Scotland with the nine succeeding ones thereby introduced . . . are incorrect.

In the Beckford descent Devorgilda, wife of John Baliol, was heir to her mother and coheir to her father. Cases exist where someone is heir or coheir only to her mother when her father has a son by another marriage. L 15 states that in such a case an heiress may quarter her father's paternal coat, but no quarterings to which he was entitled, with her mother's arms. This is not satisfactory, as there is nothing to indicate that she is not heir to her father, who may not have been entitled to any quarterings anyway.

In the seventeenth century the practice changed, and Martin Leake suggests that Dugdale was responsible when Norroy. At the Visitation of Staffordshire in 1664, the poet Charles Cotton recorded a

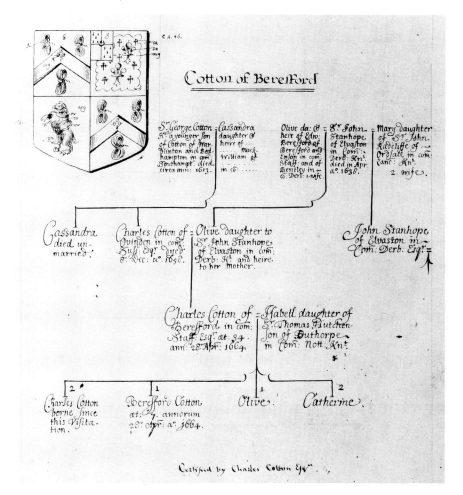

Cotton of Beresford

Cotton pedigree recorded at Visitation of Staffordshire 1664, showing a system probably invented by Dugdale to denote a woman who was heiress to her mother but not her father, where the latter's arms appear on a canton (Coll. Arms, C 36, fo. 114).

pedigree and arms. His mother was heiress to her mother, a Beresford, but not her father Stanhope. Cotton is shown quartering Beresford with Stanhope on a canton on the Beresford quartering. An example on an eighteenth-century Patent is the grant of supporters to Thomas (Villiers), Baron Hyde and subsequently 1st Earl of Clarendon of the present creation. He married Lady Charlotte Capel, daughter of the 3rd Earl of Essex and coheir to her mother Lady Jane Hyde, daughter of the 4th and last Earl of Clarendon of the first creation. Hyde is shown on an escutcheon of pretence with a canton of Capel. This is the current English system.

The popularity of Names and Arms clauses in Wills from the mid-eighteenth to the mid-nineteenth century resulted in many grants of quartered arms made pursuant to a Royal Licence permitting a rearrangement of the natural scheme. The arms of the adopted name were placed in the first quarter, and if more than one surname was retained the adopted surname was placed last. In time this practice

Record of grant of supporters dated 9 June 1756 to Thomas (Villiers), 1st Baron Hyde, where his wife is shown as heiress to her mother, née Lady Jane Hyde, but not her father, the Earl of Essex, whose arms are on a canton (Coll. Arms, Grants 10, p. 55).

changed, so that the first quarter related to the first name. In either case, such grants created indivisible or impartible coats, which remain quartered together when marshalled with other coats. If quarterings brought in before the grant of the impartible coat are to be used, the first quarter shows the impartible coat, the second the paternal coat, which is probably repeating part of the first quarter and then any quarters brought in by it, then the other part of the grand quarter is repeated if it is a maternal coat and brings in quarterings. Finally, any quarterings brought in after the creation of the impartible coat are shown. In 1794 Charles (Anderson-Pelham), 1st Baron Yarborough, whose paternal grandfather Francis Anderson had married Mary, sister of Charles Pelham of Brocklesby, Lincolnshire, had a grant of quarterly arms with Pelham in 1 and 4 and Anderson in 2 and 3. His grandson, Charles Alfred Worsley (Anderson-Pelham), 2nd Earl of Yarborough, recorded a quartered coat with the 1794 grant in the first quarter, Anderson the paternal arms in the second quarter, a quartering of Anderson recorded in 1634 in the third quarter, and the first quarter of Pelham and Anderson repeated in the fourth quarter. Such impartible quarters as in the first and fourth quarters are known as grand quarters.

There was a late sixteenth-century theory that if a woman was an heraldic heiress and married twice, only the issue by the husband who produced the son and heir quartered the arms, so that, unless there were daughters by both husbands, only one family of children quartered the arms. This was not the earlier practice, and Augustine Vincent, Windsor Herald (died 1627) noted several cases in the fifteenth century where both families quartered the arms. Examples noted by Vincent were the children of Eleanor, daughter of Richard (Beauchamp), Earl of Warwick, by her two husbands Thomas (de

Ros), Lord Ros, and Edmund (Beaufort), Duke of Somerset, who all quartered Beauchamp, and the children of Isabel (called Elizabeth by Vincent), daughter of Thomas (Le Despencer), Earl of Gloucester who married in 1411 Richard (Beauchamp), Lord Bergavenny, subsequently Earl of Worcester, and in 1423 as his second wife Richard (Beauchamp), Earl of Warwick. If this was a rule it would seem to have been of short duration, as Martin Leake dismisses it as an aberration.

In the fourteenth and fifteenth centuries heraldry evolved in Wales by the attribution of arms to ancestors who lived in a pre-heraldic period. An example is the arms of the XV Noble Tribes of North Wales. Tribe is used to mean descendants, usually in the male line, of a particular man, and identification in a society which did not use surnames was by blood and descent. Although the names attributed to the arms were retrospective fictions, in so far as the ancestors would have had no knowledge of the arms, the arms are of historical significance as regards their use by descendants. In a society where property was always divided between brothers, younger sons would remain on the land and have the means to support families, so that the Tribes were much larger than the corresponding families of descendants in the male line of a Norman feudal overlord of the twelfth century, when seven of the fifteen ancestors whose names are given to the Tribes lived. The remaining eight lived between AD 800 and 1100. The size of the Tribes and lack of social mobility, apart from general decline, led to far fewer coats of arms, since in North Wales, with the exception of newcomers, there were only fifteen alternatives. When a system of quartering was applied, the result was coats with many quarters and endless repetition of the same shields in the quarters. One of the most celebrated is that of Lloyd of Stockton, Shropshire, with 323 quarters, the uneven number perhaps emphasizing its un-English appearance. W. A. Lindsay, QC, Portcullis subsequently Clarenceux, produced a Special Report on the Lloyd quarterings in January 1894 (C.B. 16, 22). No action was taken to change College policy, but the text of the Report is perhaps a suitable conclusion to the difficult subject of quartering in Wales. It is as follows:

I ask leave to state that in deference to the past practice of the College of Arms as evidenced by schemes of Quarterings entered in volumes of the Norfolk Series of Pedigrees, I have allowed to Mr. Lloyd a number of quarterings alleged to represent various Welsh Kings & Lords whose pedigrees are given in the Collections of Vincent & Philpot and others. The Kings & Lords referred to are said to have lived many of them, centuries before the introduction of armorial bearings into England, but there is no satisfactory evidence that they ever lived at all. Their existence rests upon oral tradition and the myths relating to them are interesting. If however a scheme of quarterings is intended to mean, as I have hitherto supposed, that the person to whom the scheme is allowed represents in blood persons to whom particular coat armour belonged, I must express my personal dissent from the system on which the Lloyd scheme is founded. I have no belief that the majority of the Welsh pedigrees on which the Lloyd scheme of quarterings is based, are genuine, nor in the existence of the persons quarterings for whom are allowed, and I am reasonably certain that if such persons ever existed they did not bear coat armour. I must therefore ask leave to be exonerated from all responsibility for the Lloyd scheme of quarterings in respect of any quarter-ings more ancient than those admitted in G.9 ('Heralds' Visitation of Shropshire' 1569) and I respectfully protest against the system in deference to which I have approved the scheme tendered herewith.

(signed) W. A. Lindsay, Portcullis, Jan 1894.

VIII Heraldic Authority in Great Britain

OST of the surviving monarchies and even some of the republics of Europe maintain some form of official heraldic authority. Holland, Belgium, Denmark, and Eire, for instance, have individual working heralds. In Spain, the Chronicler King of Arms is responsible for marshalling the arms of the nobility, although the power to create new arms is retained by the Sovereign, while the Heralds themselves are titular and hereditary in certain noble families, taking part only in state ceremonial such as the Opening of Parliament. At the Vatican, the design of papal arms is the province of a prelate who is specially interested in the subject, at present Archbishop Heim. But only in England does there survive a fully fledged College of Arms on the medieval model.

The College of Arms remains a vigorous institution and an aspect of that part of the English Constitution which Bagehot classified as the 'Dignified'. It is a hierarchical corporation of thirteen members: three Kings of Arms, six Heralds, and four Pursuivants; there are also, at present, seven Extraordinaries who take part on ceremonial occasions but are not part of the corporation. All are members of the Royal Household, appointed by the Crown (the Officers in Ordinary by Letters Patent under the Great Seal and the Officers Extraordinary by Royal Sign Manual) on the recommendation of the Duke of Norfolk, who presides over the College as hereditary Earl Marshal.

The Officers of the College were instituted at different dates, some originating as private Heralds in noble households, some being Royal from the start. The office of Garter King of Arms was instituted by King Henry V in 1415 just before he sailed to France. In doing so the King created two precedents, for it was the first time that a King of Arms was appointed in England for the service of an Order of Chivalry, and it was the first time that the holder of a particular title was designated *ex officio* Doyen of the Officers of Arms. Clarenceux King of Arms, whose province is all England south of the River Trent, is the senior Provincial King. His title is derived from the Earldom of Clare and the earliest reference is in 1334. Norroy and Ulster is the junior Provincial King and has a province north of the Trent (as well as the six counties of Northern Ireland since 1943). The name is a corruption of *Nord* and *roy*. The earliest reference occurs in 1276. The six Heralds—York, Chester, Windsor, Richmond, Lancaster, and Somerset—derive their names from the titles of those whom they originally served, except for Windsor, which is called after the Royal castle. They were instituted at different dates in the fourteenth and fifteenth centuries. The four Pursuivants, or junior Heralds, comprise Rouge Dragon and Portcullis, both of whom were instituted by Henry VII and take their names from Royal badges, Bluemantle and Rouge Croix, who first appear in the reign of Henry V and take their names from the mantle and badge of the Order of the Garter. The Officers Extraordinary take their names from the Earl Marshal's titles and were created at different dates for ceremonial purposes.

The history of the Heralds as part of the Household goes back to the thirteenth century, well before they were first constituted into a corporation by Richard III in 1484, and there have been many vicissitudes since. Henry VII on his accession at first denigrated the Heralds and confiscated their building, but their potentially useful role was soon recognized, and is seen not only in the granting of arms to new men but also in the surveys known as the Heralds' Visitations which began in 1530. Queen Mary and King Philip renewed their Charter in 1555 and gave them Derby House in the City, the site which they still occupy, although the old house was burnt in the Great Fire and rebuilt between 1671 and 1688 to the design of Maurice Emmett, Master Bricklayer to the Office of Works under Sir Christopher Wren. Under the Stuarts in the seventeenth century the College enjoyed a golden age. Those would-be rulers by Divine Right were particular about anything which pertained to the dignity of the Crown, and the Heralds themselves were at the forefront of the great surge of antiquarian and historical study at that time. They included among their numbers both Elias Ashmole and Sir William Dugdale. In the early eighteenth century the College, like so many ancient institutions, languished in a state of comfortable decay, but the late eighteenth century and the nineteenth century saw a revival which ran parallel to the romantic interest in the Middle Ages, and the rise of scientific historical scholarship. The twentieth century has seen an Indian summer, not unconnected with the general inflation of honours and a widespread public interest in ceremonial, pageantry, and genealogy. The College of Arms thus survives as the only part of the English Establishment which has never been reformed by Parliament.

As a result of its long history, the various functions of the College are rather complicated. Some are vested in the corporation or Chapter of the College, others in the Kings of Arms, others in the Officers of Arms individually, and certain supervisory functions in the Earl

Marshal, who sits as the judge in the Court of Chivalry. The College is
almost entirely self-financing, and is not the recipient of any regular
public funding, though its officers do have official salaries which were
last raised in the reign of James I, but reduced again under William IV.
At present these amount to £49.07 per annum for Garter King of
Arms, £20.25 for Clarenceux and Norroy and Ulster, £17.80 for
Heralds, and £13.95 for Pursuivants. Nor, unlike many ancient
institutions, does the College of Arms have any endowments of its
own. George IV, with grandiose generosity, provided a regular
income for the maintenance of the building and records based on a
grant of augmented fees of Honour, but these, unfortunately, were
abolished by the Liberal Government in 1905, as part of its unsuccess-
ful attack on the House of Lords and the hereditary principle. By a
mixture of frugality and luck, however, the College has so far
managed to keep its head above water. It is perhaps fortunate that
Robert Abraham's palatial design for a large new college building in
Trafalgar Square was never executed and that the smaller seventeenth-
century building was retained.

Of the functions of the Heralds today, the most obvious to the
general public is the ceremonial. Dressed in court uniform and tabards
embroidered with the Royal Arms, they are responsible for marshalling and leading the processions on State occasions, and for proclaiming the accession of the Monarch. They also form the Earl
Marshal's staff during the preparations for State funerals and Coronations. On average, the English Heralds turn out in full uniform twice

a year, for the Garter Service at Windsor in early summer and for
the State Opening of Parliament in the autumn. Though the most
spectacular, this is the least time-consuming part of the Heralds' lives,
and they are engaged for most of the year in routine work connected
with honours and dignities, armorial matters, and genealogy, including much historical research. The Kings of Arms have the special
function of granting arms by Letters Patent. Any subject of the Crown
desirous of bearing arms can apply for a Grant of Arms. The Kings of
Arms are authorized by the Sovereign in their Patents of Appointment
to grant arms to 'eminent men, subject to the consent in writing of the
Earl Marshal first given'. If an applicant is considered 'eminent' an
Earl Marshal's Warrant is issued, the arms are designed according to
the strict rules of heraldry (no two Grants of Arms may be identical),
and eventually an illuminated Patent is issued and signed by the Kings
of Arms. The rule of thumb applied to eligibility to bear arms has
latterly been at least the possession of a civil or military commission,

or a university degree, professional qualification and/or evidence of public service. The definition of 'eminence', however, is essentially a matter of common sense; there are no hard and fast rules.

In addition to new Grants of Arms, the College is also responsible for proving the right to arms by descent, designing supporters to their arms for new peers, supervising the production of banners for High Sheriffs, and authorizing the assumption of arms in accordance with a change of name by Royal Licence (usually as a result of a conditional inheritance).

Establishing a right to arms by descent can be a complicated and expensive business, as it requires a standard of evidence that would be acceptable as proof in a court of law. For this reason a certain amount of legal knowledge is a useful qualification for a Herald, and two or three of the present generation of Officers of Arms are trained lawyers, though most are historians. John Ferne in *The Glory of Generositie* (1586) wrote in answer to the question what sort of men ought to be Heralds: 'he ought to be a Gentleman and an old man . . . not admitting into that sacred office everie glasier, painter & tricker, or a meere blazonner of Armes: for to the office of a herald is requisite the skill of many faculties and professions of literature, and likewise the knowlege of warres.' William Flower, Norroy, aged 88 in 1586 and a Poor Knight of Windsor may have been Ferne's ideal Herald, but Garter and Clarenceux were aged 44 and 55, and of the Heralds whose ages are known three were in their forties and two in their fifties. Similarly, not all Heralds are old today, and though their talents must be varied they are not necessarily exactly as envisaged by the sixteenth-century writers. Gerard Leigh in *The Accedence of Armory* (1562) states that, when designing new arms, the Herald 'must have a singular respect to the face of him that should have the Armes, where he shall well perceive in what season of the yeere, his owne complexion will serve him to doe best service in and thereby give him token according'. Apes coloured green were recommended for spring, and their absence from English Armory suggests that even in the sixteenth century Heralds did not comply with the wilder advice of writers on the subject and study the faces of grantees.

As has been discussed already, peers are entitled to supporters to their arms as an integral part of the traditional dignity of their rank. The College was keen that life peers, not just hereditary peers, should take advantage of this privilege, and many have applied for supporters. The names taken as titles by new peers have to be agreed with Garter King of Arms, and he also assists in the introduction of new peers into the House of Lords, either in person or through another Officer of Arms acting as his deputy. The 'Knights' Roll' is kept at the College, and has to be signed by new Knights. Inspectorates of badges of the

Armed Forces are also vested in Officers at the College. The fees charged for Grants of Arms and other services are divided between the Herald who acts as agent, the painter and scrivener involved in the work, and the College itself, according to a precisely laid down set of rules. The lion's share goes to the College, and is the source of income for the upkeep of the building.

It is an offence for a person to assume arms or other honours to which he is not entitled, and this can lead to prosecution in the Court of Chivalry. In the past, much of the activity of the Heralds was directed to 'policing' the use of arms. In the sixteenth and seventeenth centuries, under Commissions from the Crown, they embarked on regular Visitations of English counties to ensure that there was no unauthorized use of arms. These were discontinued in 1689. Since then, the College itself has not taken the initiative in these matters, but leaves it to the rightful possessor of arms to bring an action against anybody using them unlawfully. The most recent occasion was in 1954 when Manchester Corporation successfully sued a local theatre for illegally using the Corporation's arms. This was a case of assumption of existing arms. It is also an offence to assume an original device of heraldic appearance. Proceedings known as 'causes of office' were promoted either by the King's Advocate, whose powers are now vested in the Attorney-General, or by a private person known as the promoter. There has been no cause of office since the eighteenth century, but there is no reason to believe that it would no longer be possible for one to be promoted.

All Officers in Ordinary of the College have the right to conduct an individual practice in heraldry and genealogy, and can earn money by this. The extent to which individual officers practise varies; some specialize in particular aspects of heraldry or genealogy. There is a rotation whereby the Heralds and Pursuivants take turns 'in waiting' for a week at a time. Their own banner flies from the College porch for that week, and indicates who is on duty. It is the custom of the College that all enquiries, whether written and not addressed to a particular Herald, or in person, which are received that week become the business of the Officer in waiting. An applicant thereby becomes the client of the individual Officer from whom he first commissions work. In this way a Herald can build up his own independent practice, rather like a barrister. This work does not just comprise Grants of Arms, recording pedigrees, or genealogical research, but also includes identifying coats of arms or crests on works of art. Very often, for instance, it is possible to identify the sitter in a sixteenth-century portrait from the arms displayed in a corner, or to discover the original provenance of pieces of old silver or china. Officers are also able to design heraldic decoration for clients, such as book-plates or memorial tablets.

Theise Armes Creast and Supporters rightly
belonging to the right honorable Philippe Erle
of Arundell, Lord Maltravers and of Clun, wer
for him described and set foorth by me Robert
Cooke Esquire alias Clarencieulx king of
Armes and principall Herald of the South
parts of England to be by him and his posterity
vsed

18. Confirmation of arms, crest, and supporters, dated 28 May 1580, by Robert Cooke, Clarenceux, to Philip (Howard), Earl of Arundel, surprisingly omitting the arms of Howard. The sinister supporter is an heraldic antelope (Coll. Arms, R 22, fo. 75).

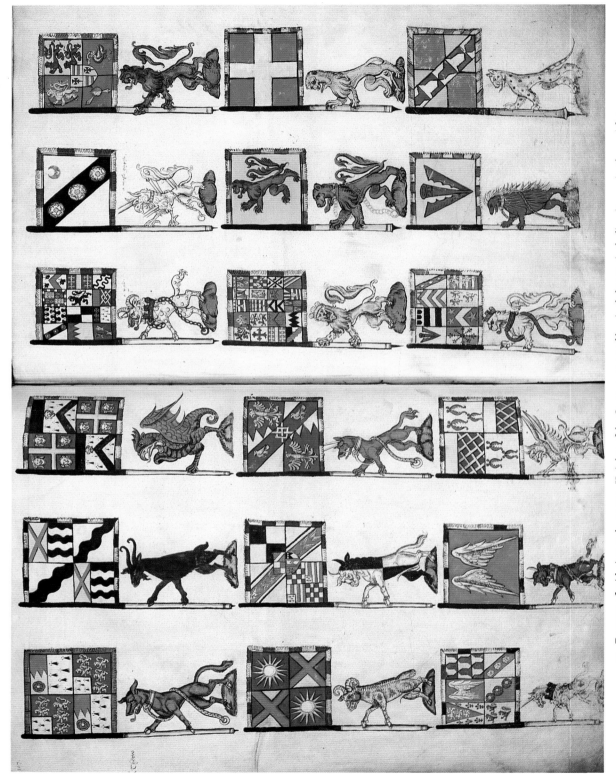

19. Banners of mid-sixteenth-century Knights of the Garter supported by single beasts, including (*top row*) a theow (*first on left*), cockatrice (*third from right*), yale (*third from right*), male griffin (*second from right*); and (*bottom row*) a unicorn (*first on left*)

20. College of Arms record of armorial bearings of the Princess of Wales with a sinister supporter derived from the dexter supporter of her father, Edward John (Spencer), 8th Earl Spencer. The dexter impalement shows the arms of the Principality of Wales on an escutcheon of pretence ensigned by a Prince's Coronet (Coll. Arms, I 84, p. 118).

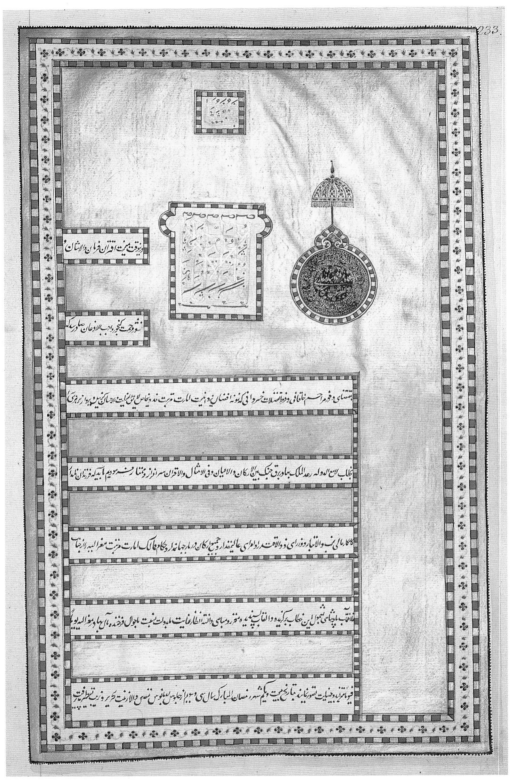

21. College of Arms 1806 enrolment of patent from the Emperor of Hindustan, creating Major General Vere Warner Hussey a Noble or Omrah of the Mogul Empire (Coll. Arms, I 37, p. 233).

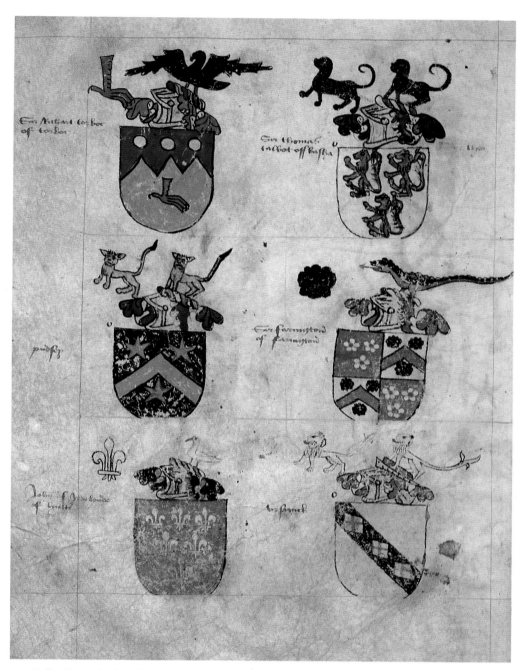

22. 'Ballard's Book': late fifteenth-century badges with arms and crests of families of Torbock, Talbot, Pudsey, Farrington, Ireland, and Urswick (Coll. Arms, M 3, fo. 37v).

23 (*right*). College record dated 27 June 1767 of John (Perceval), 2nd Earl of Egmont, impaling the arms of his two wives on one shield. The shield shows Perceval in 1 and 4 quartering 2 and 3 *Lovel Barry nebuly of six Or and Gules*, impaling to the dexter Cecil for his first wife, and to the sinister Compton for his second wife (Coll. Arms, Peers I, p. 2).

24 (*below*). Scheme of thirty quarterings registered at the College of Arms in 1808 by William Beckford, of which ten were disallowed in 1879 (Coll. Arms, Norfolk 2, p. 176).

See report as to Quarterings XVI–XXV with Order of Chapter [Chapter Book XIV, pp. 81-2]

I. BECKFORD.	XVI. SCOT.
II. HAMILTON.	XVII. SCOTLAND.
III. LESLY.	XVIII. SAXON KINGS.
IV. ABERNETHY.	XIX. WALTHEOF.
V. ROSS.	XX. ALDRED.
VI. COMYN.	XXI. KEVELIOC.
VII. QUINCY.	XXII. GERNONS.
VIII. BELLOMONT.	XXIII. MESCHINES.
IX. MELLENT.	XXIV. LUPUS.
X. GWADYR.	XXV. ALGAR.
XI. FITZ OSBORNE.	XXVI. CAITHNESS.
XII. YVERY.	XXVII. DOUGLAS of Dalkeith
XIII. GRANTESMESNIL.	XXVIII. READING.
XIV. GALLOWAY.	XXIX. COWARD.
XV. MORVILLE.	XXX. HALL.

DE · DIEU · TOUT

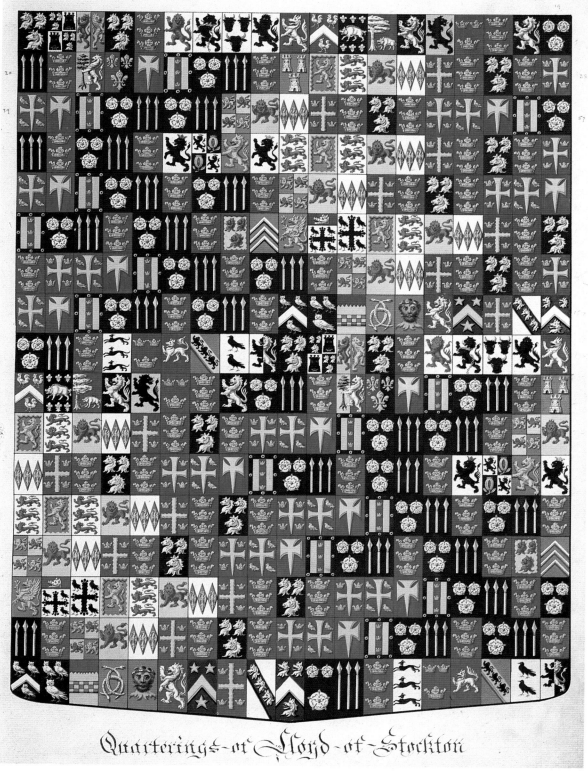

25. Three hundred and twenty-three quarters of Lloyd of Stockton, Shropshire, 1894 (Coll. Arms, Norfolk 16, p. 47).

26 'Vincent's Precedents': early seventeenth-century painting of the officer about to be created Garter King of Arms surrounded by heralds holding the objects to be used in the ceremony (his Patent, the book on which he is to swear his oath, his robe as an officer of the Order of the Garter, his sword, a cup of wine for baptizing him, etc.) (Coll. Arms, Vincent 151, fo. 30v).

27 (*facing*). Funeral certificate of Sir John Spencer of Althorp, Northamptonshire, Kt., d. 9 Jan. 1599/1600, showing a standard, guidon, helm, mantling and crest, shield, and tabard, painted by Richard Scarlett (d. 1607) (Coll. Arms, I 16, p.82).

Sʳ John Spencer.

Mihi Chr̃us Vita

dieu defende le Droit

Thō paynter mỹ
Garlott

28. The coffin of the Electress Sophia of Hanover, d. 8 June 1714 (mother of George I), from *The Genealogy of the Sovereigns of the Most Honourable Military Order of the Bath*, compiled by George Nayler, Genealogist and Blanc Coursier Herald, subsequently Garter (Coll. Arms, *Bath Book*, p. 98).

29. Armorial bearings of HH The Maharao of Kota, designed by Robert Taylor of the Bengal Civil Service for the Imperial Assemblage at Delhi 1877 (Coll. Arms, *The Princely Armory*, no. 52).

30. Flag of Kota on which the preceding arms were based (Coll. Arms, *The Princely Armory*, pt. 2, no. 29).

31. Robes and other insignia of the nobles of the Province of Carolina, recorded in 1705 (Coll. Arms, I 9, fo. 200).

32 (*facing*). Catafalque of Edward (Stanley), 3rd Earl of Derby (d. 1572), from 'Vincent's Precedents', showing heraldic display at a noble funeral including a standard, tabard with the deceased's arms, and banners of the family alliances (Coll. Arms, Vincent 151, fo. 366).

33. Tomb of George (Talbot), 6th Earl of Shrewsbury (d. 1590), in Sheffield Cathedral, lavishly decorated with shields of arms, which include Talbot and Ogle impaled coats (Coll. Arms, I 1, p. 7).

34. A selection of eighteenth-century Chinese Export armorial plates (Christie's).

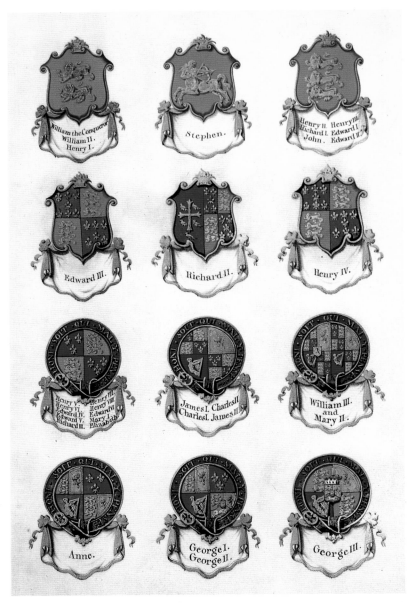

35. An early nineteenth-century view of the evolution of the Royal Arms. There is no evidence that the coat attributed to William I and II and Henry I was ever used by them. It is sometimes attributed to Normandy, and two lions appear on the surcoat worn by Robert Curthose, Duke of Normandy, in the sketch of his tomb in Gloucester Cathedral by Robert Cooke, Clarenceux (see p. 174). Matthew Paris shows a blank shield for Normandy, and gives three lions passant guardant for William the Conqueror and his sons, as illustrated for Henry II and his successors. He also gives the same shield for King Stephen rather than *Gules a Sagittary Or*, first suggested as three sagittaries by Nicholas Upton in *de Studio Militari* in about 1400. The symbolism of the sagittary relates either to the fact that Stephen landed in England and was crowned under the zodiacal sign of the sagittary in 1135, or possibly to the victory of his archers. France ancient quartered by Edward III is shown in an unusual form, since with any coat that is semy it is customary to show parts of the charges visible in base and chief, and at the sides where they disappear off the shield. Although Richard II used the same arms as his grandfather Edward III on his Great Seal, elsewhere they sometimes appear as illustrated, impaled with the attributed arms of Edward the Confessor, said by Froissart to have been adopted to please the Irish who had a high regard for Edward the Confessor. Henry IV used both France ancient and modern quartering England. The arms of the later Sovereigns are shown accurately. Impaled arms are given for William and Mary, appropriate till her death in 1694. The arms used by Queen Anne between 1707 and 1714 are shown, and the arms of George III are as used between 1801 and 1816 (Coll. Arms, *Bath Book*, p. 11).

Armorial book-plates are a particularly attractive form of heraldic decoration, and the College has a long tradition in this field.

Each Officer has his own set of rooms opening off a staircase, as at Oxford or Cambridge, and the College also provides accommodation for a number of heraldic painters and scriveners. They fully maintain the tradition of their ancient crafts, painting and engrossing patents of arms, pedigrees, and such like for the College's own records, as well as for clients. The College has through the centuries maintained a high standard of heraldic painting and elegant straightforward lettering, mercifully free from the transient fashions of graphic design.

The basic working tool of the Heralds is their library, and the College archive is the most important heraldic accumulation of its kind. Its history goes back to the original charter of incorporation in 1484, but in the first hundred years it suffered many vicissitudes. It is likely that the College had a collection of books at the start. Certainly the heralds of France, who provided the model for the English College of Arms, had been given the Church of St Antoine le Petit in Paris in 1407 as a place to house their records. In the early days, however, individual officers kept their own books and records, some of which were probably bequeathed to their successors in the College, but a number unfortunately passed out of official custody. To control this abuse, Elizabeth I's Earl Marshal, Thomas, 4th Duke of Norfolk, laid down strict regulations in 1568 for the future conduct of the College including its records. A special room was to be set aside for a library, and none was to be allowed to enter unless accompanied by a Herald. The execution of the Duke in 1572 (for aspiring to marry Mary, Queen of Scots) thwarted these good intentions, and neglect of the library continued until 1597, when there was a further attempt at reform. This proved successful, and since 1597 the history of the library has been continuous. In that year it proved possible to retrieve from William Dethick, Garter, and his heirs a number of heraldic volumes which were deemed to be the official records of the College, and these form the nucleus of the present records. They were catalogued in 1618 by Sampson Lennard, Bluemantle, and this inventory is the oldest extant record of the College library.

An important aspect of the work of the Tudor and Stuart Heralds, as has been seen, were the Visitations of particular counties in order to 'remove all false arms and arms devised without authority', and 'to take note of descents'. The fruits of the Visitations are an invaluable corpus of genealogical and heraldic information. The reports, bound and stored at the College, include, as well as notes and family trees, pen-and-ink or coloured sketches and drawings of arms copied from tombs, stained-glass windows, charters, seals, and banners. They are of unique historical interest, as many of the things which they record, especially the more fragile church furnishings, were destroyed in the Civil War. Several of the Tudor and Stuart Heralds had wide antiquarian interests, and they often included material which was not exclusively heraldic, such as views of towns and old buildings, or even Roman ruins. Parallel to the Visitation Books were the pedigrees of great families, and these have been continued on a voluntary basis down to the present day.

When the College was rebuilt after the Great Fire, in the 1670s, special provision was made for the library, which was fortunately saved from the conflagration. The Great Fire having started at the other end of the City, the Heralds had a day in which to rescue their library before the flames reached it. The books were taken to Whitehall, probably by boat along the river, and only returned to the College in 1674. They were then placed in the new library next to the Earl Marshal's Court.

Since 1673 all English patents of arms have been recorded in a single continuous series, and this is still current. These volumes of grants of arms form the second important block of heraldic records. Before 1673 the docquet books of patents of arms are less complete, but gaps have been filled wherever possible by abstracts and transcripts. The medieval arms of families who did not fail in the male line are exhaustively covered by the Visitations.

The library is divided into two categories: Records and Collections. The former comprise the canonical sequence of heraldic records built up since the sixteenth century. They have legal significance, being accepted *per se* as evidence in court cases over peerage claims and disputed descents. The Collections are subsidiary genealogical and

Prospect of Richmond, from a volume of church and other notes compiled during Visitation of Yorkshire 1666. Sketch by Gregory King (1648–1712), Dugdale's Clerk and subsequently Lancaster Herald (Coll. Arms, Dugdale's Yorkshire Arms, fos. 192v–193).

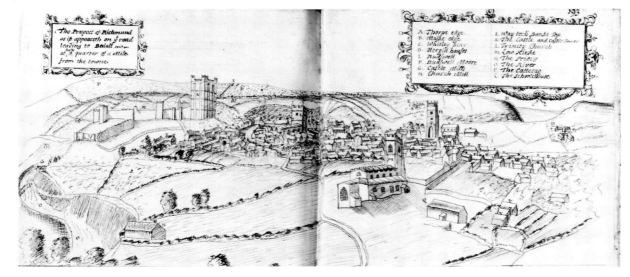

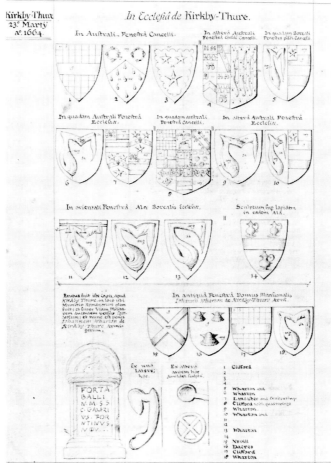

(*top left*) Sketch of a window in the nave of York Minster, from Dugdale's Church Notes (Coll. Arms, Dugdale's Yorkshire Arms, fo. 96c).

(*top right*) A page from Dugdale's Visitation of Westmorland 1664, showing arms in the church at Kirkby Thure (Kirkby Thore), and also a Roman altar (Coll. Arms, C 39, p. 6).

(*bottom right*) Prospect of the castle and chapel at Bishop Auckland drawn by Gregory King, dated 4 Sept. 1666, during Dugdale's Visitation of Durham (Coll. Arms, C 41 [2], fo. 10c).

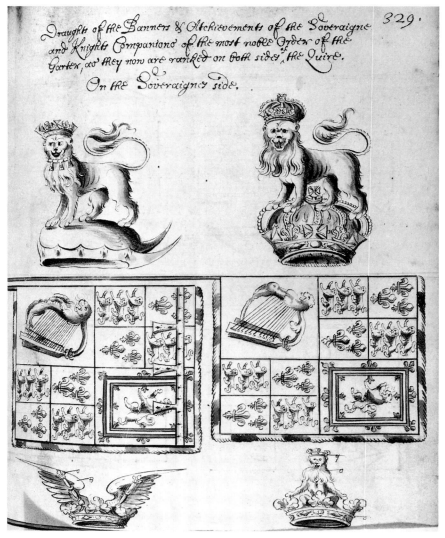

Visitation of Berkshire, 1664–6; garter banners and crests from St George's Chapel, Windsor, showing banners of Charles II and James II as Duke of York. The Visitation was carried out by Elias Ashmole (1617–92), Windsor Herald as Deputy to Clarenceux (Coll. Arms, C 12, pt. 2, fo. 329).

heraldic material accumulated since the late seventeenth century, by gift, bequest and purchase, in order to assist in the day-to-day work of the College.

The division of the library into Records and Collections goes back to the early eighteenth century, and follows a legal opinion 'that office books made by Heralds in the execution of their offices were evidence', but that other books were not.

In 1800, a return by the Heralds to a Select Committee on Public Records in the United Kingdom specified eight categories in the Records section, namely: Visitation Books; Modern Pedigrees; Peers' Pedigrees, Baronets' Pedigrees; Funeral Certificates; Records of Royal Marriages, Coronations, and Funerals; the Earl Marshal's Books; Books of Arms of the Nobility and Knights of the Garter and the Bath;

Shields in the Friars of Carmarthen and in the College of Abergwili, recorded at the Visitation of Wales 1530. The Visitation was carried out by William Fellow, Lancaster Herald (subsequently Norroy), on behalf of Thomas Benolt, Clarenceux (Coll. Arms, H 8, fo.22).

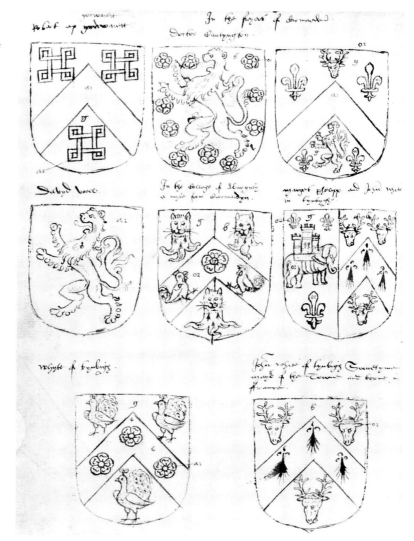

and Records of Grants of Arms. A further four categories were added to the Records in the nineteenth century. These are: Lists of Knights; Pedigrees of Knights of the Bath; Scotch and Irish Registers; and Partition Books.

The Funeral Certificates fill eighteen volumes, and record the ceremonial funerals of the sixteenth and seventeenth centuries, until they went out of fashion in the late seventeenth century, although there are a few later entries of State and other funerals such as those of Evelyn (Pierrepont), Duke of Kingston (1773), William (Pitt), Earl of Chatham (1778), Horatio (Nelson), Viscount Nelson of The Nile (1805), William Ewart Gladstone (1898), and Alan Francis (Brooke), Viscount Alanbrooke (1963). They depict the banners, escutcheons of arms, and achievements of the deceased carried in funeral processions, as well as accompanying particulars of the deceased and their families. It is the latter details which make them a valuable source for genealogical research.

The Earl Marshal's Books begin in the reign of Elizabeth I, and continue to the present day. They contain entries of warrants under Royal Sign Manual as relating to the Royal Arms, licences for changes of name and arms, grants of foreign honours, grants of precedency, and 'whatever relates to that part of the office of Earl Marshal which concerns the superintendance of the College'.

The Records of the Order of the Bath are largely the work of the Order's own genealogist in the late eighteenth and early nineteenth centuries, Sir George Nayler. They were deposited at the College in 1861 by order of the Prince Consort. Nayler's *magnum opus* was *A History of the Sovereigns of the Most Honourable Military Order of the Bath*, a sumptuously illustrated volume with much decoration in gold leaf. This is of outstanding interest for the illustrations of the golden coffins in the Chapel Royal at Hanover, including that of the Electress Sophia, mother of George I and ancestress of the present British Royal Family. It was prepared for King George III; but he refused to pay the £2,000 bill, and the volume passed to Nayler's daughter, and eventually came to the College through her cousin Robert Laurie, Clarenceux King of Arms.

The Collections, as opposed to the Records, are formed of the gifts and bequests to the College since the late seventeenth century. They comprise copies of charters, patents, abstracts of records, and miscellaneous documents. The nucleus of these is the group of Arundel Manuscripts given to the College in 1678 by Henry, 6th Duke of Norfolk, and being that part of the library of his grandfather, the 'Collector' Earl of Arundel, which was to do with history and heraldry. They comprise fifty-three volumes, including a fifteenth-century manuscript of the Statutes of the Order of the Garter, and Descents of King Alfred the Great and Edward IV from Adam. The 6th Duke of Norfolk also gave the College the Talbot Family Letters and Papers, now in Lambeth Palace Library.

Many other collections have followed, including Sir Edward Walker (Garter)'s gifts of Patents and assorted heraldic materials, and Ralph Sheldon's bequest in 1684 of two hundred and sixty-eight volumes of Visitations, local pedigrees, and the like largely formed by Augustine Vincent, Windsor Herald till his death in 1626. A small bequest of the late seventeenth century was the five manuscript volumes given in 1686 by George Holman of Warkworth from the library of Hector Le Breton, King of Arms of France, a post in which he had succeeded his cousin, Denis Le Breton, in 1615. In the early eighteenth-century doldrums, little was added, although John Hare,

Frontispiece to pedigree book of the family of Lentilhac-Sedière, an example of the revived late-eighteenth-century interest in heraldry as an aspect of the Gothic Revival (Coll. Arms, *Généalogie de la maison de Lentilhac-Sedière*).

Richmond, who committed suicide in the College in 1720, left the College a small collection including eight volumes of papers of the Lancashire antiquary Richard Kuerden. In 1759 Edward, Duke of Norfolk, purchased manuscripts for the College at the sale of John Warburton, Somerset Herald. But in the nineteenth century there was a greater influx by gift and purchase, including a substantial part of the genealogical library of a notable scholar, Colonel Joseph Lemuel Chester, which included useful extracts from parish registers as well as a large collection of American material. In 1828 the College acquired the Protheroe Collection of twenty-eight volumes of Welsh gene-alogy, which form the most authoritative corpus of material on the subject in existence. In this century the Collections have continued to be enriched, largely by the bequest of their own libraries by individual Heralds. In particular, the great Burke Collection acquired on the death of Sir Henry Farnham Burke, Garter, in 1930, included not only one hundred and eighty-four volumes of his own correspondence and pedigrees, but also sixty-nine volumes of his father Sir Bernard Burke (died 1892), Ulster King of Arms's genealogical collections, and thirty-three volumes of his Irish pedigrees. These are of importance, as much material on which they were based was destroyed with the

Irish Public Records in 1922. An unusual collection acquired in the present century are the arms of the Ruling Chiefs of India, designed by Robert Taylor of the Bengal Civil Service for the Imperial Assemblage held at Delhi on 1 January 1877. The arms are based on the sketches of banners or symbols which were submitted by the Indian rulers. For instance, the arms of the Maharao of Kota are blazoned *Gules Garud Or vested of the same plumed Vert holding a mace of the second* [i.e. Or] *in dexter and a Conch in sinister*. This is based on a sketch of a flag that was submitted, and the arms of Jhalawar, a State carved out of Kota in 1838, are very similar. Both States have dragon supporters but the crests differ, the demi-man of Kota being based on Chohan emblems whereas the Star of Jhalawar is said to be the emblem of a wise counsellor. The arms and original sketches provide an unusual and evocative synthesis of East and West.

The Court of the Lord Lyon, as the authority on all matters heraldic in Scotland, is among the most ancient and important of Scottish national institutions, and one which occupies a unique position in the national life of the kingdom. Scots heraldry has long enjoyed a high reputation, and has preserved to a considerable degree through the centuries the standards of simplicity in design and scientific accuracy of medieval armory. This is partly because heraldry in Scotland has developed as a branch of the law, and also because interest in the subject is deeply imbedded in the national character. In the old Scottish kingdom heraldry, honours, and titles enjoyed a much wider distribution than in England or the European kingdoms. At the time of the Act of Union in 1707, for instance, Scotland, with a population of only one and a quarter million souls, had one hundred and fifty-four peers while England, with a population of five and a half million, had one hundred and sixty-four peers. In addition to the peerage, ten thousand other lairds enjoyed picturesque territorial designations which were recognized as titles by the courts. It has been computed from this that one out of every forty-four people in the country was either 'of somewhere' or else related to such a 'house'.

Unlike the English Kings of Arms, the Lord Lyon is not subordinate to the Earl Marshal but is himself a great officer of state responsible for many of the functions which in England are shared between the Earl Marshal and the Lord Chamberlain. In Scotland the Lord Lyon is responsible for the preparation, conduct, and record of all State, Royal, and public ceremonial. To him has also been entrusted the whole of the Crown's jurisdiction in armorial matters, and he is the official adviser to the Secretary of State for Scotland on many aspects of Scottish honours and ceremonial. As controller of Her Majesty's Messengers at Arms, he is also the head of the Executive Department of the Law of Scotland. He has, in addition, always held the appointment of King of Arms to the Order of the Thistle, whose chapter and ceremonies he attends.

The Lord Lyon is not only a Minister of the Crown but also a judge of the realm, and almost all Scottish heraldic business is today conducted on judicial lines through the machinery of the Court of the Lord Lyon which exercises both a civil and a penal jurisdiction under Scottish common law and a series of Acts of Parliament. In this the Lyon Court differs considerably from the English College of Arms. It was, and is, a part of the Scottish judicial system and functions entirely as a court of law. It is not, and never has been, a corporate body like the English College of Arms. Searches for evidence to satisfy Lyon are normally made by people outside his office on behalf of the petitioners themselves, as part of the evidence submitted for his judgement on genealogical or heraldic matters.

The Court of the Lord Lyon operates like any other court of law, with lawyers pleading a case before a judge (the Lord Lyon himself). The judicial duties of the Lyon Court, as they are exercised today, fall into two categories. On the one hand they comprise establishing rights to arms and pedigrees. When satisfactory evidence is produced by a petitioner, Lord Lyon grants a warrant to the Lyon Clerk to register the arms in the 'Public Register of All Arms and Bearings in Scotland' which is maintained at the Lyon Court. In the case of new arms, Lyon issues a warrant to the Lyon Clerk to prepare Letters Patent granting the arms. Secondly there is the penal jurisdiction concerned with protecting the rights of private individuals and the Crown in heraldic matters. The Lyon Court has a Procurator-Fiscal, or public prosecutor, like any other Scottish Court, and he can bring proceedings against those who improperly usurp armorial bearings. Such a prosecution is analogous to an Inland Revenue case, the armorial offender having cheated the exchequer out of the fees payable on the matriculation or grant of arms.

In order to understand the Court of the Lord Lyon as it exists today it is necessary to know something of the history of the Scottish Heralds, who claim greater antiquity than the English, although a Norroy King of Arms is known in England in 1276 before the earliest surviving record of a Herald in Scotland. The office of Lyon in Scotland to which there is a reference in 1318 does pre-date that of Garter King of Arms in England, as the latter was only instituted in 1415. The Scottish Heralds are known by name from the early fourteenth century. Froissart records that, in 1327, Robert the Bruce defied Edward III by the mouth of a Herald called Douglas, and in 1333, when Edward was at Alnwick, a Herald called Dundee came before the King to announce that he had been sent to parley by the Scottish lords and bishops.

Unlike England, however, which came to have three Kings of Arms in addition to Heralds and Pursuivants, Scotland only ever had the one, Lord Lyon, who derives his name from 'the national escutcheon'. The precise date of his institution is not known. He is not recorded at the Coronation of Alexander III at Scone on 13 July 1349, but played a prominent role at that of Robert II on 26 March 1371. In the early days he was probably subordinate to the Marshal and Constable, but his dependence on them ceased early, and he came to hold his office immediately from the Sovereign. His jurisdiction in matters heraldic had already developed by the mid-sixteenth century, but the first legislative enactment which directly bestows on Lyon a jurisdiction in questions of armorial bearings was a Statute of 1592 which empowered him to inspect the arms of all noblemen, barons, and gentlemen to distinguish them with proper differences, to matriculate them in his Register, and 'to put inhibition to all the common sort of people not worthy by the law of arms to bear any signs armorial'. His jurisdiction was more fully set out following the Restoration in an Act of 1661, but this was repealed the following year. The title of Lord Lyon King of Arms, however, dates from 1662. A further Act of 1672 renewed and confirmed the powers granted in 1592, ordered the matriculation of all arms in Scotland, and expressly authorized Lyon to grant armorial bearings 'to virtuous and well-deserving persons', and his authority in these matters was reserved entire in the nineteenth article of the Treaty of Union.

The duties and powers of Lyon under the Statutes of 1592 and 1672 are sevenfold: to assign suitable differences to cadets of armigerous families; to record genealogies; to determine all disputes between heraldic claimants; to grant arms to 'virtuous and well-deserving persons'; to matriculate in the official Register all arms used in the kingdom; to furnish extracts from the same; and to enforce penalties imposed on unlawful users of arms by proceedings in his own court. Following the Act of 1692 a 'Register of arms in Scotland' has been maintained to the present day, in vellum-bound folios. Earlier than this, however, the records are rather sparse, and the Lyon Court does not possess a great heraldic archive and historic library comparable to that of the English College of Arms. It is traditionally recorded that all the early heraldic records were taken to England by Cromwell and lost at sea on their return in 1661. Further documents were lost in a fire in about 1670 or were retained in their own possession by later officials of the Court. The earliest Scottish heraldic register is the 'Book of Blazons' compiled by Sir David Lindsay of the Mount in 1542. Today this is preserved in the Advocates' Library in Edinburgh, and not at the Court of the Lord Lyon.

Following the Act of Union there came a century of quiet decline.

The office of Lord Lyon became a sinecure, and much of the day-to-day judicial and heraldic work was performed by a deputy, the 'Lyon-Depute'. From 1796 for over half a century, the office of Lord Lyon was filled successively by the 10th and 11th Earls of Kinnoull. The later nineteenth-century revival was an offshoot of George IV's State Visit to Edinburgh in 1820, which led to the general renaissance of Scottish public ceremonial thanks to the inspiration of Sir Walter Scott. The Scottish Heralds were provided with new tabards for the occasion. There was an official report on the Court of the Lord Lyon in 1822 which made recommendation for reform, notably that the Lyon-Depute should be a member of the Faculty of Advocates of 'not less than a year's standing at the Bar'; that all fees should be fixed and paid to the Treasury, not to individual Officers; and that the staff of the Lord Lyon's Court should become salaried public officials. This followed criticism of the high fees, which had increased five times between 1804 and 1814. 'The extraction of fees, displayed in a hundred capricious vagaries, is the ruling characteristic of the establishment, not one member of which, from the Lyon to his meanest cub, has ever produced a work or exhibited any skills in the sciences of Heraldry, Genealogy, or the cognate accomplishments', wrote one particularly acerbic critic. In fact, nothing was done during the reign of the 11th Earl of Kinnoull, who was Lord Lyon from 1804, when he succeeded his father at the age of 19, until his death in 1866. The long-deferred reform was finally carried out in 1867 when an Act of Parliament (30 31 Victoria C17) put the Court on a new footing. All fees were thenceforth paid to the Treasury, and the Lord Lyon King of Arms, Lyon Clerk, and the Heralds and Pursuivants were paid salaries and received no fees. At the same time the number of Officers of Arms was halved. From 1500 to 1866 there were six Heralds and six Pursuivants in Scotland (compared to six Heralds and four Pursuivants in the Corporation of the English College of Arms). Their descriptions are very ancient and of local origin, many of them being the names of the castles of the Scottish monarchy. The Heralds were Islay, Rothesay, Marchmont, Albany, Ross, and Snowdon. The Pursuivants were Kintyre, Dingwall, Carrick, Bute, Ormond, and Unicorn. Now there are only three of each—at present Albany, Marchmont, and Rothesay Heralds, and Carrick, Kintyre, and Unicorn Pursuivants. They are members of the Scottish Royal Household, and their principal function is ceremonial, attending Royal Proclamations, and State and public cermonies, on which occasions they wear tabards with the Royal Arms as used officially in Scotland, i.e. with the Scottish lion in the first quarter rather than the second (a reversal of the Royal Arms as used in England).

American Heraldry

EGULATED heraldry in what became the United States of America began early, developed slowly, and just as it was beginning to flourish was cut off by the Revolution. The beginning was a probable grant to the City and Corporation of Ralegh in Virginia in 1586, probable because only three rough drafts of the text survive. The grant is interesting because not only does it assign arms of *Argent a Cross Gules in the first quarter a Roebuck proper* to the city but arms are also given to the Governor, John White, and the twelve Assistants in the same Patent. All these latter coats contain fusils and the tincture Gules derived from the arms of Sir Walter Raleigh, *Gules five Fusils in bend Argent*. In the case of White, the coat granted, *Ermine on a Canton Gules a Fusil Argent*, was an augmentation to his existing arms, and borne in the first quarter. In the other shields the arms are unquartered; thus Roger Baylye was granted *Gules a Cross paty between four Fusils Argent*, and Dionyse Hartye *Gules a Bear rampant between four Fusils Argent*. Other coats include *Ermine on a Chief Gules three Fusils Argent* for Roger Pratt, John Nicholes's *Per bend Argent and Gules five Fusils counterchanged*, and *Gules a Cross engrailed between four Fusils Argent* granted to Ananias Dare whose daughter Virginia was the first child of English parentage born in America. One draft names nine of the twelve Assistants, the others in addition to Baylye, Hartye, Pratt, Nicholes, and Dare being Christopher Cooper, William Fullwood, George Howe, and Simon Ferdinando; the other draft adds Richard Hakluyt, presumably the distinguished geographer, and two almost illegible names which may be Coningsby and Delves. The drafts refer to the grant as being by William Dethick, Garter, and states that by a Royal Charter of 1584 Sir Walter Raleigh was licensed to find heathen and barbarous lands not possessed by any Christian Prince. Ossomocomuck, alias Wyngandacoia alias Virginea, as it is described in the Patent was the first such place and Raleigh appointed a Governor and Assistants for a city of Ralegh. The settlement failed and its site is that of the town of Manteo, North Carolina. Sketches by its Governor, John White, of Virginian Indians published in 1590 by Theodore de Bry were the basis of a rough sketch of possible supporters for John (Holles), 1st Earl of Clare, though they do not seem to have been granted as his descendants bore different supporters.

On 1 January 1637/8 Sir John Borough, Garter, granted to

(*top left*) Proposed Virginian Indian supporters and crest for John (Holles), 1st Earl of Clare, with arms of Holles quartering (2) Stopham, (3) Hanham, (4) Denzell, (5) Wenlock, (6) Archdeacon, (7) Skewis, (8) ? (Coll. Arms, R 22, fo. 16v).

(*top right*) Arms, crest, and supporters granted by Sir John Borough, Garter, to Newfoundland on 1 Jan. 1637/ 8. The arms are derived from the Royal supporters and the supporters show two Beothuk Indians described as 'Savages of the clyme' (Coll. Arms, Miscellaneous Grants 4, fo. 7).

Newfoundland arms of *Gules a Cross Argent between in the first and fourth quarters a Lion passant guardant crowned Or and in the second and third quarters a Unicorn passant Argent armed maned unguled and gorged with a crown whereunto is affixed a chain passing between his forelegs and reflexed over the back all Or*. The tinctures of the mantling do not follow the wreath, and the crest granted was *Upon a helm mantled Gules doubled Argent with a wreath Or and Gules an Elk passant proper* with supporters of *Two Savages of the clyme proper armed and apparaled according to their guise when they go to war*. The text of the Patent states that: 'for the greater honor and splendor of that countrey and the people therein inhabiting it is and will be necessary that there be proper and peculiar Armes thereunto belonging to be used in all such cases as Armes are wont to be by other nations and countries'.

Despite these sentiments, the progress of heraldry in North America was scarcely apparent, and the Seal for Virginia dated 9 August 1662 is of the Royal Arms within the Garter all encircled by a ribbon inscribed *En dat Virginia Quintum*. This contrasts with the new design of arms, crest, and supporters granted to Jamaica in the previous year. North America was not an unknown continent to all members of the College of Arms in the seventeenth century. William Crowne, appointed

Seals for Jamaica and Virginia, granted by Royal Warrant in 1661 and 1662 (Coll. Arms, Walker Grants 2, p. 5).

Rouge Dragon by Charles I, was one of the Officers to support Parliament, and obtained a joint grant of the province of Nova Scotia from Cromwell. In 1657 he went there, returning to England at the Restoration to try to obtain a confirmation of his grant. He attended Charles II's Coronation as Rouge Dragon, resigned a month later, and returned to America in 1662; any hopes he had regarding Nova Scotia went when it was ceded to France in 1667, and he died in Boston, Massachusetts, in 1683. John Gibbon, who was appointed Bluemantle in 1670, spent fifteen months in Virginia from October 1659 to February 1660/1. His kinsman Edward Gibbon wrote that 'in this remote province his taste, or rather passion, for heraldry found a singular gratification at a war-dance of the native Indians'. In his *Introductio ad Latinam Blasoniam* (1682) John Gibbon wrote,

the Dancers were painted some Party per pale Gu. and Sab. from forehead to foot (some Party per fesse of the same colours) and carried little ill-made shields of Bark, also painted of those colours (for I saw no other) some party per Fess, some per pale (and some barry) at which I exceedingly wondered, and concluded That Heraldry was ingrafted naturally into the sense of humane Race.

Crowne's connection with America came at the end of his career at the College, but Gibbon was an Officer of Arms for forty-eight years till his death in 1718. His influence at the College was perhaps slight, as he was never promoted beyond Bluemantle and wrote in College books criticizing the learning and behaviour of his colleagues.

It was not till twenty-three years after Gibbon's appointment that the first person resident in North America petitioned for a grant, and on 1 March 1693/4 arms and a crest were granted by the brothers Thomas and Henry St George, Garter and Clarenceux, to Francis Nicholson, described as 'Captain General and Governor in Chief of Their Majesty's Province of Maryland One of the Chief Governors of a College or University now to be erected or founded in Virginia'. The arms granted contained suns, which are common to many Nicholson coats, and are blazoned *Azure on a Cross Argent between four Suns Or a Cathedral Church Gules*, the latter presumably being a reference to the College. The crest is blazoned *On a wreath of his colours (i.e. Argent and Azure) a demy Man habited in a close coat Azure the buttons and cuffs of his sleeves turned up Or his face and hands proper armed with a headpiece and gorget Argent the beaver open holding in the right hand a sword erected proper hilt and pomel Or and in the left a Bible opened the clasps Argent*. Two months later, on 14 May 1694, the trustees for what became the College of William and Mary in Virginia, of whom Nicholson was the first named, were granted arms of *Vert a Colledge or Edifice mason'd Argent in chief a Sun rising Or the hemisphere proper*. As is sometimes the case with corporate grants, no crest was granted. The Patent was endorsed on 18 October 1698, permitting the transfer of the Armorial Bearings from the trustees to the President and Masters when the College was erected.

The next opportunity for the development of heraldry in America came with the appointment of Carolina Herald in 1705. Pursuant to the Royal Charter of Charles II establishing the form of government in the Province, it was provided 'that there be a certain number of Landgraves and Cassiques, who may be and are the Perpetual and Hereditary Nobles and Peers of our said Province'. By the Patent of 1 June 1705, registered at the College, the Lords Proprietors appointed Laurence Cromp, York Herald, to be President of their Court of Honour and Principal Herald of the whole Province of Carolina with power to grant to the Landgraves and Cassiques such arms and crest as he should think proper, the arms to be set upon the face of the sun, and the crest to be surmounted with a coronet formed of the rays of the sun. The Patent depicts the robes of scarlet embossed with gold and other marks of honour to be borne by the nobles of the Province. There is no evidence of any grant of arms by Cromp as Carolina Herald; on his Patent of appointment the Lords Proprietors used a seal showing arms of two cornucopiae in saltire which were not granted by the Kings of Arms, so he may have had a hand in this. Cromp died insolvent in 1715, ten years after his appointment, so he may not have been an ideal choice to promote heraldry in America, though he was not the only York Herald to be insolvent. His predecessor but one,

Obverse and reverse of the seal of the Lords Proprietor of the Province of Carolina. The reverse shows the personal arms of the Lords Proprietor (Coll. Arms, I 9, fo. 194).

John Wingfield, died in the King's Bench prison in 1678, and his successor, Thomas Whitwick, died insolvent in 1722. Although Cromp does not seem to have granted any arms, the Lords Proprietors did create Abel Ketelby of the Middle Temple a Landgrave of Carolina by Patent dated 24 March 1708/9. The grant was to him and his heirs for ever. A pedigree registered at the College shows that he died without male issue in 1744, and the descent of the title till Independence appears to be to his only child Mary, wife of Robert Johnston of the Middle Temple, Serjeant-at-Law, who took the name and arms of Ketelby by Act of Parliament. They had one child, Abel Johnston Ketelby who died before his mother, leaving an only daughter Maria Statira Elizabeth Farquharson Johnston Ketelby, who married Thomas Rundell of Bath, surgeon, on 30 December 1766. The eldest surviving son of the marriage in 1785, when the pedigree was registered, was Thomas Hodgetts Rundell, born at Bath in 1771. Abel Ketelby, whom the pedigree describes as having the honour of Landgrave of Carolina conferred on him by Queen Anne rather than by the Lords Proprietors, was entitled to arms by descent recorded at the Heralds' Visitation of Shropshire in 1663.

The only other record of the conferment of the title of Landgrave or Cassique appears to be a patent of 11 April 1715 creating William Hodgson of the Six Clerks Office, a brother-in-law of a deceased Lord Proprietor William (Craven), Lord Craven, both a Cassique and Landgrave. The limitations, unlike the Ketelby grant, are to the grantee's heirs male, though there is no stipulation that they must be of his body, i.e. descended from him. Hodgson thought he was entitled to arms by descent, and like Ketelby was not granted arms by Cromp. A subsequent examination of the College records revealed that, although his father recorded a pedigree at the 1664–5 Visitation of Cumberland, his claim to arms was respited. Consequently the son had a grant of arms and a crest from the English Kings of Arms in 1730.

The first half of the eighteenth century was devoid of grants to Americans till William Pepperell was created a Baronet in 1746. His father had gone over to New England about seventy years earlier, and on 4 December 1746 Pepperell was granted arms of *Argent a Chevron Gules between three Pineapples* [i.e. pine cones] *Vert with the augmentation of a Canton Gules charged with a Fleur-de-lis Argent.* The augmentation referred to victories over the French, and he was also granted a crest.

In 1759 Isaac Heard was appointed Bluemantle, and was promoted to Lancaster in 1761; he remained at the College till his death, aged 91, in 1822, when he had been Garter King of Arms for thirty-seven years. But for American Independence Heard would probably have established a regulated heraldic system both by new grants and registration of pedigrees proving a right to arms by descent throughout North America. He was well placed to do this as he had traded as a merchant between Bilbao in Spain and Boston for five years before coming to the College, and his wife Katherine was a native of Boston, being a daughter of Andrew Tyler by his wife Miriam, sister of Sir William Pepperell, the 1746 grantee. The first grant to an American after Heard's appointment is dated 5 May 1764, but the only record is among the papers of Stephen Martin Leake, Garter, as it was 'never delivered nor entered not having been paid for'. The grantee Joseph Hopkins of Maryland was Commandant of the Queen's Regiment of American Rangers and was the first officer who landed at Louisburgh on 8 June 1758, where he scalped the Chief of the St John Indians, taking from him an honorary medal given him by the French. The design is cluttered, which suggests the influence of Heard, and the symbolism is far from concealed. The arms are blazoned *Sable on a Chevron between two pistols Or and a silver Medal with a French Kings bust incribed Louis XV a laurel Chaplet in the centre a Scalp on a staff on the dexter and a Tomahawk on the sinister proper a Chief embattled Argent.*

In 1767 a short run of grants began with one to John Williams of Boston (1722–82), Inspector General of the American Board of Customs Commissioners and son of Jonathan Williams of Salem. Williams was in London in 1767 to receive his Commission as Inspector General, and in the same year had a grant of arms. In 1783, the year after his death, a pedigree was registered at the College. He also probably purchased the coffee pot, now in the San Diego Museum of

Arms and crest which would have been granted to Joseph Hopkins of Maryland in 1764 if the Patent had been paid for. Hopkins was Commandant of the Queen's Regiment of American Rangers, and the scalp on the shield represents that of the Chief of the St John Indians, whom he scalped at Louisburgh where he landed 8 June 1758 (Coll. Arms, SML 34, p. 14).

Silver coffee-pot with arms granted to John Williams of Boston in 1767 (San Diego Museum of Art: Gift of William B. Miller).

Art, made in 1767–8 by the partners Thomas Whipham and Charles Wright of London, and engraved with his armorial bearings which are blazoned in the Letters Patent, *Or a Lion rampant Gules on a Chief Azure two Doves rising Argent* with a crest of *On a wreath of the colours an Eagle the wings expanded proper reposing the dexter claw on a Mound Or*. As an office-holder one would expect Williams to have been a Tory, but he and most of his family were strongly pro-American Whigs. His brother Jonathan Williams (1717–96), who was married to a niece of Benjamin Franklin, was a Boston Justice of the Peace and Moderator of the Boston Assembly of 1774 that resulted in the Boston Tea Party. His nephew Jonathan Williams was for a time law clerk to John

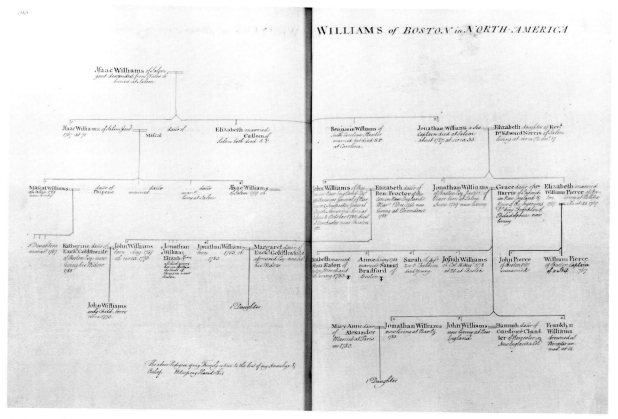

Pedigree of Williams of Boston recorded in 1783, the year after the death of John Williams, granted arms and a crest in 1767 (Coll. Arms, 6 D 14, pp. 313–14).

Adams, and subsequently the first Director of the Military Academy at West Point. The inventory prepared after the death of John Williams includes a coffee pot, and in his will he refers to his silver 'mark't with the crest of my family Arms'.

In 1768 arms and a crest were granted to Daniel Heyward of the parish of St Luke in Granville County, South Carolina, on the petition of his son Thomas Heyward of the Middle Temple, and a pedigree was recorded. There is an American element in the crest, which is blazoned *On a wreath of the colours a dexter Arm embowed habited Gules in the hand proper a Tomahawk*. In 1771 a grant was made to Daniel Huger of South Carolina, Esquire, the crest being blazoned *On a sprig a Virginia Nightingale proper*. The family had quitted France at the Revocation of the Edict of Nantes, and the motto shown was *Ubi Libertas Ibi Patria*, which might be translated as 'Where there is liberty there is my homeland', an interesting choice on the eve of a revolution. Huger also recorded a pedigree but unlike Williams and Heyward he came to the College to sign it, the witness being Isaac Heard. Heard also witnessed a pedigree recorded in 1773 by William Henry Ricketts of Canaan in Jamaica, twenty-third but only surviving child of the twenty-seven of Major-General George Ricketts, also of Canaan. In the same year Ricketts had a grant and the limitations were extended to include the descendants of his uncle William Ricketts of the Jerseys in North America. In 1774 Heard, who was by then Norroy, had a grant of arms for his wife, and the limitations were extended to include with a crest the descendants of her father and uncle, Andrew and William Tyler. A Tyler pedigree witnessed by Heard was recorded in 1778. The last grant to an American before Independence was dated 31 March 1775, and was to Andrew Pepperell Sparhawk, subsequently Pepperell, the son of Mrs Heard's first cousin, who obtained a Royal Licence in February 1775 to take the name and arms of his maternal grandfather, Sir William Pepperell.

After 1775 there are occasional references to America in grants to those who left after the Revolution. The limitations of some of the grants were extended to include members of the grantees' families still resident in America. In 1783 Heard, by then Clarenceux, in testimony of the sincere regard he bore to William Foster of Boston in New England but then resident in London, and of the warm friendship and affection which had existed for a great number of years between him

Pedigree of Foster of Boston recorded in 1783, including arms and crest in which there is a Virginia Nightingale (Coll. Arms, 6 D 14, pp. 311–12).

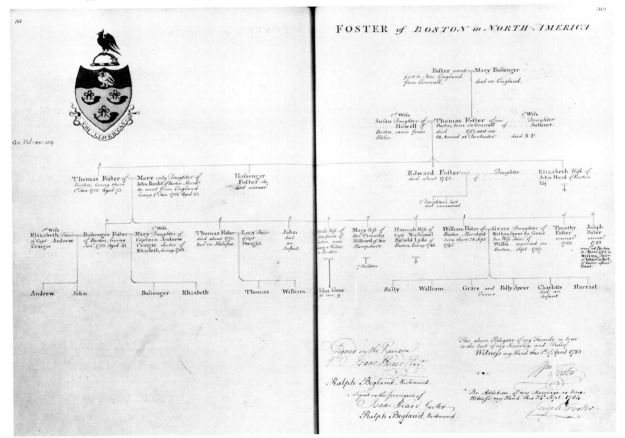

and Foster's uncle by marriage, John Hurd of Boston, petitioned for grants to the two families. These were made in one patent, the limitations being extended to include the descendants of Thomas Foster, father of William Foster, and Jacob Hurd, father of William Hurd. The Virginia nightingale appears in the crest granted to Thomas Foster which is blazoned *A bugle Horn inverted Vert garnished Or thereon a Virginia Nightingale rising proper*. In 1788 arms and a crest were granted to Ebenezer Jessup of Fludyer Street, Westminster, late Lieutenant-Colonel Commandant of the King's Loyal American Regiment, third son of Joseph Jessup of Fairfield, Connecticut. Two years later the grantees for 1790 include James Woodmason, described as only surviving issue of the Reverend Charles Woodmason, formerly Vicar of St Mark in the Province of South Carolina. In 1798 Charles Moulton, described as of New York, merchant, obtained a Royal Licence that his infant sons Edward Barrett Moulton and Samuel Barrett Moulton might assume the name and arms of Barrett; the arms had been granted to their maternal uncle Samuel Barrett and the descendants of their grandfather Edward Barrett of Cinnamon Hill, Jamaica, in 1792. The elder son was subsequently the father of Elizabeth Barrett Browning, and as Edward Moulton Barrett of Hope End, Herefordshire, an estate he was forced to sell for financial reasons, he obtained a grant of arms for his father, Charles Moulton, in 1815, when the latter was of Wakefield, Jamaica.

In 1802 Alexander Macleod, Senior East India Company Merchant at Madras, obtained a grant of arms on assuming his mother's maiden name of Hume, his maternal grandfather being described as of South Carolina. In the following year a grant was made to James Putnam then of Halifax, Nova Scotia, but formerly of 'the town and County of Worcester in the late Province (now State) of Massachusetts Bay in New England'. In 1807, Sir George Nugent, Bt., obtained a grant for his wife Maria, and the Patent included the other descendants of her deceased father Cortlandt Skinner, sometime Attorney-General of the Province of New Jersey. In the next year James Carsan of the City of London, only child of James Carsan of South Carolina, obtained a Royal Licence to bear the name and arms of Porter, his stepfather. In 1812 a grant was made to Jahleel Brenton, a post captain in the Royal Navy, the son and grandson of men of the same name, the former having been a Rear-Admiral of the Blue Squadron, and the latter of Rhode Island, in North America. The limitations of the grant included the descendants of the grantee's grandfather, Jahleel Brenton of Rhode Island, and those listed as resident in America were Benjamin Brenton, Frances, wife of Solomon Townshend, and Frances, wife of Robert Brown, all of Newport, Rhode Island, and Mary, wife of Leslie Stewart of New York, merchant. One of the English beneficiaries was

John Brenton, then Flag-Lieutenant of HMS *Victory*. A grant with extended limitations was made to James Russell of Clifton, Gloucestershire, in 1820. He is described as only surviving son of James Russell, late of Charlestown in the Province of Massachusetts, and grandson of Daniel Russell of the same place, and the grant included James and Charles Russell of Boston, grandsons of the Petitioner's uncle Richard Russell. An 1823 grant to Joseph Pringle Taylor, an army captain on half-pay, included the other descendants of his father William Taylor, late of Amboy in the Province of New Jersey. This was the first grant to someone with an American connection made after the death of Sir Isaac Heard in 1822 and it was almost the last such grant to be made in the nineteenth century. The only later similar grant was in 1828 to Sir James Alexander Wright, Bt., of Carolside, Berwickshire, only son of James Alexander Wright of Charlestown, South Carolina, and grandson of Alexander Wright of the same place. His great-grandfather James Wright, Governor of the Province of Georgia, was created a baronet in 1772. Sir James Alexander Wright died unmarried in 1837, when he should have been succeeded as 4th Baronet by his first cousin John Wright, son of his uncle John Izard Wright. The entry for the family last appears in the 1882 edition of *Burke's Peerage*, after which it seems to have been removed for apparent lack of information about the 4th Baronet or his younger brother Alexander.

After the 1828 grant there is one of American interest in 1838 when Granville Penn of Stoke Park, Buckinghamshire, only surviving son and heir of Thomas Penn of the same place, and grandson and heir male of William Penn, sometime proprietor and first settler of Pennsylvania, had a grant pursuant to a Royal Licence of *Argent on a Fess Sable three Plates and on a canton of honourable augmentation Gules a Crown proper representing the Royal Crown of Charles II*. Thereafter the only nineteenth-century grant that has been found in which any mention is made of America is one in 1876 to Edward Denman Thornburgh-Cropper, who married Virginia Shepherd, only child of William Butler Thornburgh of San Francisco, and was granted a quartering for Thornburgh.

The armorial bearings of the United States were decided upon by Congress in 1782. In accepting the need for such insignia it is unfortunate that Congress did not establish its own heraldic authority. Eugene Zieber's *Heraldry in America* (1909) quoting the *Journals of Congress*, iv. 39, blazons the armorial bearings as follows:

Arms *Paleways of thirteen pieces, argent and gules; a chief, azure; the escutcheon on the breast of the American eagle displayed proper, holding in his dexter talon an olive branch, and in his sinister a bundle of thirteen arrows, all proper, and in his beak a scroll, inscribed with this motto 'E pluribus Unum'. Crest Over the head of the Eagle, which appears above the escutcheon, a glory, or, breaking through a cloud, proper, and surrounding thirteen stars, forming a constellation argent on an azure field.*

Punctuation marks, which would not be in an English blazon, are used, and where there is an odd number of paly pieces in England it would be blazoned *Argent six Pallets Gules*. The English scheme of capital letters for tinctures and principal charges is also not followed. What is called the crest, though it is not borne on a helmet, is of the type considered now to be bad heraldry as it floats above the head.

Accompanying the blazon adopted by Congress is a section entitled 'Remarks and Explanation' which perpetuates the nonsense of English writers in attributing virtues to charges and tinctures. It states,

The Escutcheon is composed of the chief and pale, the two most honourable ordinaries. The pieces, paly, represent the several states all joined in one solid compact entire, supporting a chief, which unites the whole and represents Congress. The Motto alludes to this union. The pales in the Arms are kept closely united by the chief and the chief depends on that union and the strength resulting from it for its support, to denote the Confederacy of the United States of America; White signifies purity and innocence, Red, hardiness and valour, and Blue, the colour of the chief signifies vigilance perseverance & justice. The Olive branch and arrows denote the power of peace and war which is exclusively vested in Congress. The Constellation denotes a new State taking its place and rank among the sovereign powers. The Escutcheon is born on the breast of an American Eagle without any other supporters, to denote that the United States ought to rely on their own virtue.

Five pointed stars, or mullets as they are blazoned in England, appear in the arms of Washington as recorded at the Heralds' Visitation of Northamptonshire in 1619. George Washington did not record a pedigree establishing his right to these arms by descent, although he and Heard corresponded about his ancestry in 1791 and 1792 and Washington used an armorial book-plate with these arms. He eventually appeared on an undated pedigree registered at the College in the mid–1970s. The closest Heard got to recording Washington was in a pedigree of Gale which Heard witnessed on 31 December 1776, and which includes Washington's step-grandfather, George Gale, who married his grandmother, Mildred Warner.

Heraldry of both a personal and corporate nature was in frequent use in America both before and after Independence in seals, book-plates and on monuments. Much of the personal heraldry was of English origin, and corporate heraldry tended to be borne without any official sanction from the English Kings of Arms; for instance, the arms of Harvard College were first adopted in 1643 by the Overseers as a seal design without tinctures. The arms then appeared as three books, those in chief being open with the letters '*VE*' and '*RI*' upon them with that in base face down and inscribed '*TAS*' producing the motto '*VERITAS*'. Later in the seventeenth century a chevron was placed between the three books, and was used until the nineteenth century, when a seal was adopted without one but with all three books face upwards.

In 1866 an American, John Von Sonnentag Haviland, later de Haviland, was appointed Rouge Croix, and he became York Herald in 1872. He was born in 1826, probably in Philadephia where his father, an architect who specialized in designing prisons, practised. De Haviland served as a Brigadier-General in Spain under Don Carlos in 1875 when a Herald, and was a soldier of fortune whose medals included the Iron Cross. Like his predecessors as York, Wingfield, Cromp, and Whitwick, he was in financial difficulties at the time of his death in 1886; of particular interest is his evidence to the Earl Marshal's Inquiry of 1869, in which he stated that, despite the wishes of Americans to trace their descent from English families, the College now refused to register their pedigrees. This would seem to mark the low point of the College's dealings with independent America. The general interest in family origins in mid-nineteenth-century America can be seen in the founding of the New England Historic Genealogical Society. Publication of its Register began in 1847, its first stated aim being to comprehend 'Biographical Memoirs sketches, and Notices of persons who came to North America especially to New England before 1700'. By 1985 one hundred and sixty-nine volumes had been published, and there were one hundred and sixteen volumes of the *New York Genealogical and Biographical Record*, first published in 1870. Notable American genealogists such as Colonel Joseph Lemuel Chester worked in England, and Chester's papers were acquired by the College of Arms. This interest led many Americans to come to the College in pursuit of English ancestors, both armigerous and non-armigerous. For those not entitled to arms by descent the only way to obtain a grant from the English Kings of Arms was to find a remote cousin who could petition for a grant with extended limitations to include descendants of the common ancestor. Thus, in 1917 a grant was made to Arthur John Lewis Delafield, a British subject, and to the descendants of his great-great-grandfather. These included an American, John Ross Delafield of New York, born in 1874, who was described in 1932 as a Brigadier-General, Ordnance Department Reserve, and graduate of Harvard Law School. In 1916 J. R. Dela-field's mother, whose maiden name was Livingston, descended from an emigrant Robert Livingston born at Ancrum in Scotland in 1654, had obtained a grant of arms for Livingston from Lord Lyon. Following the 1917 grant, J. R. Delafield had several grants of quarterings from the English Kings of Arms. These began with a grant of arms for Hallett in 1919 in respect of his great-grandmother, born in 1766, the daughter of Joseph Hallett of New York, merchant. Subsequent grants were for Schuyler and Beckman in 1927 and Vanbrugh in 1932. J. R. Delafield was not a subject of the Crown, but perhaps his inclusion within the Limitations of a grant to someone who was enabled him to receive later grants in the normal form.

At what seems to be an unrecorded date, and not as the result of any minuted decision or a general Warrant from the Earl Marshal, the English Kings of Arms began to make honorary grants of Armorial Bearings to eminent Americans descended in an unbroken male line from subjects of the British Crown. These grants are recorded in the same series as other grants, the only difference being the inclusion of the word 'Honorary'. The restriction as to descent means that this must be in the male line from an ancestor resident in America at the time Britain recognized American Independence (the Treaty of Paris 1783), or from a subsequent emigrant. An early example of an honorary grant is that to Alain Campbell White of Litchfield, Connecticut, in 1920. In 1964 Garter stated to the Chapter of the College that the Kings of Arms would not in future be prepared to make honorary grants on the basis of British descent unless the pedigree establishing the descent was registered at the College.

Honorary grants enabled a limited number of Americans to receive grants from England, and the twentieth century has seen the registration of American pedigrees connecting with seventeenth-century or earlier records. Extensive pedigrees have, for instance, been registered for families of Randolph and Pell, the former linking on to one recorded at the Heralds' Visitation of Northamptonshire in 1681, and Robert E. Lee appears on a pedigree dated 6 November 1957. Honorary grants have also been made to Honorary Knights such as Douglas Fairbanks, Jun., but corporate bodies have not received honorary grants. This was remedied in part by a Warrant of the Earl Marshal to the Kings of Arms dated 25 July 1960, stating that the Kings of Arms had been requested by the Councils of certain towns in the United States of America to devise Armorial Bearings for them, and as it appeared expedient that they should devise such arms they were authorized to do so. Devisals, as opposed to grants of armorial bearings, have consequently been made to American towns since 1960. The consent of the Governor of the State is first obtained in all such cases, and the records are entered in a College series entitled *Foreign Arms* rather than the main grants series. A subsequent Earl Marshal's Warrant of 1 February 1962 extended the jurisdiction to devise arms to include American bodies corporate other than Town Councils. Devisals cannot be made to American subjects of non-

British descent as an alternative to an honorary grant. Fewer than forty devisals have been made since 1960; the first two were to the cities of Hampton, Virginia and Kingston, North Carolina, both dated 20 December 1960. London (1968), King and Queen (1975), Charles City (1975), Prince George (1976), Powhatan (1978), and King William (1979) Counties in Virginia have had devisals, as have the Commonwealth of Virginia (1976) and the Senate of the Commonwealth of Virginia (1979). Georgia State College (1968), Middle Georgia College (1983), and Winthrop College, South Carolina (1980) are representatives of another group, as are the Cathedral Church of the Advent, Birmingham, Alabama (1985) and St Thomas's Church, New York (1975). Only three devisals were made to commercial companies between 1962 and 1987; these were all in 1967 to Mill Brothers Company of Chattanooga, Tennessee, Barclays Bank of California, and Rich's Incorporated of the City of Atlanta, Georgia. The most unusual devisal is that to the Mescalero Apache Tribe in 1986. A circular Apache shield was used, following immediate precedents of grants to African subjects of the Crown such as the former Colony of Kenya which have used African shield shapes, and the arms are ensigned with an Apache Crown following the precedent of some English Civic heraldry where the arms can be ensigned with a mural crown. The unusual shield shape also emphasizes the point that the shield is only a vehicle to display the arms, and its exact shape is not significant. The supporters are two Mescalero Apache spirit dancers, and the arms contain tribal motifs.

American heraldry regulated from England began in 1586 with the grant to the City of Ralegh, then in the Colony of Virginia, and almost four hundred years later the Town of Manteo, North Carolina, which occupies the site of the proposed city of Ralegh, petitioned the Kings of Arms for a devisal which they received in 1983. The arms devised were *Argent on a Cross Gules six Lozenges conjoined palewise of the field in dexter chief a Roebuck statant also Gules.* This varied the 1586 grant by the addition of lozenges to the cross, an allusion to Sir Walter Raleigh, and the alteration of the tincture of the roebuck from proper or its natural colour to Gules. Although in the United States there is only a comparatively small body of new authorized heraldry from England, the extensive use there of, for instance, personal arms since the seventeenth century is indicative of the existence of heraldry in all states derived from Europe. Even though the devisal system is of slight financial benefit to the College of Arms it is perhaps time that the United States recognized the need for at least properly regulated municipal or corporate heraldry, and established its own heraldic authority.

Record of devisal of armorial bearings made in 1986 to the Mescalero Apache Tribe (Coll. Arms, Foreign Arms 2, p. 176).

X *The Use of Heraldry as Decoration*

THE PURELY decorative use of heraldry can be traced back to the middle of the thirteenth century, about a hundred years after its invention, and like so much else in medieval art the initial inspiration may have been French, though England can claim to be the first country in Europe to adopt heraldry as part of the vocabulary of architecture rather than as a form of temporary decoration or pageantry. The fashion for architectural heraldic decoration in England was first stimulated by the example of King Henry III, and became increasingly strong as the Middle Ages progressed. Henry had a passion for heraldry all his life. He was, therefore, greatly impressed by the decoration at a banquet given for him in the Temple by Louis IX on a visit to Paris in 1254. On that occasion Louis hung the walls of the Great Hall with painted wooden shields bearing the arms of the great noble families of France, thus adapting the trappings of a tournament to make a form of indoor embellishment. On his return to London Henry decided to copy this idea, but in permanent carved stone rather than temporary painted wood. In 1258 he ordered that the spandrels of the aisle arcades at Westminster Abbey should be adorned with carved stone shields representing his own arms and those of the Royal houses with which he was connected by marriage, namely the arms of Edward the Confessor, of England, the Empire, France, Provence, and Scotland, together with those of his principal vassals, the great English Barons: Clare, Bigod, Montfort, Warenne, Bohun, Arundel, de Quinci, de Lacy, Richard, Earl of Cornwall, and one unidentified. When coloured these shields must have made a grand display of royal and baronial glory, and the idea soon came to be widely copied elsewhere.

Even before his visit to France Henry had made use of coats of arms to adorn metalwork, tiles, and painted wall decoration. As early as 1237, for instance, he commissioned a silver platter ornamented with the Royal Arms as a present for the Queen. In 1240 he ordered his arms to be painted on the window shutters of his Great Chamber at the Tower of London, and in 1266 extended the practice to all the doors and shutters of the New Hall and Chamber at Winchester Castle. The

North aisle of the nave of Westminster Abbey. The shields in the spandrels, including those illustrated which show France Ancient and an Eagle displayed, survive from Henry III's original scheme, and are the earliest known example of the permanent use of heraldry as a form of architectural decoration. The early eighteenth-century monuments, including one to the musician John Blow, all contain shields of the arms of the deceased (Royal Commission on Historical Monuments, NMR CC70/209).

Great Hall at Rochester Castle and the Chapel at Havering were likewise embellished with heraldic stained glass at about the same time. The latter depicted not just Henry's own arms but also those of his father-in-law, the Count of Provence. And in 1268 Henry instructed the Keeper of the Works at Westminster to send to the Palace of Havering twenty glass windows decorated with forty shields of arms for the Queen's Chamber. At Westminster Abbey, apart from the carved stone shields in the aisle arcades, the floor of the Chapter House had been decorated with heraldry in about 1253, and the floor tiles of the Westminster Chapter House have the earliest surviving representation of the King's Arms in architectural decoration.

The Sovereign's example was soon widely emulated by the barons and great ecclesiastics, and there was a rapid spread of heraldic decoration in the later thirteenth century. This can be seen as an aspect of the growth of courtly romanticism at that time, and a manifestation of the more secular trends of the age, heraldry taking some of the place hitherto occupied by religious symbolism. Within a short time coats of arms became the standard form of embellishment on the tombs of both the laity and the clergy, at first modestly, and then with increasing elaboration and decorative fancy. For instance, the early thirteenth-century figure in Gloucester Cathedral of Robert Curthose, Duke of Normandy (died 1134), of which Robert Cooke, Clarenceux, made a sketch in about 1569, shows the hero of the first Crusade lying cross-legged wearing a coat of arms on a tomb decorated with ten shields. Nor was the use of heraldic decoration confined to the architecture of churches, palaces, houses, and tombs. Heraldry soon found its way into the illumination of manuscripts, where medallions

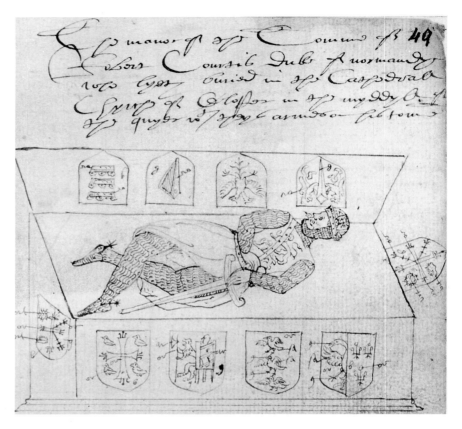

of arms took their place alongside religious, naturalistic, and grotesque decorations in the coloured borders and initial letters. *The Arundel Psalter* in the British Library, with its diaper pattern of heraldic lions and fleurs-de-lis, or the *Ormsby Psalter* (Douce 366) in the Bodleian at Oxford, with its shields of arms, are typical late thirteenth-century examples. Sometimes the shields in the borders of manuscripts were suspended from painted loops or twigs, creating very attractive patterns.

Heraldry made its mark on needlework too. Much has disappeared, but it is likely that secular decorative hangings and tapestries were often enlivened with coats of arms, and Church vestments certainly were; bishops and abbots, for instance, enjoying the right to display their own arms on the orphreys of their cope or at the bottom of the cross on the back of their chasuble. The Syon Cope in the Victoria and Albert Museum is a very good surviving example of a late thirteenth-century vestment with heraldic needlework orphreys (though the latter are now thought to have been made up out of a Stole).

Heraldry provided the artist with an easy repertory of ready-made motifs, and full advantage was taken of this, notably by painters and stained-glass makers, the patterns and colours of coats of arms lending

The heraldic orphreys of the late-thirteenth-century Syon Cope (Victoria and Albert Museum, Q 1241).

themselves to glazing. Surviving medieval stained glass, such as that in York Minster of about 1300, contains much elaborate heraldic decoration; the windows in the Chapter House for instance contain royal arms in medallions, including the fleurs-de-lis of France, the castles of Castile, and the chalices of Galicia, while the nave windows have borders displaying the arms of the royal and noble benefactors of the Minster and of the great northern families. The display of heraldry in stained glass, in both secular and religious buildings, has continued to be one of the most popular decorative uses of heraldry down to the present day, perhaps reaching its most extensive manifestation in the windows of the great town halls of Victorian England.

The development of heraldry as a form of artistic and architectural embellishment in the thirteenth century received a further fillip from Edward I's military ideals and cult of chivalry. In Edward's reign the whole of court life seems to have been touched by a romantic glamour reflected in rich pageantry, new ceremonial, and the general elaboration of heraldry. This was a European-wide development at the time, but the impact probably went deeper in England than in other countries, and the use of heraldic decoration was sometimes taken to extremes. The canopy over the tomb of Edmund Crouchback in Westminster Abbey, for instance, was painted with no fewer than one hundred and fifty coats of arms, while the Gatehouse of Kirkham Priory (*c.*1300) in Yorkshire was entirely covered with the arms of the founders and benefactors of the Priory, while at Butleigh Priory in Suffolk the coats of arms adorning the gatehouse filled no fewer than seven closely packed rows, like a sheet of postage stamps.

The decorative fancy and exquisite craftsmanship of late thirteenth-century heraldic art is seen in its most fully developed form in the Eleanor Crosses which Edward erected to commemorate the funeral procession of his wife, Eleanor of Castile, who died in Nottinghamshire in 1290. Her twelve-day funeral journey from Harby to Westminster Abbey was given a permanent memorial in the form of a stone cross at each place where the coffin rested overnight. Each of them was decorated on the sides with shields of the arms of England and Castile, as can be seen still on the surviving examples at Geddington and Hardingstone in Northamptonshire and Waltham Cross in Essex. The cult of the pageantry of death and the employment of heraldry for the purpose probably had its origins in France, Edward being influenced by the pomp and circumstance that had surrounded the return of the body of St Louis of France from Tunis to the Abbey of St Denis. The stations of the last stages of the funeral procession of St Louis had been marked by similar ceremonial, and the erection of stone crosses known as the Montjoies of St Louis.

The fashion thus started reached its culmination in the later Middle

The gateway of Kirkham Priory in Yorkshire (built c.1300), embellished with the arms of founders and benefactors (Royal Commission on Historical Monuments, NMR BB86/ 7420).

Detail of the Eleanor Cross at Hardingstone in Northamptonshire carved with coats of arms (Royal Commission on Historical Monuments, NMR B45/986).

Drawing by Henry Lilly (1589–1638), Rouge Dragon Pursuivant, of the fourteenth-century font and cover (now lost) at East Winch in Norfolk, with carved and painted Howard and other arms (Duke of Norfolk).

In East Winch Church in Com. Norfolk

A faire Font antientlie erected after this manner in the saide Church by S.ͬ Robert Howard knight as appeareth by his and his wiues Armes thereon the being in fine one of the Colsens and heires of the Baron Scales of Neufells. the saide S.ͬ Robert Howard died A.ᵒ 12.ᵒ Rici. 2.ͩ

Ages in the elaborate etiquette of royal and noble funerals. The burials of the great became grandiose heraldic spectacles, with the lying-in-state, the funeral procession, and not least the catafalque itself all being used to display the crests, coronets, arms, supporters, badges, and mottoes of the deceased. A late but well-recorded example is that of Thomas Howard, 2nd Duke of Norfolk, the victor of Flodden, who died on 21 May 1524, and was given the last great funeral of the Middle Ages. 'No nobleman was ever to be buried in such style again.' The chamber of state, the great hall, and the chapel at Framlingham Castle, the principal Howard seat in Suffolk, were hung with black cloth and numerous escutcheons of arms, while the Duke's body lay in state there for a month. On 22 June the Duke's coffin set out on the 24-mile journey to Thetford Priory, Norfolk, the ancestral burial place of the Duke's family. The coffin, drawn on a chariot, was bedecked with gold escutcheons and accompanied by nine hundred mourners, including black-hooded torchmen, friars, the gentlemen of his household, and Heralds. His helmet with crest was borne by Windsor Herald, and hatchments displaying his armorial achievements were carried by Carlisle Herald and Clarenceux and Garter Kings of Arms. At Thetford Priory the coffin was placed on a fabulous catafalque in the centre of the choir for the funeral service. This catafalque was an enormous heraldic fantasy of black and gold, adorned with seven hundred lights, black-gowned wax effigies holding eight 'bannerols', and no fewer than a hundred achievements of his arms. The funeral service itself was marked by a series of heraldic ceremonies, including a procession of the Heralds bearing achievements of the Duke's arms, and, most awesome of all, the dramatic entry into the church of a knight on horseback wearing the dead Duke's armour with the visor closed and carrying his battleaxe head-down.

Though this kind of ceremonial funeral with heraldic display reached its apogee in the later Middle Ages, the fashion lingered on in a reduced form into the seventeenth and eighteenth centuries, and the habit of displaying the hatchments of the arms of the deceased, in the form of a single one over the front door of his residence, still occurs from time to time in the twentieth century at the odd Oxford college or country house in Lincolnshire. Such hatchments were usually displayed for a year on the house and then deposited in the local church. Many, dating from the eighteenth and nineteenth centuries, are a familiar sight hanging aloft diamond-wise in the old parish churches and family chapels of England; they are painted on square wooden boards or canvas with simple black frames. Where the deceased was married his arms are shown impaled with those of his wife, and if the widow outlived him, only the half behind the deceased's arms is painted black, the background of his living spouse being painted white, unless the wife is divorced, when her arms no longer appear.

A full account of a grand later funeral is Francis Sandford's *Funeral of the Great Duke of Albemarle* in 1670. The lying-in-state took place at Somerset House in the Strand, where three rooms were hung with black velvet and decorated with escutcheons of arms. The Duke lay on a black velvet bed of state under a large hatchment, and at his feet was placed an arrangement of heraldic banners and bannerols, and a table with his coat of arms, sword, targe, helm and crest, gauntlet, and spurs. The 1st Duke of Marlborough's funeral in London in 1722 is also well recorded. On that occasion five rooms at Marlborough House were decorated for the lying-in-state, hung with black, and embellished with heraldic devices and badges of the Order of the Garter. The Heralds usually attended and recorded the funerals of the nobility, but this practice gradually fell into desuetude in the course of the eighteenth century. Today the Heralds only take part in the Sovereign's funeral, that of the Earl Marshal, or a State funeral like Sir Winston Churchill's; on the latter occasion they carried shields of the deceased's arms and his banner in the procession in St Paul's Cathedral. Heraldry, however, continues to be one of the chief forms of decoration on memorial tablets and tombs, as it has been since the thirteenth century.

Just as the use of heraldry became standardized as part of the trappings of a noble funeral, so in the later Middle Ages its architectural manifestation became increasingly uniform. In churches, coats of arms and crests embellished the bosses of the vault, the stained glass in the windows, the spandrels of the arches, the panels of screens, and tomb chests. In houses, colleges, and secular buildings it also became the norm to have a grand heraldic display over the gatehouse, on fireplaces, and on the metal vanes of the roof, as can be seen in the colleges at Oxford or Cambridge. The architectural use of heraldry in Gothic architecture reached its ultimate prominence in the decoration of King's College Chapel at Cambridge. There, all the stone carving is devoted to dynastic display; there is no religious imagery in the stonework at all; everywhere six feet high rampant greyhounds and dragons support the Royal Arms. Immense and deeply undercut roses and portcullises are set off against the bare Perpendicular stone panelling. This triumphant heraldic expression on the part of the new Tudor Monarchy was part of an international architectural development in the later Middle Ages, and can be paralleled, for instance, at San Juan de los Reyes at Toledo, where huge crowned escutcheons of the arms of Ferdinand and Isabella enliven the stonework, or the façade of the University of Salamanca, perhaps the most superb specimen of heraldic sculpture in Europe.

In the sixteenth and seventeenth centuries there was a considerable diminution in the use of heraldry in architecture. The Renaissance brought with it a new vocabulary of Italian classical decoration which ousted the more Gothic excesses associated with the architectural use of heraldry. Heraldry tended to be once more associated with temporary decorations for royal and other pageantry, rather than permanently executed in stone. Thus, for the marriage of Prince Arthur to Catherine of Aragon in 1501, very elaborate wooden and canvas arches were erected, embellished with paintings of the Royal Arms, badges, devices, and supporters. And these temporary arches and other forms of 'stage scenery' became a standard item of royal ceremonial at coronations, marriages, receptions for foreign ignitaries, and so forth. In the seventeenth century heraldry played little or no part in the decoration of the houses and palaces of Inigo Jones or Wren. Even Vanbrugh, who was himself a Herald, made little use of heraldic devices in his buildings. In the eighteenth century heraldry was usually confined, on the outside of buildings, to the embellishment of pediments, and was strictly curtailed by the overall discipline of the classical architecture. A good example is the display of the Devonshire arms in the pediment over the entrance to the stables

Early seventeenth-century book binding stamped with the arms of Henry (Howard), Earl of Northampton, quartering Brotherton, Warenne, and Fitzalan. The little crescent in the centre of the shield is a cadency mark for a second son (Duke of Norfolk).

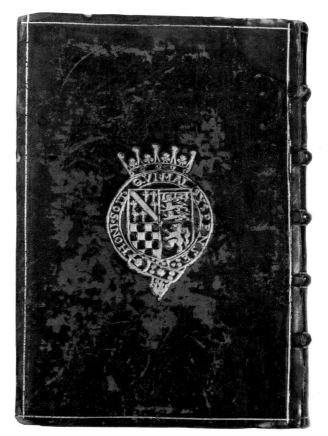

designed by James Paine at Chatsworth in 1758. There the life-size stone stags supporting the Cavendish arms have real antlers.

Inside Georgian houses the convention was to confine the display of heraldry to the entrance hall, where the family's crest was usually painted on the wooden backs of the un-upholstered hall chairs, and sometimes was also used as a decorative emblem in the plaster frieze; where the frieze is Doric, the crest is often used for the metopes between the triglyphs, as at Norfolk House, Shugborough, Sledmere, and many other places. At Kedleston, the seat of the Curzon family since Norman times but rebuilt in the mid-eighteenth century, heraldry is restricted to miniscule, and inaccurate, marble tablets in the chimney-pieces of Adam's entrance hall. There are exceptions to this general rule, of course: at Boughton in Northamptonshire, for instance, there is a charming mid-eighteenth-century chinoiserie staircase, each tread of which displays a shield bearing the family arms of the Dukes of Montagu, referred to by Horace Walpole in a typical pun as the 'descent of the Montagues'.

Walpole himself was one of the revivers of heraldic architectural decoration, as well as of Gothic in general, at his famous house

Strawberry Hill in Middlesex. The two things went hand-in-hand in the late eighteenth and early nineteenth centuries. Wherever mock battlements or traceried windows or pinnacled skylines raised themselves, so also could be expected a proud display of, occasionally bogus, heraldry. William Beckford's Fonthill Abbey, for instance, was bedecked with all the heraldry he could command or imagine in plaster, stone, and stained glass. The early nineteenth century saw the enthusiasm for the Middle Ages manifested in such projects as the grandiose reconstruction of Windsor Castle, combined with a more scholarly approach in the work of designers like Thomas Willement, 'Heraldic Artist to George IV', who was responsible for reviving medieval-style heraldic painted decoration and stained glass, a revival perfected by A. W. N. Pugin who, just as he introduced a note of high seriousness into the Gothic Revival, so also helped to instil a scholarly note into architectural decoration. His heraldic display in the Houses of Parliament is exemplary, and would have won the approval of Henry III himself. It set the standard for much of the Victorian revival of architectural heraldic decoration, which soon outdid even the fourteenth century in scale and prolixity. To Pugin, for instance, goes the credit for reviving the heraldic encaustic tile, as well as brasses and enamelwork. A typically Victorian development was heraldic carpet, examples of which survive at Charlecote (Warwickshire) decorated with the 'luces' of the Lucy family, and at Carlton Towers (Yorkshire), woven with the Beaumont lion. It would be hard to think of more thoroughgoing and scholarly schemes of heraldic decoration than those conceived in the 1870s by Charles Alban Buckler, Surrey Herald Extraordinary, for the 15th Duke of Norfolk at Arundel Castle, or by General de Havilland, York Herald, at Carlton Towers for the 9th Lord Beaumont. In these vast Gothic houses nearly every window glows with heraldic stained glass, every fireplace is lined with heraldic tiles, nearly every ceiling and cornice sports an array of carved and painted shields, coronets, quarterings, crests, and supporters.

The fashion for heraldic decoration in the nineteenth century was not just an aspect of the Gothic Revival and new medieval historical scholarship; it was also a manifestation of the seigneurial pride of the English upper classes after the French Revolution and Waterloo. The early nineteenth century in England saw the manufacture of endless Norman pedigrees, the medievalizing of surnames and titles—de Freyne, de Ramsey, Wyatville—and the indiscriminating enjoyment of all the trappings that went with such sonorous medievalisms. Thus, the landowner marked all the tied cottages on his estate with tablets bearing his crest or coat of arms. At Holkham in Norfolk, the iron door of every cottage oven was embossed with the ostrich crest of the Cokes. At Arundel, the cast-iron bollards in the streets of the town

(*top left*) Chimney-piece in the drawing room at Arundel Castle, designed in 1870 by Charles Alban Buckler (1824–1905), Surrey Herald Extraordinary, and carved by Thomas Earp. The larger heraldic achievement shows the arms of the 15th Duke of Norfolk impaled with those of his wife Flora (Abney-Hastings). The small shields depict the principal medieval quarterings inherited by the Duke, while the Minton tiles in the fireplace bear the Howard, Fitzalan, and Warenne arms (Duke of Norfolk).

(*top right*) Date-stone of 1821 on a cottage at Inverbrora on the Dunrobin Castle estate, Sutherland, with the arms of (Leweson-Gower) 1st Marquess of Stafford, and those of his wife, Countess of Sutherland in her own right.

bear the ducal lion of the Norfolks, and even the tokens for the toll bridge at Shoreham, built by the 12th Duke, were stamped with the Norfolk crest. Humphry Repton, in the *Red Book* for improving the park at Tatton in Cheshire, advised his client there, Wilbraham Egerton, to decorate all the milestones along the public roads on the estate with the Egerton arms. The heraldic inn sign, which became widespread in this period, continues to be so common a sight in England as to be taken for granted. Nearly every village and town has at least one pub displaying the arms of a past or present local family. They even continue to be augmented. In 1955 the Green Dragon at Downham in Lancashire, for instance, changed its name to the Assheton Arms on the elevation of the local squire, Sir Ralph Assheton, to the peerage as the 1st Lord Clitheroe, and its façade was suitably embellished with a large heraldic signboard to match. More recently the pub at Hainton in Lincolnshire changed its name from the Hainton Inn to the Heneage Arms.

The use of heraldry has always been a mark of livery, and though partly practical (to enable a man's servants and dependants to be recognized), this was always largely decorative. In the Middle Ages great magnates clad their servants and followers in liveries based on their heraldic colours, despite repeated attempts by the Crown to control this abuse. Armorial Bearings were used as a symbol of a man's authority on all he owned and directed: on his seals, his plate, his horse trappings, his servants, his gaming counters, his dogs, and so forth. In the eighteenth and nineteenth centuries this had its most spectacular manifestation in the decoration of carriages, family silver, and footmen's livery. Whole armies of coach painters were employed in painting heraldic panels for carriages, and some well-known artists began in this particular line. The architect William Kent, for instance, began life as an apprentice to a coach painter in Hull, before a group of local gentlemen, struck by his talent, clubbed together to pay to send him to Italy to train as a proper painter. Many heraldic coach panels survive, as they were often cut out and kept when the coach itself was broken up. Coachmen's and footmen's livery also made great decorative play on the family heraldry, usually being in the family colours, with the silver buttons bearing the full achievement or the crest alone. Some liveries went even further in the heraldic line. The footmen of the Leghs of Lyme of Cheshire, for instance, wore a spare sleeve flapping at the back of their coats to represent the standard-bearing arm of the augmentation in the family arms (granted in 1575 on the

(*bottom left*) Obverse and reverse of mother-of-pearl gaming counters of Henry (Hyde), Viscount Cornbury by courtesy (d. 1753), showing arms of Hyde and incorrectly a viscount's coronet, as he was only summoned to Parliament in his father, the Earl of Clarendon's, lifetime as a baron (private collection).

(*bottom right*) Seal matrix (enlarged) of quartered arms, supporters, and coronet of rank of a baron, of John (Arundel), 4th Lord Arundel of Trerice. Arms quarterly one and four *Sable six swallows close three, two, and one Argent*, two and three *Sable three chevronels Argent*; supporters *two panthers guardant Or spotted of various colours and incensed Proper* (private collection).

Book-plate of Sir Alfred Scott-Gatty (1847–1918), with his own arms and those of his office as Garter King of Arms (private collection).

basis of the muddled tradition of descent from a hero of Crécy). The use of arms on table china and silver varies from an engraving of the crest to three-dimensional representations. At Chatsworth much of the plate is supported by the Cavendish stags, or has the Cavendish snakes as handles. At Woburn, the silver salt cellars take the form of the Russell goat crest. The use of heraldry to decorate tableware perhaps had its most attractive expression in the eighteenth-century armorial porcelain produced in China for European clients. Whole dinner services were painted with coats of arms, depicted with greater or lesser accuracy. The stories of written instructions on the original sketch—'This is Gules, this is Vert'—being painstakingly reproduced by an oriental painter on a hundred plates are not apocryphal. Such painting on Chinese Export porcelain was usually done from heraldic book-plates which the client sent out with his order. Book-plates themselves are, of course, an attractive seventeenth-century heraldic creation, and one which is still a popular form of heraldic decoration today.

The use of heraldry to mark the owner's possessions, as a form of display, was so widespread that it was taxed in the eighteenth century as a form of income tax, and licences to display arms, similar to the dog licence, survived until 1945. The comparison with dog licences is not entirely coincidental, because dogs were often used for heraldic

Dog-collar of the 6th Duke of
Devonshire's mastiff, Hector,
with the Cavendish crest and a
Duke's coronet applied in silver
by Robert Garrard II, 1832
(Duke of Devonshire and the
Trustees of Chatsworth
Settlement).

display themselves, their collars being embellished with the family
arms or crest. A good example survives at Chatsworth: the collar of
the 6th Duke of Devonshire's mastiff, Hector, which sports a ducal
coronet and the Cavendish snake crest in silver. And Siegfried Sassoon
tells us that his uncle, at the beginning of this century, had his poodle's
coat cut with the family crest!

While most people might perhaps consider an heraldic poodle a bit
showy, a refined version of this tradition is the chief decorative
expression of heraldry today. The use of the crest or full achievement
in book-plates, on table silver, on signet rings, or on writing paper is
the main outlet for heraldic art in the late twentieth century; and there
is even a recent fashion for painting arms on the lids of lavatory seats—
as can be seen at Renishaw and other flourishing country houses.
There are no hard and fast rules about the decorative display of
heraldry. It is very much a matter of individual taste, though carried to
extremes it can look ridiculous, as in the case described by Upton
Sinclair in his book *The Great Metropolis*: 'Mrs Winnie had a coat of
arms; he had noticed it upon her auto, and again upon the liveries of
her footmen, and yet again upon the decanter of Scotch. And now—
incredible and appalling—he observed it branded upon the delicately
browned sweetbread.'

The Royal Arms of Great Britain

THE best known example of heraldry in Britain is undoubtedly the Royal Arms as depicted on coins, seals, Acts of Parliament, government circulars, royal warrants on shop fronts, the banner which flies over the Queen's houses when she is in residence, and, in its various historic forms, in churches and many public buildings throughout the land. It is not an exaggeration to claim that the Royal Arms are the most frequently displayed of all heraldic achievements, so much so that they tend to be taken for granted. Yet they are of the greatest historical interest, and their design reflects the many stages in the evolution of the British monarchy, as well as changes in the development of heraldic practice and design from the earliest centuries to the present day.

The Royal Arms as used today quarter the three Kingdoms of England, Scotland, and Ireland. Of these, the arms of the Kingdom of England, *Gules three Lions passant guardant Or* are the most ancient, and date back to the reign of King Richard I in the late twelfth century. Their earliest known representation is on his second Great Seal, brought into use in 1198, which shows the King on horseback holding a shield of these arms. He was the first English King to use the three lions, though from the time of Matthew Paris in the thirteenth century these arms were 'backdated', and sometimes attributed to all the English Kings from William the Conqueror onwards. The fashion for inventing legendary arms for great figures of the past who lived before heraldry was invented was a popular pastime in the later Middle Ages throughout Europe, and is seen in an extreme form in the arms attributed to Christ and the Apostles or even Adam. The arms of Edward the Confessor, which were much used by Henry III in his building works at Westminster in the mid-thirteenth century, and which can be seen, for instance, all over Westminster Abbey, are an example of such legendary posthumous arms. It seems likely that the use of arms by the Kings of England goes back no further than Henry II, the father of Richard I. There is literary evidence (though no surviving physical evidence) that Henry II bore *Gules a Lion rampant Or*. Richard Cœur de Lion's first Great Seal had a single lion rampant, which substantiates the claim that these were the arms borne by his father. The seal of Richard's younger brother John as Lord of Ireland and Count of Mortain, struck in 1177, had a shield with two lions passant guardant, and it is possible that the arms with three lions on the second seal of Richard I was derived from that. It was believed by the seventeenth-century antiquaries and Heralds such as Elias Ashmole that the third lion was added to represent Aquitaine (Richard being the immediate heir to the Dukedom of Aquitaine through his mother Eleanor), the other two lions representing England and Normandy.

The arms of the Kings of England retained the form assumed by Richard Cœur de Lion down to 1340, when Edward III quartered the arms of France (ancient), *Azure semy of Fleurs de lis Or* as part of his claim to the French throne, a claim which caused the outbreak of the Hundred Years War. At some time in the first decade of the fifteenth century (the exact date is not clear) the French quartering in the Royal Arms was altered to France (modern), *Azure three Fleurs de lis Or* in order to bring it into line with current French practice. The new arms of France quartered with England appear on Henry IV's second Great Seal which came into use during November 1406, thought it is possible that the change had occurred a year or so before that. Froissart records that Edward III quartered the French arms at the insistence of his Flemish allies, who made it a condition of their support for his claim to the French throne. The reason was that they were bound by a pledge of two million florins to the Pope not to make war against the legitimate King of France. At a Council in Brussels they told Edward that if he bore the arms of France (to which he was lawfully entitled in right of his mother), they would regard him as the rightful King of France, and this would release them from the consequences of their pledge if they fought for him. The quartered coat thus became the *arms of England*, not of England and France together. The gold and silver coins minted after Henry VI was crowned King of France in Paris depict two escutcheons, one containing the French arms only and the other the quartered arms of England; the point being that the quartered arms were not those of France and England but of England only.

Apart from the reign of Queen Mary in the mid-sixteenth century, when the arms of England were sometimes shown impaled with those of her husband King Philip II of Spain on seals and coins, France modern quartered with England remained the Royal Arms down to 1603 and the accession of James I, an event which led to further modifications in order to incorporate the arms of Scotland. At that time the quartered arms of England and France were placed in the first and fourth quarters, the arms of Scotland, *Or a Lion rampant within a double Tressure flory counterflory Gules* were placed in the second quarter, and the arms of Ireland, *Azure a Harp Or stringed Argent*, were introduced into the third quarter for the first time. The arms of Ireland were, therefore, not introduced into the Royal Achievement until the reign of James I, so as to balance Scotland, despite the fact that the Kings of England had been Lords of Ireland since the reign of John, and hereditary Kings of Ireland since the assumption of that title by Henry VIII in 1541.

During the Commonwealth the Royal Arms, along with other trappings of monarchy, were abolished, but apart from this interruption the Royal Arms remained the same from 1603 till the flight from the throne of James II in 1688. Charles II, however, seriously considered dropping the French quartering from the arms of England in order to satisfy the vanity of Louis XIV of France, but was dissuaded on antiquarian and political grounds by Elias Ashmole, Windsor Herald, who set out his arguments in a letter to the King dated 16 June 1661 (preserved in a transcript by John Anstis at the College of Arms). As this has never been published it might be of interest to quote from the relevant paragraph:

The premises considered, I must humbly propose to your Majesty's judgment and wisdom, whether the Present Arms of England (which upon such solid reasons of state were composed of France and England, by King Edward the 3rd, and throughout the succession of our Kings have hitherto been inviolably preserved from alteration and which, upon 2nd thoughts, and further deliberation, were confirmed by your Royal Grandfather, and so continue to this day) may by your Majesty be voluntarily disquartered without manifest prejudice to ye Title and Claim to France. And therefore, that your Majesty will please in an affair of so Publick and high a Concern as this both is and may prove to be, to weigh exactly the interest of England and France together, which such other considerations, as may naturally and Politickly arise therefrom, before you determine any thing therein.

Charles II took Ashmole's advice, and left the arms as they were. In the event, the French quartering remained part of the English heraldic achievement till 1801, when it was omitted in compliance with one of the articles of the Treaty of Paris, George III renouncing his title of King of France at the same time.

Part of Ashmole's argument was that the Arms of England and France were an impartible coat representing England. Some support for this can be found in the arms assigned to illegitimate children of various Sovereigns, who were not granted the Arms of England alone, suitably differenced, but a differenced version of the Royal Arms as borne by their parent. Although there is the added point that France and England were borne as a Grand Quarter by Charles II's father and grandfather, and subsequently by him and his brother

James II, Ashmole's argument cannot be taken particularly far as it might be argued that the Arms of England and the quarterings borne with it are Arms of Dominion, representing countries of which the King or Queen is Sovereign, and that it is consequently inappropriate to treat it as if it was a quartered personal coat.

After the departure of James II, the Royal Arms changed several times during the reign of his daughter Mary and her first cousin and husband William of Orange. William and Mary were proclaimed King and Queen in February 1689, and until the Scottish Parliament recognized them in April 1689 they bore a Grand Quarter in one and four of *Quarterly France modern and England* with Ireland in two and three and an escutcheon overall for Nassau, namely *Azure billetty and a Lion rampant Or*. In April 1689 a coat was briefly adopted and appears on some coinage of (1) England, (2) Scotland, (3) Ireland, (4) France, with an escutcheon of Nassau overall. This disregarded the impartible aspect of England and France and lasted only a few months. Thereafter the arms as used by the first four Stuart Sovereigns of England were re-adopted, namely (1 and 4) a Grand Quarter of France modern and England, (2) Scotland, (3) Ireland, with Nassau over all. This coat could also be impaled with a similar one omitting the escutcheon of Nassau over all to signify joint monarchs till the death of Mary, aged 32, in 1694. On the death of William and the accession of Mary's sister Anne in 1702, the escutcheon over all for Nassau was dropped, and Queen Anne bore till 1707 the traditional Stuart Royal Arms as borne by her father, uncle, grandfather, and great-grandfather. The Act of Union of 1707 destroyed Ashmole's impartible coat of France and England. Thereafter, the Union was signified by an impaled coat of England and Scotland in the first and fourth quarters, with France modern in the second quarter, and Ireland in the third.

On the accession of George I in 1714 the first three quarters remained the same. The fourth, which had been identical to the first, was replaced by three coats tierced per pale and per chevron for Hanover comprising (1) *Gules two Lions passant guardant Or* for Brunswick, (2) *Or semy of hearts Gules a Lion rampant Azure* for Luneburg, (3) *Gules a Horse courant Argent* for Westphalia, with over all *an Escutcheon Gules charged with the Crown of Charlemagne Or* for the Arch-Treasurership of the Holy Roman Empire. This fourth quarter has also been blazoned as Brunswick impaling Luneburg with West-phalia, also known as Saxony ancient *entre en pointe and in an escutcheon sur tout Gules the Crown of Charlemagne Or*. There was no further change in the Royal Arms till 1801 when, as we have seen, the French Arms finally disappeared. At that time the Arms of England were placed in the first and fourth quarters, Scotland in the second, and Ireland in the third, with the Arms of Hanover (as above) placed on an escutcheon over all surmounted by the Electoral Bonnet. In 1816 Hanover became a Kingdom and the Bonnet was replaced by a Royal Crown. This form of the Royal Arms survived until the accession of Queen Victoria in 1837. As a woman she was unable to succeed to the Throne of Hanover (governed in these matters by the Salic Law which enforced a strict male succession, to which the Throne of England of course was not subject) and the Hanoverian escutcheon and crown were consequently removed. Since 1837, the Royal Arms of England have remained unchanged in the form that is now generally known. As well as changes to the shield itself, the supporters of the Royal Arms have also undergone variations, but this was discussed in the chapter on supporters.

English and Scottish Kings of Arms

GARTER KINGS OF ARMS

1415–50	William Bruges.
1450–78	John Smert.
1478–1504	John Wrythe.
1505–34	Sir Thomas Wrythe, alias Wriothesley (son of John Wrythe).
1534–6	Thomas Wall.
1536–50	Sir Christopher Barker.
1550–84	Sir Gilbert Dethick.
1584–6	vacancy (Robert Cooke, Clarenceux appointed Acting Garter).
1586–1606	Sir William Dethick (son of Sir Gilbert Dethick).
1607–33	Sir William Segar.
1633–43	Sir John Borough.
1643–4	Sir Henry St George (son of Sir Richard St George, Clarenceux).
1645–77	Sir Edward Walker.
1643–60	*Sir Edward Bysshe, intruded c. 1643, confirmed by Parliament 20 Oct. 1646, deposed at Restoration 1660 (subsequently Clarenceux).*
1677–86	Sir William Dugdale.
1686–1703	Sir Thomas St George (eldest son of Sir Henry St George).
1703–15	Sir Henry St George (second surviving son of Sir Henry St George).
1715–18	vacancy (disputed Gartership).
1718–44	John Anstis.
1744–54	John Anstis (son of above and joint Garter with his father 1727–44).
1754–73	Stephen Martin Leake.
1773–4	Sir Charles Townley.
1774–80	Thomas Browne.
1780–4	Ralph Bigland.
1784–1822	Sir Isaac Heard.
1822–31	Sir George Nayler.
1831–8	Sir Ralph Bigland (nephew of Ralph Bigland, 1780–4).
1838–42	Sir William Woods.
1842–69	Sir Charles George Young.
1869–1904	Sir Albert William Woods.
1904–18	Sir Alfred Scott Scott-Gatty.
1918–30	Sir Henry Farnham Burke.
1930–44	Sir Gerald Woods Wollaston (subsequently Norroy and Ulster).
1944–50	Sir Algar Henry Stafford Howard.
1950–61	The Hon. Sir George Rothe Bellew.
1961–78	Sir Anthony Richard Wagner (subsequently Clarenceux).
1978–	Sir Alexander Colin Cole.

CLARENCEUX KINGS OF ARMS

*c.*1334	Andrew ———.	1773–4	Thomas Browne (subsequently Garter).
*c.*1383	Richard Spenser.	1774–80	Ralph Bigland (subsequently Garter).
*c.*1419	William Horsley.		
*c.*1425	John Cosoun.	1780–4	Isaac Heard (subsequently Garter).
1435–60	Roger Legh or Lygh.		
1461–76	William Hawkeslowe.	1784–1803	Thomas Lock.
1476–85	Sir Thomas Holme.	1803–20	George Harrison.
1485–7	vacancy (possibly filled by John More as Normandy King of Arms).	1820–2	Sir George Nayler (subsequently Garter).
		1822–31	Ralph Bigland (subsequently Garter).
1487–93	Sir Thomas Holme.	1831–8	William Woods (subsequently Garter).
1493–1510	Roger Machado.		
1510–11	Christopher Carlill.	1838–9	Edmund Lodge.
1511–34	Thomas Benolt.	1839–46	Joseph Hawker.
1534–6	Thomas Tonge.	1846–8	Francis Martin.
1536–57	Thomas Hawley.	1848–59	James Pulman.
1557–67	William Hervy.	1859–82	Robert Laurie.
1567–93	Robert Cooke.	1882–94	Walter Aston Blount.
1594–7	Richard Lee or Leigh.	1894–1911	George Edward Cokayne.
1597–1623	William Camden.		
1623–35	Sir Richard St George.	1911–19	Sir William Henry Weldon.
1635–46	Sir William Le Neve.		
1646–50	*Arthur Squibb, appointed by vote of Parliament 20 Oct. 1646.*	1919–22	Charles Harold Athill.
		1922–6	William Alexander Lindsay.
1650–5	*Edward Bysshe, appointed by Parliament 12 June 1650 (as well as Garter).*	1926–7	Gordon Ambrose de Lisle Lee.
		1927–54	Sir Arthur William Steuart Cochrane.
1658–61	*William Ryley, intruded c. Sept. 1658.*	1954–5	Archibald George Blomefield Russell.
1661–79	Sir Edward Bysshe (previously intruded Garter).	1955–67	Sir John Dunamace Heaton-Armstrong.
1680–1703	Sir Henry St George (subsequently Garter).	1968–78	John Riddell Bromhead Walker.
1704–26	Sir John Vanbrugh.	1978–	Sir Anthony Richard Wagner (formerly Garter).
1726–41	Knox Ward.		
1741–54	Stephen Martin Leake (subsequently Garter).		
1755–73	Charles Townley (subsequently Garter).		

NORROY KINGS OF ARMS

*c.*1276	Peter (?de Horbury).	1593–7	vacancy.
*c.*1323	William de Morlee.	1597–1604	William Segar
*c.*1338	Andrew ——.		(subsequently Garter).
*c.*1386	John Lake or Othelake, alias March.	1604–23	Richard St George (subsequently Clarenceux).
temp. Ric. II	? Roger Durroit.	1623–33	John Borough (subsequently Garter).
*c.*1399	Richard Bruges or Del Brugge.	1633–5	William Le Neve (subsequently Clarenceux).
*c.*1426	John Ashwell.		
1436	William Boys.	1635–43	Sir Henry St George (subsequently Garter).
*c.*1450	William Tyndale or Tendale.	1643–5	Edward Walker (subsequently Garter).
*c.*1462	William Grimsby.		
1464–76	Thomas Holme (subsequently Clarenceux).	1646–58	*William Ryley (intruded 20 Aug. and confirmed by Parliament 20 Oct. 1646).*
1477–8	John Wrythe (subsequently Garter).		
1478–85	John More.	1658–60	*George Owen (intruded c. Sept. 1658).*
1485–93	Roger Machado (subsequently Clarenceux).	1660–77	William Dugdale (subsequently Garter).
1494–1510	Christopher Carlill.	1677–80	Sir Henry St George (subsequently Clarenceux and Garter).
1510–11	Thomas Benolt (subsequently Clarenceux).		
1511–16	John Yonge or Young.	1680–86	Sir Thomas St George (subsequently Garter).
1516–22	Thomas Wall.		
1522	John Joyner.	1686–1700	Sir John Dugdale.
1522–34	Thomas Tonge (subsequently Clarenceux).	1700–4	Robert Devenish.
		1704–29	Peter Le Neve.
1534–6	Thomas Hawley or Halley (subsequently Clarenceux).	1729–41	Stephen Martin Leake (subsequently Clarenceux and Garter).
1536	Christopher Barker (subsequently Garter).	1741–51	John Cheale.
		1751–5	Charles Townley (subsequently Clarenceux and Garter).
1536–47	William Fellow.		
1547–50	Gilbert Dethick (subsequently Garter).		
1550–7	William Hervy (subsequently Clarenceux).	1755–61	William Oldys.
		1761–73	Thomas Browne (subsequently Clarenceux and Garter).
1557–61	Laurence Dalton.		
1562–88	William Flower.		
1588–92	vacancy.	1773–4	Ralph Bigland (subsequently
1592–3	Edmund Knight.		

	Clarenceux and Garter).	1859–82	Walter Aston Blount (subsequently Clarenceux).
1774–80	Isaac Heard (subsequently Clarenceux and Garter).	1882–94	George Edward Cokayne (subsequently Clarenceux).
1780–1	Peter Dore.		
1781–4	Thomas Lock (subsequently Clarenceux).	1894–1911	William Henry Weldon (subsequently Clarenceux).
1784–1803	George Harrison (subsequently Clarenceux).	1911–9	Henry Farnham Burke (subsequently Garter).
1803–22	Ralph Bigland (subsequently Clarenceux and Garter).	1919	Charles Harold Athill (subsequently Clarenceux).
1822–38	Edmund Lodge (subsequently Clarenceux).	1919–22	William Alexander Lindsay (subsequently Clarenceux).
1838–9	Joseph Hawker (subsequently Clarenceux).	1922–6	Gordon Ambrose De Lisle Lee (subsequently Clarenceux).
1839–46	Francis Martin (subsequently Clarenceux).	1926–8	Arthur William Steuart Cochrane (subsequently Clarenceux).
1846–8	James Pulman (subsequently Clarenceux).	1928–30	Gerald Woods Wollaston (subsequently Garter and later Norroy and Ulster).
1848–9	Edward Howard Gibbon, afterwards Howard-Gibbon.		
1849–59	Robert Laurie (subsequently Clarenceux).	1930–43	Algar Henry Stafford Howard (subsequently Garter).

NORROY AND ULSTER KINGS OF ARMS.

1943–4	Algar Henry Stafford Howard	1966–71	Richard Preston Graham-Vivian.
1944–57	Sir Gerald Woods Wollaston (formerly Garter).	1971–80	Walter John George Verco.
1957–66	Aubrey John Toppin.	1980–	John Philip Brooke Brooke-Little.

LORD LYON KINGS OF ARMS

1399–	Henry Greve.
1410–21	—— Douglas.
1471–	Laird of Woodhead.
1481–	unknown.
1489–	Sir Andrew Murray of Truim.
1496–1512	Henry Thomson of Keillour.
1512–19	Sir William Cumming of Inverallochy.
1522–	Thomas Pettigrew of Magdalensyde.
1542–55	Sir David Lindsay of the Mount.
1555–67	Sir Robert Forman of Luthrie.
1567–8	Sir William Stewart of Luthrie.
1568–91	Sir David Lindsay of Rathillet.
1591–1620	Sir David Lindsay of the Mount.
1620–30	Sir Jerome Lindsay of Annatland.
1630–54	Sir James Balfour of Denmilne, Bt.
1658–60	*Sir James Campbell of Lawers.*
1660–3	Sir Alexander Durham of Largo.
1663–77	Sir Charles Erskine of Cambo, 1st Bt. (father of next).
1672–1727	Sir Alexander Erskine of Cambo, 2nd Bt. (joint Lyon with his father, father of next).
1701–?	Sir Alexander Erskine, younger of Cambo (joint Lyon with his father, whom he predeceased).
1727–54	Alexander Brodie of that Ilk.
1754–95	John Hooke Campbell of Bangeston, Co. Pembroke.
1795–6	Robert Boswell (interim Lyon).
1796–1804	Robert Auriol (Hay-Drummond), 10th Earl of Kinnoull.
1804–66	Thomas Robert (Hay-Drummond), 11th Earl of Kinnoull.
1866–90	George Burnett.
1890–1926	Sir James Balfour Paul.
1927–9	Captain George Sitwell Campbell Swinton.
1929–45	Sir Francis James Grant.
1945–69	Sir Thomas Innes of Learney.
1969–81	Sir James Monteith Grant.
1981–	Malcolm Rognvald Innes of Edingight (son of Sir Thomas Innes).

The dates of tenure of some of the earlier holders of the Office are unknown.

Glossary of Heraldic Terms in General Use

Addorsed Back to back.

Affronty Facing the spectator.

Ancient The arms formerly borne (in fact or legend) by a country or family, now out of date or obsolete; as opposed to *Modern*.

Annulet A ring.

Antelope, Heraldic A monster with the body of an antelope, two horns, a mane, and long tail.

Appaumé or **Appaumy** With the palm of the hand facing the spectator.

Arched Used of an *Ordinary* that is bowed in the form of an arch.

Argent Heraldic term for silver or white.

Armed As a term of *blazon* refers to a creature's offensive and defensive weapons; in the case of birds, beaks and talons, but not legs, although as a term of falconry it includes the scaly part of legs.

Attired With antlers.

Augmentation An additional *charge* to arms, *crest*, *badge*, or *supporters*, usually as a mark of honour.

Azure Heraldic term for blue.

Badge A free-standing heraldic device. In the fifteenth century a distinction can be made between personal badges, which were often beasts and survived in the Royal Beasts, and retainers' badges, which were simple, often inanimate *charges*.

Bar A horizontal stripe on the shield; a diminutive of the *fess*.

Bar gemel Two thin *bars* borne together; visually identical to a *voided* bar.

Barbed With *roses* this refers to the leaves enclosing the bud which appear between the petals of an open rose, and if *blazoned* proper *Vert* is shown. Alternatively, the point of a sharp weapon.

Barry Said of a *field* or *charge* divided horizontally into an even number of stripes.

Base The lower portion of the shield.

Baston or **Baton** A *couped bend*.

Bearing Originally synonymous with a *charge* borne on a shield, it now occurs most frequently in 'armorial bearings', which is used generally to mean as much of a full achievement as is depicted—although 'armorial ensigns' might be more appropriate, ensigns (insignia) being a more suitable word if a *crest*, *supporters*, or *badge* are included.

Bend The fourth Honourable *Ordinary*; a diagonal stripe drawn across the shield from the *dexter chief* to the *sinister base*.

Bendwise Said of *charges* when shown at the same angle as a *bend*. This is to be contrasted with 'in bend', where charges are arranged across the shield diagonally but the angle at which they stand is not specified.

Bezant A gold *roundel*.

Bezanty *Field* or *charge* powdered with *bezants*.

Barry of six

Bend

Bordure and diaper

Stag's head **caboshed**

Canton

Chequy

Chevron

Chief

Cockatrice

Blazon The written description of armorial *bearings*.

Bleu celeste Sky blue. Emerged in response to wartime requirements of the Royal Air Force.

Bordure A border round the edge of the shield.

Caboshed Animal's head, often stag's *affronty*, without a neck.

Cadency mark Device to distinguish the arms of junior members of a family.

Canting arms Arms containing *charges* which allude punningly to the name of the bearer.

Canton A square division, the same depth as a *chief*, in one of the upper corners of the shield, usually in *dexter* chief and often *charged* and used as an *augmentation*.

Chaplet Synonymous with floral wreath, e.g. chaplet of roses.

Charge A *bearing* or figure represented on the shield.

Chequy, Checquy, or **Checky** A term applied to a *field* or *charge* divided into three or more rows of small squares of alternate *tinctures* like a chess board (see *gobony*).

Chevron The seventh Honourable *Ordinary*, representing two rafters of a house meeting at the top like an upturned V.

Chevronel A *chevron* of half the usual width.

Chevronny The *field* divided into an equal number of *chevron*-shaped areas.

Chief The second Honourable *Ordinary*, created by drawing a horizontal line across the shield, and occupying at most the upper third of the shield.

Cinquefoil *Charge* similar to five-leaved clover.

Cockatrice A two-legged *dragon* or *wyvern*, with a cock's head.

Colours The principle colours are blue (Azure), red (Gules), black (Sable), green (Vert), and purple (Purpure). See also *tinctures*.

Combatant Two *rampant* beasts facing one another with raised paws, as if in a pugilistic attitude.

Compartment An optional addition, being the area beneath an English peer's arms, usually depicting a piece of solid land on which the shield rests and *supporters* stand.

Compony or **Gobony** Composed of a single row of squares of two alternate *tinctures*; said of a *bordure, bend*, etc. Cf. *chequy* and *countercompony*.

Coronet There are five different coronets of rank which may surmount the arms of British peers. The so-called ducal coronet, used either with or instead of a *crest* wreath, implies no rank, and the term crest coronet is preferred today.

Duke

Marquess

Earl

Viscount

Baron

Coronets of Rank

Ducal or crest **coronet**

Lion's head **couped**

Cubit arm

Covered **cup**

Dentilly

Dimidiation of lion and ship

Dragon

Eagle displayed

Cotise A diminutive of the *bend*, one quarter its width, and only borne in pairs on either side of the bend.

Couchant A beast lying on all fours with its head erect like the sphinx.

Couché Of a shield, means it is shown at an angle.

Counterchanged When the field is divided between a *metal* and a *colour*, and those *charges* or parts of charges which fall upon the metal are of the colour and vice versa, the charges are said to be counterchanged.

Countercompony or **Countergobony** A double row of squares of alternating *tinctures*, cf. *compony* and *chequy*.

Couped With the end cut off. When used of an Honourable *Ordinary* it means the ends do not touch the sides of the shield.

Courant or **Current** Running.

Coward Used of a beast or monster with its tail between its legs.

Crancelin A crown in the form of an ornamental arched *bend*, said to be derived from a *chaplet* of rue, and found in the arms of Saxony.

Crescent Can be either a *charge* or a *cadency mark*.

Crest A device mounted on the *helmet* in the days of chivalry, and still so displayed in modern heraldry.

Crined Used to describe the hair of a human head, or beast's mane, when of a different *tincture* from the body.

Cross The first Honourable *Ordinary*. Many variations exist (see overleaf).

Crusily *Field* or *charge* powdered with *cross* crosslets.

Cubit Arm cut off below the elbow, usually shown *palewise*.

Cup Usually shown covered, and often seen in the heraldry of families named Butler.

Dancetty A zigzag line of partition, similar to but larger in size than *indented*. This distinction was not drawn in medieval heraldry.

Demi or **Demy** The upper half of a beast, bird, etc.

Dentilly A line of partition which is *indented bendwise* like the teeth of a ratchet wheel, derived from Guernsey French 'dentelé', meaning jagged.

Dexter Right as opposed to left (*sinister*) when describing *charges* on the shield. All *blazon* assumes one is standing behind the shield. The dexter half of the shield consequently is the left-hand side to the spectator.

Diapering An optional patterning with scrollwork or flourishes on uncharged parts of a shield executed in the same *tincture* to relieve the surface.

Difference To make an addition or alteration to arms and *crest*, usually to mark a distinction between the coats of arms of closely related persons whose shields would otherwise be the same.

Dimidiation Cutting two coats of arms in half by a vertical line, and uniting the *dexter* half of one with the *sinister* half of the other. Precursor of *impale*ment.

Displayed Used of birds with outstretched wings, like imperial *eagles*.

Dormant A beast in a sleeping position.

Doubled Used of the lining of *mantling*, usually *Or* or *Argent*.

Dragon The four-legged monster of mythology.

Eagle The bird which occurs with greatest frequency in early heraldry, usually shown *displayed*.

Crosses
 (1) cross pommy
 (2) cross paty or patonce
 (3) cross bottony
 (4) passion or Latin cross
 (5) cross formy quadrate
 (6) Tau cross
 (7) Celtic cross
 (8) cross formy floretty
 (9) plain cross
 (10) Patriarchal cross
 (11) cross recercely
 (12) cross formy fitchy
 (13) cross potent
 (14) cross crosslet fitchy
 (15) cross flory
 (16) Egyptian cross
 (17) Fylfot or swastika
 (18) Maltese cross
 (19) cross gyronny

Arm **embowed**

Lion's head **erased**

Escallop

Embattled Crenellated.

Embowed Bent at the elbow.

Embrued With blood on its point.

Enfile An object is enfiled by a *charge* which it pierces or threads.

Engrailed *Indented* in a series of curves with the points outward to make a concave pattern.

Erased Cut off with a jagged base line, as compared to *couped* which is a straight cut.

Ermine One of the *furs*, black tails on white; variants: Ermines, Erminois, and Pean.

Escallop A shell and pilgrim's *badge*.

Escarbuncle Central boss with radiating decorated spokes, often terminating in *fleurs-de-lis*.

Escutcheon Shield. When used as a *charge*, synonymous with *inescutcheon*.

Fess

Fleur-de-lis

Lion's **gamb**

Griffin

Male **griffin**

Escutcheon of Pretence The small shield of an heraldic heiress placed in the centre of her husband's shield, instead of being *impaled* with his arms. The same device may be used by a Sovereign or Prince to denote one of his dominions.

Estoile A star with wavy limbs.

Fess The fifth Honourable *Ordinary* is a band taking up the centre third of the *escutcheon*, and formed by two horizontal lines drawn across the shield.

Field The background *colour*, *fur*, or *metal* of the shield, always mentioned first in a *blazon*. It can be of more than one *tincture* if patterned.

Fimbriated Edged.

Fitchy Pointed, terminating in a point. Usually used with forms of *cross*.

Flasque A narrow *flaunch*.

Flaunch A convex segmental *Ordinary* on either side of the shield.

Fleur-de-lis Stylized flower based on lily or iris, seen in the French Royal Arms, and borne in those of England till 1801.

Flory counterflory Denoting that the flowers with which an *Ordinary* (usually a *tressure*) is adorned have their heads placed inward and outward alternately, as in the Scottish Royal Arms.

Foil Generic term for group of flower-like *charges*, including *trefoil*, *quatrefoil*, *cinquefoil*.

Forcene *Salient* when used of horses.

Forchee or **Forchy** Forked; normally occurs as *queue* forchee, a forked tail.

Fountain A *roundel barry wavy Argent* and *Azure*.

Fret *Mascle* interlaced by a *saltire*.

Fretty A pattern of *frets*.

Fur The principal furs are Ermine (black tails on white) and Vair (a pattern of blue and white). See also *tincture*.

Fusil An elongated *lozenge*.

Gamb A paw, usually a lion's or bear's.

Garb A sheaf, often of wheat.

Gobony or **Compony** A single row of squares of alternate *tinctures*.

Gorged Collared.

Goutte A drop, for instance of water (d'eau) or blood (de sang); different terms are used depending on the *tincture*.

Griffin Winged monster with foreparts of an eagle and hindparts of a lion with a beard and ears. A male griffin has no wings, and spikes emerge from the body.

Guardant Used of a beast looking out at the spectator rather than seen in profile.

Gules Heraldic term for red.

Gutty Powdered with or *semy* of *gouttes*.

Gyronny Said of a *field* that is divided into triangular parts or gyrons, created by halving *quarters* diagonally.

Hatching A system for identifying *tincture* in monochrome by lines and dots.

Haurient A fish shown vertically.

Helmets
(1) Royal Helm and crest
(2) Peer's Helm
(3) Baronet's and Knight's Helm
(4) Melbury Helm, 15th cent.
(5) Close Helm, 16th cent.
(6) Barrel Helm, 14th cent.

Helmet The helmet bears the *crest* and differs according to rank. It can also be used as a *charge*.

Humetty *Couped.*

Hurt An *azure roundel.*

Impale To arrange two coats of arms side by side in one shield divided (or parted) per *pale*, normally to display arms of a husband (to the *dexter*) and his wife (to the *sinister*), or of Office (dexter) and the Office-holder (sinister).

Indented A line of partition resembling the blade of a saw.

Inescutcheon A shield when borne as a *charge* on another shield.

Invected The reverse of *engrailed, indented* with a series of curves pointing inward.

Issuant Used of beasts or monsters, unless they are winged, when rising (see also *rising*).

Jessant de lis With *fleurs-de-lis* issuing from the mouth and head.

Knot Occurs as a *charge*, such as Bowen, Bourchier, Cavendish, Dacre, Harington, Heneage, Hungerford, Lacy, Stafford, and Wake Knots, named after the families who bore them and each of a different shape. Many derive from *badges*.

Label A horizontal *bar*, usually *couped*, and normally with three or five dependent points. A label of three points now normally denotes an eldest son in the lifetime of his father.

Langued Tongued.

Leopard Term used in medieval heraldry for *lion passant guardant*. Now used for the natural beast.

Lined With a line similar to a leash, usually attached to a collar.

Lion Most frequently found beast in heraldry; occurs in many positions, of which the most usual are *rampant* and *passant*.

Lioncel Diminutive of *lion*, occasionally used if several on shield.

Lodged Deer are lodged when *couchant*.

Lion
(1) lion rampant
(2) lion dormant
(3) sea lion
(4) lion passant
(5) lion rampant regardant
(6) lion sejant coward
(7) lion passant guardant

Lymphad

Lozenge A diamond shape used both as a *charge* and instead of a shield to display the arms of single women and peeresses in their own right.

Lucy A pike (fish).

Lymphad A type of ship.

Mantled Refers to the outside rather than the lining (doubled) of *mantling*.

Mantling Represents slashed cloth worn over head and shoulders, often stylized as acanthus leaves.

Marshal To combine coats of arms on a single shield by *quartering* or other means (see chapter on marshalling).

Martlet A legless bird, sometimes said to represent the swift or swallow.

Mascle A hollow diamond-shaped device or *voided lozenge*.

Masoned Used when lines of pointing are of a different *tincture* from the building on which they appear.

Maunch A device representing a medieval sleeve.

Metal Two metals are used, gold (Or) and silver (Argent).

Millrind The iron retaining piece fixed at the centre of a millstone.

Modern The arms borne by a country or family in present and recent times; opposite to *ancient*.

Monster For obscure monsters see *The Heraldic Imagination* by R. O. Dennys.

Mullet A figure resembling a star with straight limbs, usually of five points in England.

Naiant Swimming, usually for fish which are *fess*wise.

Nebuly A form of *wavy* now like a row of jigsaw tongues. No distinction was made between this and wavy in medieval heraldry.

Ogress Synonymous with *pellet*, a black *roundel* or roundel *Sable*.

Or Heraldic term for gold or yellow.

Ordinary Any one of the major armorial geometrical *charges*, also known as Honourable Ordinaries. Heralds differ as to the number but nine are usually given, namely *cross, chief, pale, bend, fess, inescutcheon, chevron, saltire, bar*. Sub-Ordinaries or plain Ordinaries without the prefix Honourable are *gyron, orle, pile, quarter*, quarter *sinister, canton*, canton sinister, *flasque, flaunch*. Some writers add *fret, lozenge, fusil*, and *mascle*.

Orle A *voided escutcheon* a *bordure's* width from the edge of the shield. *Charges* placed in orle follow the line of the orle as on the illustrated seal of Aymer (de Valence), Earl of Pembroke.

Ounce Synonymous with the post-medieval *leopard*.

Pairle Said of the shield divided in the form of a *pall*, or of *charges* so arranged.

Pale The third Honourable *Ordinary*. A vertical stripe in the middle of the shield occupying at most one third of the shield.

Palewise Said of *charges* when vertical. It does not relate to the relationship between charges which might be 'palewise in *bend*' if arranged diagonally across the shield, although pointing upwards. When charges are above one another the term 'in *pale*' is used.

Pall

Pantheon

Panther

Phoenix

Pile

Tudor **rose**

Salamander

Pall A Y-shaped *charge*.

Pallet A narrow vertical stripe on the shield, half the width of a *pale*.

Paly Divided into an even number of vertical stripes of equal width, in alternating *tinctures*.

Panache An arrangement of feathers on the *helmet*, one of the precursors of the *crest*.

Pantheon Monster resembling a hind powdered with *estoiles* or *mullets*, usually with a bushy tail.

Panther The beast is depicted heraldically with flames issuing from ears and mouth and with body powdered with multi-coloured spots.

Passant Four-legged beast or monster depicted with the *dexter* foreleg raised as if walking.

Pegasus Term often used for the winged horse.

Pelican Usually shown 'in her piety' pecking her breast to feed her young with her blood.

Pellet A *roundel Sable*, also known as an *ogress*.

Pellety *Field* or *charge* powdered with *pellets*.

Pheon An arrowhead.

Phoenix Usually shown as a *demi-eagle* emerging from flames.

Pierced Refers to a circular hole in a *charge* through which the *field* shows unless another *tincture* is specified, cf. *voided*.

Pile A triangular sub-*Ordinary*.

Pineapple The pine-cone rather than the fruit.

Plate A *roundel Argent*.

Pomme A *roundel Vert*.

Pommel The spherical end of a sword.

Proper Depicted in natural colours.

Purpure Heraldic term for purple.

Quarter To divide the shield into four or more compartments of equal sizes.

Quatrefoil *Charge* similar to four-leafed clover.

Queue Tail of a beast.

Raguly Designating a *charge* or *Ordinary* jagged or notched like the trunk or limbs of a tree lopped of its branches. Also a line of partition.

Rampant Beast or monster standing on one hind leg.

Regardant Applied to any beast, bird, or monster looking back over its shoulder.

Rising Used of birds when rising, but not for beasts or monsters (see *issuant*).

Rose In England the rose is usually stylized, the most noted being those of Lancaster (red) and York (white), and the Tudor rose (white on red).

Roundel A circle. Can be called a *bezant* when *Or*, *plate* when *Argent*, *hurt* when *Azure*, *torteau* when *Gules*, *pellet* when *Sable*, and *pomme* when *Vert*.

Sable Heraldic term for black.

Salamander Shown as a reptile in flames.

Salient A beast jumping, leaping, or rearing.

Talbot

Thunderbolt

Trefoil

Unicorn

Wyvern

Saltire The eighth Honourable *Ordinary*, depicted in the form of a St Andrew's Cross.

Segreant *Rampant* when used of *griffins*.

Sejant Beasts and monsters seated erect.

Semy or **semée** Scattered or powdered as in semy de lis (strewn with *fleurs-de-lis*).

Sinister Left as opposed to right (*dexter*) when describing *charges* on the shield. All *blazon* assumes one is standing behind the shield. The sinister half of the shield is consequently the right-hand side to the spectator.

Slipped With a stalk; term is used with flowers and *foils*.

Supporter Either of a pair of figures standing one on each side of and supporting the shield.

Talbot Medieval hunting dog.

Tenné Heraldic term for orange.

Theow A monster resembling a wolf with cloven hooves.

Thunderbolt A winged column with flames at either end and stylized lightning crossing behind the centre of the column in *saltire*.

Tincture The general designation for *colours*, *metals*, and *furs*.

Torse Synonymous with the *crest* wreath, and normally of six visible twists of cloth wound round the *helmet*. Often shown under the crest without a helmet.

Torteau A *roundel Gules*.

Trefoil A stylized leaf resembling a three-leaved clover. It is termed a trefoil *slipped* if it has a stalk.

Tressure A diminutive of the *orle* appearing as a narrow band near the edge of a coat of arms, often ornamented with *fleurs-de-lis*, as in the Scottish Royal Arms.

Tricking System of indicating *tincture* in uncoloured records by abbreviation.

Trippant Used of deer when *passant*.

Undé or **undy** See *wavy*.

Unguled Hooved, of beasts or monsters.

Unicorn Monster shown as a horse with a twisted horn, lion's tail, and hooves.

Urchin Heraldic term for a hedgehog.

Vair A fur depicted in various stylized patterns of blue and white.

Vairy Used for *Vair* in *tinctures* other than blue and white.

Vert Heraldic term for green.

Voided With a hole in the centre of the same shape as the *charge* (see also *pierced*).

Volant Heraldic term for flying.

Wavy or **undy** Applied to *Ordinaries* or division lines which curve and recurve like waves.

Wyvern A two-legged *dragon*.

Yale A tusked monster with cloven hooves, pointed ears, usually curved horns, and a short lion's tail.

Bibliography

THE outstanding bibliography of British heraldry is Thomas Moule's *Bibliotheca Heraldica*, published in 1822. This lists printed books on heraldry chronologically down to 1821, and was reprinted in 1966 by Heraldry Today (London). The following list is consequently principally of books published since 1821, although a few earlier books to which particular reference is made are included. Those who want a full bibliography should refer to Moule; there is at present no equivalent source for books published after 1821 of which the following are only a small fraction.

AILES, A. *The Origins of the Royal Arms of England* (Reading: Graduate Centre for Medieval Studies, Reading University, 1982).

BARRON, O. Article on 'Heraldry' in 11th edition, *Encyclopaedia Britannica* (1910).

BEDFORD, W. K. R. *The Blazon of Episcopacy* (Oxford: 1897).

BERRY, William *Encyclopaedia Heraldica* (London: Sherwood, Gilbert, & Piper, 1828), 3 vols.

BIRCH, W. de G. *Catalogue of Seals in the Department of Manuscripts in the British Museum, London* (printed by Order of the Trustees: 1887–1900), 6 vols.

BOUTELL, Charles *Boutell's Heraldry*, first published as *The Manual of Heraldry* (1863), revised ed. by J. P. Brooke-Little (London: Warne, 1983).

BRAULT, Gerard J. *Early Blazon* (Oxford: Clarendon Press, 1972).

—— *Eight thirteenth-century Rolls of Arms in French and Anglo-Norman Blazon* (Pennsylvania State University Press, 1973).

BRIGGS, Geoffrey *Civic and Corporate Heraldry* (London: Heraldry Today, 1971).

BROOKE-LITTLE, J. P. (ed.), '*The Coat of Arms*', an heraldic quarterly magazine (The Heraldry Society, 1950–).

—— *An Heraldic Alphabet* (London: Macdonald & Co., 1973).

BURKE, Bernard *The General Armory of England, Scotland, and Wales* (London: Harrison, 1884).

CHESSHYRE, Hubert *The Identification of Coats of Arms on British Silver* (London: Hawkslure Publications, 1978).

CHILD, Heather *Heraldic Design* (London: G. Bell & Sons Ltd, 1965).

CLARK, Hugh *Introduction to Heraldry*, 14th edn. (London: H. Washbourne, 1845).

CUSSANS, J. E. *Handbook of Heraldry*, 3rd edn. (London: Chatto & Windus, 1893).

DALLAWAY, James *Inquiries into the Origin and Progress of the Science of Heraldry in England* (Gloucester: Cadell, 1793).

DENHOLM-YOUNG, Noel *History and Heraldry 1254–1310: A Study of the Historical Value of the Rolls of Arms* (Oxford: Clarendon Press, 1965).

DENNYS, Rodney *The Heraldic Imagination* (London: Barrie & Jenkins, 1975).

—— *Heraldry and The Heralds* (London: Jonathan Cape, 1982).

DORLING, E. E. *Leopards of England and Other Papers* (London: Constable, 1912).

EDMONDSON, Joseph *A Complete Body of Heraldry* (London: The Author, 1780), 2 vols.

ELLIS, Roger H. (ed.), *Catalogue of Seals in the Public Record Office, Personal Seals, vol. I* (London: HMSO, 1978).

ELLIS, William Smith *The Antiquities of Heraldry* (London: 1869).

ELVIN, Charles Norton *Dictionary of Heraldry* (London, etc.: W. H. Brown, 1889).

EVANS, Sloane *Grammar of Heraldry* (London: 1847).

EVE, George W. *Heraldry as Art: an account of its development and practice, chiefly in England* (London: Batsford, 1907).

—— *Decorative heraldry: a handbook of its description and treatment* (London: Bell, 1908).

FAIRBAIRN, James *Book of Crests of the Families of Great Britain*, 4th edn. (London: Jack, 1904), 2 vols.

FERNE, John *The Blazon of Gentrie* (London: 1586).

FORD, Richard 'Spanish Genealogy and Heraldry', no. 123 of *Quarterly Review* (June, 1838).

FOSTER, Joseph (ed.) *Two Tudor Books of Arms: being Harleian Mss. 2179 and 6163* (Privately printed: de Walden Library, 1904).

FOX-DAVIES, A. C. *A Complete Guide to Heraldry* (first published 1909), rev. by J. P. Brooke-Little (London: Orbis, 1985).

FRANKLIN, Charles A. H. *The Bearing of Coat Armour by Ladies* (London: John Murray, 1923).

FRANKLYN, J. *Shield and Crest*, 3rd edn. (London: MacGibbon & Key, 1967).

FRIAR, Stephen (ed.) *A New Dictionary of Heraldry* (London: A. & C. Black, 1987).

GALBREATH, D. L. *Papal Heraldry*, 2nd edn., rev. by G. Briggs (London: Heraldry Today, 1970).

GIBBON, John *Introductio ad Latinam Blasoniam* (London: 1682).

GUILLIM, John *A Display of Heraldrie* 1st edn. (London: 1610), 6th edn. (London: 1724).

GRANT, F. J. *The Manual of Heraldry* (Edinburgh: John Grant, 1924).

HEIM, B. B. *Heraldry in the Catholic Church, its Origins, Customs, and Laws* (Gerrards Cross: Van Duren, 1978).

Heralds' Commemorative Exhibition, 1484–1934, enlarged and illustrated catalogue (London: 1936), reprinted (London: Tabard Press, 1970).

Heraldic Exhibition, Edinburgh 1891, memorial catalogue (Edinburgh: printed for the Committee, Constable, 1892).

HOPE, W. H. St John *Heraldry for Craftsmen and Designers* (London: J. Hogg, 1913).

—— *A Grammar of English Heraldry*, 2nd edn. by A. R. Wagner (Cambridge University Press, 1953).

HOWARD DE WALDEN, Thomas Evelyn (Scott-Ellis), Lord *Some Feudal Lords and Their Seals, 1301*, with an Introduction by Lord Howard de Walden (Privately printed: de Walden Library, 1904).

—— *Banners, Standards, and Badges from a Tudor Manuscript in the College of Arms*, with an Introduction by Lord Howard de Walden (Privately printed: de Walden Library, 1904).

INNES OF LEARNEY, Thomas *Scots Heraldry*, 2nd edn. (Edinburgh: Oliver & Boyd, 1956).

HUMPHERY-SMITH, Cecil R. *Anglo-Norman Armory* (Canterbury: Family History, 1973).

—— *Anglo-Norman Armory Two* (Canterbury: Institute of Heraldic and Genealogical Studies, 1984).

JONES, E. J. *Medieval Heraldry* (Cardiff: William Lewis, 1943).

LAING, H. *Descriptive Catalogue of Impressions from Ancient Scottish Seals* (Edinburgh: 1850), Supplement (1866).

LAWRANCE, H. *Heraldry from Military Monuments before 1350 in England and Wales* (London: Harleian Society, vol. 96, 1946).

LEAF, W. and PURCELL, S. *Heraldic Symbols, Islamic Insignia and Western Heraldry* (London: Victoria and Albert Museum, 1986).

LEIGH, G. *The Accedence of Armory*, 1st edn. (London: 1562), last edn. (London: 1612).

LIDDERDALE, W. A. (ed.), *A Collection of Miscellaneous Grants, Crests, Confirmations, Augmentations, and Exemplifications of Arms* (London: Harleian Society, vols. 77–8, 1925–6).

LONDON, H. S. *Royal Beasts* (The Heraldry Society, 1956).

LONDON SURVEY COMMITTEE: *The College of Arms* (London: HMSO, 1963).

LOUDA, J. and MACLAGAN, M. *Lines of Succession* (London: Orbis, 1981).

LOWER, M. A. *Curiosities of Heraldry* (London: R. Smith, 1845).

LYON OFFICE *An Ordinary of Arms, 1902–73*, vol. ii (Edinburgh: 1977).

MARKS, Richard and PAYNE, Ann *British Heraldry from its origins to c.1800* (London: British Museum Publications Ltd., 1978).

MONCREIFFE, I. and POTTINGER, D. *Simple Heraldry* (Edinburgh: Thomas Nelson, 1953).

MORGAN, S. *The Sphere of Gentry* (London: 1661).

MOULE, T. *Bibliotheca Heraldica* (London: 1822).

—— *Heraldry of Fish* (London: John Van Voorst, 1842).

NEUBECKER, O. *Heraldry, Sources, Symbols, and Meaning* (London: Macdonald and Jane's, 1976).

NISBET, A. *A System of Heraldry* (Edinburgh: 1722).

PALLISER, Mrs Bury *Historic Devices, Badges, and War-Cries* (London: Sampson Low, 1870).

PAPWORTH, J. W and MORANT, A. W. *An Ordinary of British Armorials* (London: T. Richards, 1874).

PARKER, J. and Co. *Glossary of the Terms used in Heraldry*, new edn. (Oxford: 1894).

PAUL, J. Balfour *Ordinary of Scottish Arms* (Edinburgh: Green, 1903).

PINCHES, J. H. and R. V. *The Royal Heraldry of England* (London: Heraldry Today, 1974).

PLANCHÉ, J. R. *The Pursuivant of Arms* (London: Hardwicke, 1859).

PLATTS, B. *Origins of Heraldry* (London: Procter Press, 1980).

RIETSTAP, J. B. *Armorial General*, 2nd edn. (1884), reprinted (London: Heraldry Today, 1965), 2 vols.

ROBSON, T. *British Herald* (Sunderland: 1830), 2 vols.

ROUND, J.H. *Geoffrey de Mandeville, a Study of the Anarchy* (London: 1892).

—— *Studies in Peerage and Family History* (London: Constable, 1901).

—— *Peerage and Pedigree, Studies in Peerage Law and Family History* (London: Nisbet, 1910), 2 vols.

—— *Family Origins and other Studies* (London: Constable, 1930).

RYLANDS, W. H. (ed.) *Grantees of Arms to the end of the Seventeenth Century* (London: Harleian Society, vol. 66, 1915).

—— (ed.), *Grantees of Arms named in Docquets and Patents 1687–1898* (London: Harleian Society, vols. 67–8, 1916–17).

SCOTT-GILES, C. W. *Civic Heraldry of England and Wales* (London: J. M. Dent, 1933).

—— *Motley Heraldry* (London: Tabard Publications, n.d.).

—— *The Romance of Heraldry* (London: J. M. Dent, 1965).

—— *Shakespeare's Heraldry* (London: J. M. Dent, 1950).

SETON, G. *The Law and Practice of Heraldry in Scotland* (Edinburgh: Edmonston & Douglas, 1863).

SKEY, W. *The Heraldic Calendar, a list of the Nobility and Gentry whose arms are registered and pedigrees recorded in the Herald's Office in Ireland* (Dublin: Alexander Thom, 1846).

SIMON, H. *Armorial General de l'Empire Francais* (Paris: 1812), 2 vols.

SQUIBB, G. D. *The Law of Arms in England* (London: Heraldry Society, revised edn. 1967).

—— *Reports of Heraldic Cases in the Court of Chivalry 1623–1732* (London: Harleian Society, vol. 107, 1956).

—— *Visitation pedigrees and the Genealogist* (London: Phillimore, 1964).

—— *The High Court of Chivalry; a study of the Civil Law in England* (Oxford: Clarendon Press, 1959).

—— *Munimenta Heraldica 1484–1984* (London: Harleian Society, new series, vol. 4, 1985).

STENTON, F. M. (ed.) *The Bayeux Tapestry: a comprehensive survey* (London: Phaidon Press, 1957).

SUMMERS, P. (ed.) *Hatchments in Britain* (London and Chichester: Phillimore, 1974–85), 6 vols.

SWAN, Conrad. *Canada: Symbols of Sovereignty* (University of Toronto Press, 1977).

WADE, W. C. *The Symbolisms of Heraldry* (London: George Redway, 1898).

WAGNER, A. R. *Heralds of England: a history of the Office and College of Arms* (London: HMSO, 1967).

—— *Heralds and Heraldry in the Middle Ages* (London: Oxford University Press, 1939), 2nd edn. (1956).

—— *Historic Heraldry of Britain* (London: Oxford University Press, 1939).

—— *A Catalogue of English Medieval Rolls of Arms, Aspilogia* vol. i (Oxford University Press for The Society of Antiquaries, 1950).

—— (general editor), *Rolls of Arms, Henry III, Aspilogia* vol. ii (Oxford University Press for The Society of Antiquaries, 1967).

—— *The Records and Collections of the College of Arms* (London: Burke's Peerage Ltd., 1952).

—— *Heralds and Ancestors* (London: Colonnade Books, 1978).

—— *Heraldry in England* (London: King Penguin Books, 1946).

WILLEMENT, T. *Regal Heraldry* (London: 1821).

WILLS, H. *Florentine Heraldry* (London: Dean & Son, 1894).

ZIEBER, E. *Heraldry in America* 2nd edn. (Philadelphia: Bailey, Banks, & Biddle, 1909).

Index

Note to the reader: Sovereigns appear under their country and Peers usually under their titles. Where a subject is illustrated its page reference appears in italics.